ARCHAEOLINGUA

Edited by

ERZSÉBET JEREM and WOLFGANG MEID

Series Minor

41

ZSUZSA ESZTER PETŐ

HERMITS IN THE HEART OF THE HUNGARIAN KINGDOM

Medieval Monastic Landscape of the Pauline Order in the Pilis

BUDAPEST 2018

The publication of this volume was generously funded by
the National Cultural Fund of Hungary

Front Cover

A bird's eye view of the Monastery of the Holy Spirit.
Photo credit: János László, Civertan Grafikai Stúdió

Back Cover

3D elevation model of the Pilis area on the basis of
ASTER GDEM and various maps

Volume editor

József Laszlovszky

ISBN 978-615-5766-09-1

HU-ISSN 1216-6847

2018

ARCHAEOLINGUA ALAPÍTVÁNY
H-1067 Budapest, Teréz krt. 13.

Language editing by Karen Stark
Copy editing by Zsuzsanna Renner
Desktop editing and layout by Szilamér Nemes

Printed by Prime Rate Kft.

Contents

Editor's Preface

Heremites, monachi, fratres: these are the medieval terms used for different branches of monastic people and communities, who followed various rules, represented particular lifestyles and created a wide range of buildings and landscapes as their special spaces in the earthly world. For some of them, the desert in Egypt was the proper place to live, while for others, an island in the Atlantic Ocean or a royal forest in Central Europe. The Order of St. Paul the First Hermit represents a particular case of monastic culture, as the medieval history of the Paulines incorporates, to some extent, all three approaches to monastic traditions. Furthermore, this is the only monastic order that emerged in Hungary, a country in Central Europe, which was Christianized many centuries after the appearance of the first monastic communities. Thus, this study on the Pauline order offers a new insight to the general history of monasticism.

The first version of this study was defended as a thesis for the Medieval Studies Program at the Central European University in Budapest. It was based on a wide range of sources; however, the most innovative trait of the work was the usage of spatial approaches and geographical information system (GIS) to analyze the Pauline space. This topographical study is also influenced by the concept of monastic landscape. Landscape archaeology and the interpretation of monastic landscapes have proven to be one of the most fruitful research directions during the last decades across Europe as well as in other areas of monasticism. In an earlier study, I have argued the Pauline order represents a particularly interesting case for monastic landscape studies – now, Zsuzsa Eszter Pető's work demonstrates in an excellent way, how the hilly region of the Pilis offered a unique monastic space under the influence of medieval royal power.

József Laszlovszky

Acknowledgements

I would like to express my deepest gratitude to all those who supported and helped me complete this work. First and foremost, special thanks are due to my supervisor, József Laszlovszky for his wise guidance and stimulating suggestions, and for his unfailing trust in my abilities. I am grateful to Katalin Szende, whose kind encouragement and contribution helped me write this work.

I would like to thank to Katalin Tolnai and András Harmath for their invaluable work in digitization.

I have benefited greatly from discussions with Gábor Tomka on the archaeology and research of the Pauline Order and with Viktor Lagutov on GIS methods.

My heartfelt thanks go to Erzsébet Jerem for accepting my manuscript for the Series Minor of the Archaeolingua Foundation, and to Zsuzsanna Renner and Szilamér Nemes for transforming my manuscript and figures into a book. I would like to thank my dear friend Karen Stark for proofreading the text.

I am grateful to the Pauline Order, especially to János Csóka *OSPPE* and Tamás Szentirmay, and to my dear friend, Kyra Lyublyanovics, for their support.

My most special thanks go to András Szabó for his support and help during the process of preparing this book.

Finally, I would like to dedicate this book to my Parents, who have had to live with archaeology for so long.

Zsuzsa Eszter Pető

1. Introduction

> *"...first the order was settled only in deserted, uninhabited, wooded places, far from populated areas and lived a monkish life in small cells and chapels, which can still be found at some places; but as time went by, through ones' donations the cells have been transformed into great monasteries, the chapels to splendid churches and around the monasteries several other necessary buildings were erected."*
> Pope Eugene IV to Dionysios, the Archbishop of Esztergom, in 1440

It is a multi-faceted, complex, and fascinating endeavor to recognize the large-scale changes of the space that we live in. The details of our home, the familiar shops at the corner down the street, or even whole areas in a city can change almost unnoticeably throughout a period of time. Recognizing these differences in historical space is a much bigger challenge. In addition to time, which is the strongest consideration in studying the past, space also has many layers, from a single room to a wide range of landscapes. The depth and possibilities of a survey depend on its aim, as well as the quantity and quality of the extant information.

Despite the complex challenge, a landscape archaeologist studies the ways in which people in the past constructed and used the environment around them. The landscape archaeologist aims to find structures and relations between different environments and uses a variety of tools to help read the mostly scattered traces of past human activities, which we have inherited from the past. Fragments of information in the landscape, ancient ruins, or just humps and bumps in the earth can tell us information about once cultivated lands, fishponds, mills, or vineyards. Small pieces of data from maps or in written documents can answer questions relating to past settlement structures, the borders of authorities, road networks, or even monastic sites and their estates. As was summarized in *The Archaeology of Rural Monasteries* by Lawrence Butler, one can identify four possible viewpoints of monastic space: 1. Monasteries as oases of sanctity and workshops of prayer (religious aspect); 2. Monasteries as financial corporations, holding land, and exploiting their resources (daily life); 3. Monastic buildings as potential deposits of material evidence; 4. Monastic ruins as ancient monuments, smoothed into well-ordered piles of masonry amid green lawns (heritage). As Butler continues, the first two options approach monasteries as their contemporaries saw them, while the two other options represent the modern perception of monasteries, "enunciated by the archaeologist and experienced by the visitor."[1]

Among the variety of viewpoints that define monastic space, the scholarship intends to find and reconstruct—at least some small—pieces of the medieval viewpoint. According to this horizontal, seemingly tenacious view of monasteries, a vertical perception also has validity. In particular, various levels of space should be examined, from the smallest unit of space within a monastery to a whole region, incorporating several monasteries. The final goal of complex spatial research is to understand and interpret the correlations between different perceptions (e.g. art historical, architectural, economic, social) of historical space, which can ultimately provide a comprehensive picture on medieval landscape for both academic researchers and visitors.

The medieval Order of Saint Paul the First Hermit has been studied from religious, historical, and archaeological perspectives for many decades, but these studies and ideas are also often unbalanced. Since the Paulines are the only religious order founded in Hungary, the order has always been in the center of not only scholarly interest, but also the emotionally loaded narrative of Hungarian history. The mysterious atmosphere around the Pauline Order has always been emphasized by the fact that most Pauline monasteries were established in the wilderness, among secluded hilly lands, whose appearance has remained unchanged even today. The significance of the order for Hungarian history is so important, even nowadays, that it forms the main pillar of the extensive research, along with the abundant, diverse material (ranging from liturgical aspects to architecture) that has been gathered by medieval and Renaissance polyhistors, modern scholars, and even by interested laymen.

Accordingly, the academic research on the order has had many different approaches in Hungarian scholarship.[2] However, there are significantly more general works available—the first summary of sources collected for art historical research[3]—than individual, smaller scale publications and projects. This

---

[1] Lawrence Butler, "The Archaeology of Rural Monasteries in England and Wales," in: *The Archaeology of Rural Monasteries*, ed. Roberta Gilchrist and Harold Mytum (Oxford: British Archaeological Reports, 1989), 1.

[2] In Germany and Austria there is also a long tradition of researching the Pauline Order, but the topic of this text emphasizes the Hungarian scholarship. For German, as well as Polish and Croatian research see Gábor Sarbak, ed., *Der Paulinerorden. Geschichte-Geist-Kultur* (Budapest: Szent István Társulat, 2010).

[3] Béla Gyéressy et al., *Documenta Artis Paulinorum,* vol. 1–3, ed. Melinda Tóth (Budapest: Magyar Tudományos Akadémia, 1975–1978).

phenomenon affects every study on the topic and usually indicates a comparative approach, in which individual cases are examined, focusing on the main tendencies of Pauline history. Consequently, this develops a type of argumentation in the research in which general conclusions help the understanding of single cases and individual phenomena may modify, or at least articulate, what is known in medieval Pauline history.

In this sense the research of a small region like the Pilis royal forest is unusual and changes the traditional understanding of Pauline history. Moreover, it gives us an opportunity to discover all, or at least most of the recognized aspects (i.e. religious aspects, daily practical life, material evidence, and heritage) of Pauline monastic life in its own historical and geographical context. At the same time, the Pilis area can be regarded as a particularly important area for the Pauline Order from two different viewpoints. Both were relevant in the Middle Ages and in a similar way, both are crucial for our modern understanding of this monastic community. The first concerns the crucial role of this region in the history of the order, while the second is the central position of the same region in the medieval history of Hungary. According to the tradition of the Pauline Order, the first monastery of the hermits was established in this area, thus, the birthplace and the landscape of emergence of a new order was exactly this historical region. But it was not only the first stage of the probably invented history of the order that connects the Pilis area to important aspects of medieval Hungary. In the thirteenth century, three Pauline monasteries were founded in the heart of the medieval kingdom: the Holy Cross, Holy Spirit, and the Monastery of St. Ladislaus. This area, the so-called *medium regni*, was surrounded by the most important medieval (royal, as well as ecclesiastical) seats and residences (Esztergom, Óbuda, Buda, Visegrád), so in this way it was always regarded as a special territory with a unique development and role (*Figure 1*).

All of this means that investigating the spatial features of the Pauline Order in the Pilis means examining the presence of royal power, where monasteries were the spiritual features of royal representation and dominance. Furthermore, based on the Pauline tradition, the foundation of the order took place in the Pilis, so the development and impact of the Paulines can be examined from its beginnings (including the vague circumstances of their foundation), with special regard to the connection between the royal power of the Hungarian kings and the emergence of the Pauline Order. Considering these phenomena, research on the Pauline monastic space in the Pilis has a complex meaning, which, by understanding it, reveals several layers of medieval royal and ecclesial history.

Figure 1. The main royal and ecclesial centers of the medium regni regarding the Pilis. Map based on the First Military Survey

As opposed to their well-explored customs in the establishment of monasteries, the exact character of the Pauline Order is hard to grasp, as it continuously changed through the centuries. The significance of this change of character is understood when one considers that the hermitic Paulines, after two hundred years, were allowed to do pastoral care in their churches and Pauline hermits (monks) were present at the royal court from the beginning of the order. Moreover, the Pauline Order had strong royal support from their foundation onwards, which supposedly helped the order to become—step-by-step—a major and defining religious and political power in late medieval Hungary. In this manner, they represented the religious ideal of the isolated hermit and the locally active, or even politically powerful, monk at the same time. Along this complex background, this study focuses on the era of the order's formation, first appearance, and the development of its character in the Pilis region.

However, in the fourteenth century only a few main historical events reflect the late medieval significance of the order. Nevertheless, these events strengthen the impression of the Paulines as a powerful, not so hermit-like, but rather half-mendicant, half-monastic order[4] (see the historical events of the order in the Catalogue).[5]

At this point the question of patronage must be addressed. Strong royal patronage had a definite impact on the order's history.[6] Trying to imitate the royal custom (*imitatio regni*), high nobles and the local elite were also great supporters of the order in later times. This is noticeable and evidenced in documents (only

---

4 E.g. important papal approvals, allowances, and donations in 1309, 1328, 1340, and 1401; the translation of the relics of St. Paul the First Hermit from Venice to Budaszentlőrinc in 1381; the running of the basilica Santo Stefano Rotondo in Rome from 1454. For more, see József Laszlovszky, "Középkori kolostorok a tájban, középkori kolostortájak" [Medieval monasteries in the landscape, medieval monastic landscapes], in: *Quasi liber et picture: Tanulmányok Kubinyi András hetvenedik születésnapjára* [Studies for the seventeenth anniversary of András Kubinyi], ed. Gyöngyi Kovács (Budapest: Eötvös Loránd Tudományegyetem, 2004), 348–49; Károly Belényesy, *Pálos kolostorok Abaúj-Hegyalján* [Pauline Friaries in the Abaúj Hegyalja Region] (Miskolc: Herman Ottó Múzeum, 2004), 87–89; Beatrix Romhányi, *A lelkiek a földiek nélkül nem tarthatóak fenn – Pálos gazdálkodás a középkorban* [Spirits cannot be sustained without earthly goods – Estate management of the Pauline monks in the Middle Ages] (Budapest: Gondolat Kiadó, 2010), 13–15.

5 Chapter 3 (Catalogue), 3.1 Overview of the significant medieval historical events regarding the Pauline Order and the Pilis region.

6 It is clear that King Béla IV (1235–1270) and his grandson King Ladislaus IV (1271–1290) had a key role in the foundation and also that the Angevin kings (1308–1387) and Matthias Corvinus (1458–1490) were the greatest supporters, but the gaps in time and the reasons of support are unclear in many cases.

for the high nobility) from the mid-fourteenth century, but the development of the order's monastic system (in connection with the "Pauline character"), the order's increasing power and impact, and the spread of the Paulines has not yet been thoroughly researched in a Hungarian context. These tendencies can be traced back to the period that is proposed for analysis in the present book.

Unfortunately, this idea has some stumbling blocks in terms of the research possibilities. Although a great deal of research has been done since the nineteenth century (e.g. *Figure 2*) and the quantity and quality of the sources is presently regarded as adequate, the number of medieval sources surviving in Hungary is much smaller compared to the Western European countries in general, and for the Pauline monasteries in German territories and Rome in particular.[7] In Hungary, research must

Figure 2. The view of the Virgin Mary Monastery at Márianosztra/Nosztra, drawn by Iván Ádám, Canon of Veszprém in the nineteenth century. Rainer (2016), "Ádám Iván," 44.

---

[7] Lorenz Weinrich, *Hungarici monasterii ordinis sancti Pauli primi heremitae de Urbe Roma instrumenta et priorum regesta* (Rome-Budapest: Hungarian Academy of Rome, 1999).

face this problem since the documents and physical remains of the Middle Ages have been destroyed or forgotten in the last four or five hundred years. Therefore, modern historical and archaeological research should use all efforts to reveal, uncover, collect, and interpret the documents and material remnants of the Middle Ages.

Concerning archaeological research, only a few monasteries have been excavated either partially or nearly completely, including those at Budaszentlőrinc[8]; Kesztölc[9]; Pilisszentlélek[10] in the *Medium Regni;* Gönc[11] and Martonyi[12] in

---

[8] Zoltán Bencze and György Szekér, *A budaszentlőrinci pálos kolostor* [The Pauline monastery at Budaszentlőrinc] (Budapest: Budapesti Történeti Múzeum, 1993).

[9] Júlia Kovalovszki, "A pálos remeték Szent Kereszt-kolostora (Méri István ásatása Klastrompusztán)" [The Pauline monastery of the Holy Cross (the excavation of István Méri at Klastrompuszta)], *Communicationes Archaeologicae Hungariae* (1993): 173–207. Later excavations were conducted by Pázmány Péter Catholic University, Balázs Major, and Elek Benkő. See Elek Benkő, "In medio regni Hungariae," in: *In medio regni Hungariae. Régészeti, művészettörténeti és történeti kutatások „az ország közepén"* [Archaeological, art historical, and historical researches "in the middle of the Kingdom"], eds. Elek Benkő and Krisztina Orosz (Budapest: MTA Régészettudományi Intézet, 2015), 11–27; Elek Benkő, "A Szent Kereszt remetéinek korai kolostorai a Pilisben" [The early cloisters of the hermits of the Holy Cross in the Pilis], in: *Pálosaink és Pécs* [Our Paulines and the town of Pécs], ed. Gábor Sarbak (Budapest: Szent István Társulat, 2016), 25–40.

[10] Sarolta Lázár, "A pilisszentléleki pálos kolostortemplom kutatása" [Archaeological investigation of the Pauline Monastery at Pilisszentlélek], in: *Varia Paulina. Pálos Rendtörténeti Tanulmányok* [Studies on the Pauline Order], vol. 1, ed. Gábor Sarbak (Csorna: Private Edition of Vince Árva, 1994), 177–180; Sarolta Lázár, "A pilisszentléleki volt pálos kolostortemplom kutatása 1985-86" [Archaeological investigation of the Pauline Monastery at Pilisszentlélek, 1985-1986], *A Komárom-Esztergom Megyei Múzeumok Közleményei* 5 (1997): 493–518; Sarolta Lázár, "A pilisszentléleki pálos kolostor kályhacsempéi" [The stove tiles of the Pauline monastery of Pilisszentlélek]. *A Komárom-Esztergom Megyei Múzeumok Közleményei* 8 (2001): 167-180; Sarolta Lázár, "A pilisszentléleki pálos kolostor műhelyháza [The workshop of the Pauline monastery at Pilisszentlélek], in: *Laudator Temporis Acti – Tanulmányok Horváth István 70 éves születésnapjára* [Studies for the seventeenth birthday of István Horváth], ed. Edit Tari (Esztergom: Balassi Bálint Múzeum, 2012), 213–222.

[11] Tamás Pusztai, "A gönci pálos kolostor 2004–2005. évi régészeti kutatása" [The archaeological research of the Pauline monastery at Gönc in 2004–2005], in: *Decus Solitudinis. Pálos évszázadok* [Pauline Centuries], ed. Gábor Sarbak (Budapest: Szent István Társulat, 2007), 515–536.

[12] Juan Cabello, Csaba László, and Zoltán Simon, "A Háromhegyi Boldogságos Szűz Mária Pálos kolostor régészeti kutatása" [The archaeological investigation of the Pauline monastery dedicated to the Blessed Virgin Mary of Háromhegy], *A Hermann Ottó Múzeum Évkönyve* 47 (2008): 147–168.

northeastern Hungary; and Balatonszemes[13] and Bakonyszentjakab[14] just recently.[15] Archaeology represents an essential source for uncovering Pauline daily life, but an excavation is usually a long-term method of uncovering the past, and a number of new excavations at Pauline sites can contribute to our knowledge. Otherwise, there are many, still standing, remains of secluded monasteries, for which architectural and art historical research has collected ample information since the early twentieth century. A *posthumous* publication of the collected works of Tamás Guzsik makes

---

[13] Excavations by Pázmány Péter Catholic University, conducted by András Végh. On the recent results see: "Megfejtésre vár a négy pálos betű," [The four Pauline characters still nead to be solved] *műemlékem.hu*, (Last accessed February 10, 2018), http://www.muemlekem.hu/magazin/balatonszemes_palos_kolostor_feltaras_alapko.

[14] Excavations by Eötvös Loránd University, led by Maxim Mordovin and Szabolcs Balázs Nagy. See more on this in Szabolcs Balázs Nagy, "A bakonyszentjakabi pálos kolostor feltárásának első eredményei" [The first results of the excavation at the Pauline monastery of Bakonyszentjakab], in: *Várak, kastélyok, templomok* [Forts, castles, churches], Annual Studies, ed. Pál Kósa (Pécs: Talma Kiadó, 2014), 56–59.

[15] See a short report on the excavations of St. Philip and James Monastery at Óhuta (North-East Hungary), conducted by Gábor Szörényi, "Eltűntnek hitt pálos kolostorok - Óhuta, Szent Fülöp és Jakab kolostor," *A pálos rend építészeti emlékei*, (Last accessed: March 25, 2018), http://palosepiteszet.blog.hu/2017/12/17/eltuntnek_hitt_palos_kolostorok_ohuta_szent_fulop_es_jakab_kolostor. The Holy Spirit Monastery in the region has already been researched but new information was revealed recently, see Melinda Miskolczi and Gábor Szörényi, "A miskolc-szentléleki pálos kolostor története és 2012. évi kutatása" [The history of the Pauline friary near Miskolc and its archeological excavation in 2012], in: *A Kaposváron 2012. november 22–24. között megrendezett Fiatal Középkoros Régészek IV. Konferenciájának tanulmányai. A Kaposvári Rippl-Rónai Múzeum Közleményei* 2 [Study Volume of the 4th Conference of Young Medieval Archaeologists. Studies of the 4th Conference of Young Medieval Archaeologists, 22–24 November 2012, Kaposvár], ed. Máté Varga (Kaposvár: Rippl-Rónai Múzeum, 2013), 83–9. For the St. Peter Monastery at Pogányszentpéter (South-West Hungary) also see: Róbert Müller, "A pogányszentpéteri ásatás" [The excavation at Pogányszentpéter], in: *A Thúry György Múzeum jubileumi emlékkönyve (1919-1969)* [The Jubilee Volume of the Thúry György Museum (1919-1969)], ed. Gyula Kiss (Nagykanizsa: Thúry György Múzeum, 1972), 265–282; on the very recent excavations, led by Zsuzsa Pető, see, "Eltűntnek hitt pálos kolostorok – Pogányszentpéter," *A pálos rend építészeti emlékei*, (Last accessed: March 25, 2018), http://palosepiteszet.blog.hu/2018/01/01/eltuntnek_hitt_palos_kolostorok_poganyszentpeter. The St. Nicholaus Monastery at Vállus (South-West Hungary) was excavated for the very first time by Lívia Simmer recently, see "Pálos rendi kolostor romjai Zalában," *National Geographic Hungary*, (Last accessed: March 23, 2018), http://www.ng.hu/Civilizacio/2016/09/06/Palos-rendi-kolostor-romjai-Zalaban.

available the material of his over three-decade long research, conducted mostly on the architecture of the Paulines.[16] However, in many cases, archaeology and architecture can reveal only the late medieval period of the monasteries (i.e., the fifteenth century), thus, Pauline research suffers from our limited understanding of previous periods—let alone the era of hermitages. In addition, archaeological results are usually not contextualized in local or broader medieval history.

Recognizing the limits of the written sources, the gaps in the historical research, and the limited possibility of complex excavations, attempts have been made to add new information to the results obtained through traditional methods. A new perspective, that is, the monastic space, may shed light on new data on the Paulines. An order with growing political impact, but with a hermit-like spatial distribution, must have had a complex, comprehensive power structure behind it, and therefore, the study of the spatial distribution of the monastic communities in the Pilis may answer questions on a larger scale.

Research in landscape archaeology, especially regarding the monastic space, does not have a long tradition in Hungary, only a few researchers have carried it out in the last few years. József Laszlovszky, followed by Beatrix Romhányi, highlighted the need and the relatively good circumstances for landscape studies in monastic space.[17] In their work they argued that Pauline monasteries offer a

---

[16] Tamás Guzsik, *A pálos rend építészete a középkori Magyarországon* [Pauline architecture in medieval Hungary] (Budapest: Mikes Kiadó, 2003).

[17] See Laszlovszky (2004), "Középkori kolostorok a tájban," 337–349; also Romhányi (2010), *Pálos gazdálkodás a középkorban*, 11. On the Pauline landscape see Belényesi (2004), *Pálos kolostorok Abaúj-Hegyalján*. Such studies were made on the Cistercians by József Laszlovszky and László Ferenczi recently, see László Ferenczi and József Laszlovszky, "Középkori utak és határhasználat a pilisi apátság területén" [Medieval roads and landscape management on the estate of the Pilis Abbey], *Studia Comitatensia* 1 (2014): 103–124; see also László Ferenczi, "Water Management in Medieval Hungary," in: *The Economy of Medieval Hungary* (Series: East Central and Eastern Europe in the Middle Ages, 450–1450, Volume: 49), eds. József Laszlovszky et al. (Leiden: Brill, 2018), 238–254. László Ferenczi ,"Észrevételek a topuszkói (toplicai) ciszterci apátság birtokstruktúrájával kapcsolatban" [Notes on the estate structure of the Cistercian abbey at Topuszkó (Toplica)], in: *A ciszterci rend Magyarországon és Közép-Európában* [The Cistercan Order in Hungary and Central Europe], vol. 5, ed. Barnabás Guitman (Piliscsaba: Pázmány Péter Katolikus Egyetem, 2009), 277–292; László Ferenczi, "Molendium ad Aquas Calidas. A pilisi ciszterciek az állítólagos Fehéregyházán. Történeti, topográfiai és tájrégészeti kutatás a pilisi apátság birtokán" [The Cistercians in the Alleged Village of Fehéregyháza. Topographical and Landscape Archaeological Investigations on the Estate of the Pilis Abbey], *Studia Comitatensia* 1 (2014): 145–161.

particularly good case for the study of monastic space and landscape. Previous topographical studies have also revealed some interesting examples (fishponds, mills, etc.) as landscape features of monastic complexes.[18] Therefore, the approach of this book adopts the idea and concept of monastic space developed in England,[19] its homeland, and adopts it to the Hungarian context.

Monastic space—in most of the studies—defines the smallest, local unit of monasteries. It represents the physical confines of a territory based on historical traditions and events. Monasteries were endowed from their foundation with landed properties (among other types) to establish, configure, and develop the system and conditions of their sustenance in the long run. These provided income to support the monastic community.[20] These elements (properties and holdings) and the boundary of monastic jurisdiction define monastic space, which is certainly a complex term in the case of the development of the Pauline Order. This means that because of the limited number of sources and the specific historical context—as it has been discussed recently—a broader horizontal and vertical view can lead to a better understanding of the order's site selection strategy, economy, and spirituality.

---

[18] E.g. in the volumes of *Magyarország Régészeti Topográfiája* [The Archaeological Topography of Hungary], for example see István Éri, ed., *Magyarország Régészeti Topográfiája. Veszprém megye régészeti topográfiája: A veszprémi járás.* [The archaeological topography of Hungary. The archaeological topography of Veszprém County. Veszprém district], vol. 2, (Budapest: Akadémiai Kiadó, 1969), 181.

[19] E.g., on fishponds see Michael Aston, ed., *Medieval Fish, Fisheries and Fishponds in England* (Oxford: British Archaeological Reports, 1988); and James Bond, "Water Management in the Rural Monastery," in: *The Archaeology of Rural Monasteries,* eds. Roberta Gilchrist and Harold Mytum (Oxford: British Archaeological Reports, 1989), 83–112. On mills see Richard Holt, *The Mills of Medieval England* (Oxford: Basil Blackwell, 1988); David Luckhurst, *Monastic Watermills: A Study of the Mills within English Monastic Precincts* (London: Society for the Protection of Ancient Buildings, 1964); on woodland management see Oliver Rackham, *Trees and Woodland in the British Landscape* (London: Phoenix, revised edition, 1996). On gardens, orchards, and vineyards see Paul Meyvaert, "The Medieval Monastic Garden," in: *Medieval Gardens,* ed. E. D. Macdougall, (Washington, D.C.: Trustees for Harvard University, 1986), 23–53. On monastic landscapes in general and for the bibliography and a great list of case studies and monographs see also the monograph by James Bond, *Monastic Landscapes* (Stroud: Tempus, 2004). A complex collection on the perspectives of monastic archaeology is by Graham Keevill, Michael Aston, and Teresa Hall, eds., *Monastic Archaeology: Papers on the Study of Medieval Monasteries* (Oxford: Oxbow Books, 2001).

[20] Bond (2004), *Monastic Landscapes*, 12.

Based on this idea, Károly Belényesy was the first to break fresh ground with his summary on the economic strategy and hierarchical structure of the Pauline Order, presented from a spatial perspective in a small-scale pilot project in the Abaúj-Hegyalja region.[21] His research revealed that traditionally used datasets, if handled with new methods, have the potential to reveal a more detailed and complex interpretation of Pauline history, from the point of view of medieval and modern spatial contexts (including both human-made and natural features). His results reinforce the fact that various traditional approaches may yield a large amount of data, and that most of the gaps have already been recognized.

However, the medieval history of the Pauline Order still poses many questions and contains only preliminary, rough conclusions. The present work is a small step in the research of Pauline space, in which I intend to give a systematic overview of several layers of space—from a single monastery to the entire Pilis Forest—using a variety of sources on a digital platform. This work is an example as well as an overview of the possible ways of doing research in the Carpathian Basin in the light of local research circumstances.

It is also crucial to briefly introduce the general attributes of the Pauline economy and its impact on the landscape, since it reveals most clearly the multifaceted character of the order. This aim indicates a double task. It has been partly solved in the historical research by systematically collecting a large number of sources and, based on them, defining general tendencies in the Pauline economy.[22] At the same time, the spatial impacts of the Pauline economy are poorly studied since—referring back to the general tendency in scholarship—small-scale studies are lacking and few features of Pauline monastic space have been recorded.[23] Therefore, the systematic connection of historical and spatial approaches creates a unique way of evaluating data, although—as will be discussed—the quality and quantity of sources create the limits of this investigation. These circumstances all affect the framework and structure of the present research, which focuses on the aspects of the landscape and the spatial features of the monasteries created in the Pilis region.

---

[21] Belényesy (2004), *Pálos kolostorok Abaúj-Hegyalján.*

[22] See the selected literature from Beatrix Romhányi in the bibliography.

[23] Two main studies should be emphasized: Belényesi (2004), *Pálos kolostorok Abaúj-Hegyalján*; Andrea Kékedi, "Középkori pálos kolostorok környezetátalakítása a nagyvázsonyi történeti táj példáján" [The impact of medieval Pauline monasteries in the landscape on the example of the historical landscape at Nagyvázsony] (Master's thesis, Corvinus Egyetem Budapest, 2008).

1.1 The Pilis Forest: Natural and Historical Environment

Introduction – *Medium Regni* and *Rex Ambulans*

All of the features that defined Pauline monastic space have been best preserved in wooded areas, thus the Pilis Royal Forest is an ideal such area, which has been examined generally by Péter Szabó.[24] During the Ottoman occupation, this territory—just as the wider area of Buda—was destroyed and deserted, so the medieval state of the space survived until the end of the Ottoman period. From the turn of the seventeenth and eighteenth centuries this territory was resettled by Slavic (mainly Slovakian and Serbian) peoples, but the woodlands of the Pilis were respected, almost until today. This indicates that the settlement structure is—just as in the Middle Ages—diffuse. The road-network has largely changed in modern times, but the remains of the medieval *viae magnae* can be reconstructed.[25]

In the Middle Ages, the Pilis was regarded as highly important since it lies in what was called the *medium regni.* A recent analysis of this term—used in medieval written sources—emphasizes the change in its meaning, arguing that in the Árpádian Age it meant only the area around Buda (within a day's journey on horseback), the heart of royal and ecclesial power.[26] The characteristics of this *Residentslandschaft*[27]—from the point of view of governmental institutions and centrality—were identified in the nineteenth century as the following:

1. It is closely connected to important ecclesial centers, and
2. the constantly developing centers of the royal court;

[24] This summary is also based on his observations, most of the information was extracted from chapters ten through fourteen of Péter Szabó, *Woodland and Forests in Medieval Hungary* (Oxford: Basingstoke Press, 2005), 93–117.

[25] On this topic see Szabó (2005), *Woodland and Forests,* and also Beatrix Romhányi, "Pálos kolostorok a Pilisben" [Pauline monasteries in the Pilis], in: *Laudator Temporis Acti – Tanulmányok Horváth István 70 éves születésnapjára* [Studies for the seventeenth birthday of István Horváth], ed. Edit Tari (Esztergom: Balassi Bálint Múzeum, 2012), 223–227. In the English landscape, around rural monastic sites, these features are more visible, e.g., at Stavordale (Somerset), Old Warden (Bedfordshire), and Bordesley (Herefordshire & Worcestershire). Bond (1989), *Water Management,* 83. Also see Aston (1988), *Medieval Fishponds*, vol. 2.

[26] Benkő (2015b), "In medio regni Hungariae," 11–27.

[27] Klaus Neitmann, "Was ist eine Residenz? Methodische Überlegungen zur Erforschung der spätmittelalterlichen Residenzbildung," in: *Vorträge unf Vorschungen zur Residenzfrage*, ed. Peter Johanek (Sigmaringen: Jan Thorbecke, 1990), 11–43.

3. royal coronations and burials took place in its territory;
4. it was scattered with royal residences and houses where the kings were available on great Christian feasts.[28]

The *medium regni,* including the Pilis area, was surrounded by all of the important centers in medieval Hungary. Esztergom, the seat of the archbishop and an early royal center, is located to the northwest (1.).[29] To the southeast is Óbuda, which seems to have been the focal place of early Hungarian leaders and kings until the first half of the thirteenth century (2.); later it was replaced by the most significant town, Buda. Further, in one day's journey to the southwest, there is Fehérvár, the town of Saint Stephen, the coronation and burial place of most of the medieval kings of Hungary (3.). These were joined by Visegrád in the north, a smaller royal town, which had symbolic significance and could claim to be the capital of Hungary from the early fourteenth century until the beginning of the fifteenth, when King Sigismund (1387–1437) emphasized Buda as the capital[30] (see *Figure 1*)

Moreover, there were royal curiae and manors in the forest (4.) because of the contemporary royal institutional system: the Árpádian era was the time of the itinerant kingship[31] (*rex ambulans*), when there was no such thing as a capital of the Hungarian Kingdom. Instead "the king had repeatedly to reinforce and reaffirm his sovereignty over each particular urban or monastic community."[32] This system allowed the king to demonstrate his power in public by collecting

---

[28] Benkő (2015b), "In medio regni Hungariae," 11.

[29] György Györffy, *Az Árpád-kori Magyarország történeti földrajza* [A historical geography of Hungary in the Árpádian period], vol. 2, (Budapest: Akadémiai Kiadó: 1987), 246–247.

[30] Szabó (2005), *Woodland and Forests,* 87. Earlier on this topic: András Kubinyi, "A király és a királyné kúriái a XIII. századi Budán" [The curiae of the kings and queens at Buda in the thirteenth century], *Archaeologiai Értesítő* 89 (1962): 160–171; András Kubinyi, "Főváros, rezidencia és az egyházi intézmények" [Capital, residence and ecclesial institutions], *Magyar Egyháztörténeti Évkönyv* 1 (1994): 57–70; András Kubinyi, "Előszó. Az 'ország közepétől' a fővárosig" in: *Medium Regni*, ed. Júlia Altmann et al. (Budapest: Nap Kiadó, 1999), 5–8; András Kubinyi, "A királyi vár és lakói a középkorban." *História* 9-10 (2002): 14–18, (Last accessed: January 22, 2018), http://www.tankonyvtar.hu/en/tartalom/historia/02-0910/ch04.html.

[31] For more on this see John W. Bernhardt, *Itinerant Kingship and Royal Monasteries in Early Medieval Germany, c.* 936–1075 (New York: Cambridge University Press, 1993) and Dušan Zupka, *Ritual and Symbolic Communication in Medieval Hungary under the Árpád Dynasty* (1000 - 1301) (Oxford: Brill, 2011).

[32] Zupka (2011), *Ritual and Symbolic Communication*, 117.

taxes (mostly paid by crop!)[33] and accepting gifts of honor and oaths of loyalty, rewarding them with new prerogatives or privileges or by settling disputes. This "ritual of *adventus regis* ... represented interactive symbolic actions beneficial to both parties."[34]

The institution of itinerant kingship was present until the fourteenth century, but the roots of the changes lead us to the mid-thirteenth century. King Emeric (1196–1204) donated the royal palace to the archbishop first in 1198, with whom the Castle Hill was shared by the kings from the early ages of the kingdom. This donation was repeated later by King Andrew II and Béla IV (1256). From that time the transformation of a shared royal and ecclesiastical center to an ecclesiastical seat began. After the Mongol Invasion, King Béla IV (1235–1270) founded the town of Buda, today's Castle Hill. Before this period, Óbuda—was the highly preferred royal residence from the late twelfth century. In parallel with this change, the desperate need for a settled royal court arose.[35] This process led to the foundation of capitals and residences, as well as—by the donation of royal residences—the basics of a monastic network in the medium regni. Unfortunately, the lack of information on the meaning of the term in the fourteenth century brings uncertainty into scholarship, however, later King Matthias I (1458–1490) used *medium regni* as a geographical term by broadening the physical delimitations of it.[36]

Pilis, the Royal Forest County

Geographically the Pilis is bordered by the Danube on the north and east, forming a large inverted triangle (400 km^2). The longest side of the triangle (ca. 35 km) runs from the northwest to the southeast, along which lie the Pilis Mountains. Pilis Peak, which gave its name to the whole region, has been bare for a millennia, as shown by the presence of the rare, Ice Age relict flower, *Ferula sadleriana,* which has grown on it continuously since (at least) the latest Ice Age. This is interesting because the name Pilis has Slavic origins, meaning a bare, plantless

[33] Kubinyi (2002), "A királyi vár és lakói a középkorban".
[34] Zupka (2011), *Ritual and Symbolic Communication,* 117–118.
[35] Kubinyi (2002), "A királyi vár és lakói a középkorban".
[36] For more on the idea of *medium regni*, see the references in Benkő (2015b), "In medio regni Hungariae," 3.

area. Connecting the origins with the noticeable bareness of the mountain, an active Slavic presence should be noted here.[37]

Unfortunately, the medieval history of the Pilis area has many poorly documented periods. It is clear that this region was a royal forest throughout the existence of the Hungarian Kingdom. The origins of the medieval royal domains and forests of Hungary go back to the time of King Stephen I (997–1038), when he re-organized territories that were controlled by Magyar chieftains or were uninhabited and wooded areas of the Carpathian Basin beyond the defensive, boundary area, called "gyepűelve." King Stephen organized the administrative and military county system of the kingdom, as a result of which he owned more than seventy percent of the lands, including royal forests. The emergence of the royal county system happened parallel to the creation of the first bishoprics during the reign of King Stephen. As a result of this process, the Pilis area, except the surroundings of Visegrád and Esztergom, became part of the Veszprém Bishopric.[38]

It is unfortunate for the scholarship that the phases of this evolution can be only roughly reconstructed, because there is a lack of direct written evidence. At the same time, more recent archaeological excavations have already revealed clear evidence for the importance of the region in the Carolingian period. New finds from the Sibrik-hill site at Visegrád support the idea that a late Roman fortification at the site was not only reused from the turn of the tenth and eleventh centuries, but also in the ninth century. This aspect must have played a role in the emergence of an early, but short-lived, county with its center at Visegrád, mentioned for the first time in a charter in 1009.[39]

In written sources the term *silva* denoted both woodland and forest in Hungary, while *silva regalis* meant specifically a wood belonging to the king. These royal forests were more than oversized woods; like a Western-type forest (German

---

[37] There are no other remains or evidence for this, except the name of Visegrád on the Danube bank, which means "high castle" in Slavic language. Szabó (2005), *Woodland and Forests*, 93.

[38] Tivadar Ortvay, *Magyarország földrajzi leírása a XIV. század elején* [The geographical report of Hungary in the fourteenth century], vol. 1, (Budapest: s.n., 1891), 286–289.

[39] Gergely Buzás et al., "The Issue of Continuity in the Early Medieval Middle Ages in Light of the Most Recent Archaeological Research on the Late Imperial Period Fort in Visegrád," *Hungarian Archaeology*, (Spring 2014): 1–8, (Last accessed August 3, 2014), http://www.hungarianarchaeology.hu/wp-content/uploads/2014/05/eng_buzas_14TA.pdf.

Forst),[40] it was more of a legal category, which incorporated wooded areas, as well as settlements, meadows, and arable lands. This becomes clear in the first decades of the thirteenth century when the sources usually mention these areas in the context of the *comes* and *comitatus* instead of *procurator* and *praedium*. Moreover, these new counties lacked many characteristic features of regular counties, thus they have been termed forest-counties in modern scholarship. Unlike regular counties they did not incorporate other castle districts or properties; instead, several royal castles were built in the territory of the forest-counties in the thirteenth century, most of which existed until the end of the Middle Ages.

The Pilis was a royal forest from very early on, (though the area was partially under the authority of Esztergom County),[41] which is denoted by its first appearance in written sources: "a mention of it as the king's very own forest in 1187."[42] However, before this it was the private possession of the Árpádians, which is marked several times in written sources, e.g., by the foundation of ecclesial institutions in the eleventh century. King Andrew I maintained strong ties with the Byzantine Empire, thus he founded a Greek monastery near Visegrád (1055).[43] Also, a Benedictine nunnery was founded at Esztergom–Prímás Island by royal support around the mid-eleventh century;[44] and the provostry at Dömös was founded by Prince Álmos (1107), the brother of King Coloman (1095–1116) on a *regale allodium*.[45] These marginal foundations were followed by the presence

40 The origin of the concept of royal forests came from England and then travelled to the Continent. On English forests see Rackham (1996), *Trees and Woodland*.

41 Beatrix Romhányi, "Ceperuntque simul claustralem ducere vitam. A pálos rend és a Medium Regni kapcsolata" [The relationship of the Pauline Order and Medium Regni], in: *In medio regni Hungariae. Régészeti, művészettörténeti és történeti kutatások "az ország közepén"* [Archaeological, art historical, and historical research"in the Middle of the Kingdom"], eds. Elek Benkő and Krisztina Orosz (Budapest: MTA Régészettudományi Intézet, 2015), 756.

42 Szabó (2005), *Woodland and Forests*, 93.

43 Jennifer Lawler, *Encyclopedia of the Byzantine Empire* (London: McFarland, 2004), 44. On the excavations conducted there, see the Archaeological Database of the Hungarian National Museum: "Visegrád, Szent András monostor," (Last accessed: March 23, 2018), http://archeodatabase.hnm.hu/hu/node/14308.

44 Zsuzsa Lovag, *Az Esztergom-prímás szigeti apácakolostor feltárása* [The excavation of the nunnery at Esztergom-Prímás sziget] (Budapest: Magyar Nemzeti Múzeum, 2014).

45 A fourteenth-century chronicle relates that King Béla I (1060–1063) died when his throne collapsed on him at Dömös. For more on the research, see: László Gerevich, "Dömös," *Műemlékvédelem* 36 (1992): 73–80; also László Gerenvich, "The Royal

of the Cistercians. King Béla III (1172–1196) in 1184 founded a Cistercian monastery near Pilisszentkereszt,[46] which had a different property structure than the previously founded ecclesial institutions; it acquired small properties, while taxes, vineyards, and manufacturing—like glass-production[47]—partially supported its daily life. The foundation of the first western Christian monastery in the Pilis was followed by the three Pauline monasteries in the second half of the thirteenth century.[48]

The early history of the Pilis was dominated by a dense network of royal residences for the itinerant court beside the main residences; there is data that verifies the existence of hunting lodges or manor houses near Pilisszentkereszt (later the Cistercian abbey), Kesztölc[49] (later the Pauline Monastery of the Holy Cross), Pilisszentlászló[50] (later the Pauline Monastery of St. Ladislaus), and

---

Court (Curia), the Provost's Residence and the Village at Dömös,"*Acta Archaeologica Academiae Scientiarum Hungarica* 83 (1983): 385–409. Available online: Arcanum Digitális Tudománytár. (Last accessed August 3, 2014), https://adtplus.arcanum.hu/hu/view/ACTAARCHEOLOGICA_35/?pg=398&layout=s.

46 László Gerevich, *A pilisi ciszterci apátság* [The Cistercian Abbey at Pilis] (Szentendre: Pest Megyei Múzeumok Igazgatósága, 1984).

47 József Laszlovszky, "Ciszterci vagy pálos? A Pomáz-Nagykovácsipusztán található középkori épületmaradványok azonosítása" [Cistercian or Pauline? Interpretation of the medieval architectural remains at Nagykovácsipuszta, Pomáz], in: *A ciszterci rend Magyarországon és Közép-Európában* [The Cistercan Order in Hungary and Central Europe], vol. 5, ed. Barnabás Guitman (Piliscsaba: Pázmány Péter Katolikus Egyetem, 2009), 191–208; Laszlovszky et al., "The 'Glass Church' in the Pilis Mountains," *Hungarian Archaeology*, (Winter 2014): 1–11. (Last accessed: March 23, 2018), http://www.hungarianarchaeology.hu/wp-content/uploads/2015/01/Laszlovszky_E14T.pdf.

48 NB, the concept of a Cistercian monastery surrounded by eremitic communities was not unique here, Beatrix Romhányi, for example, emphasizes the presence of Carthusians near Cistercian abbeys, like near Léoncel in France. Romhányi (2015b), "Ceperutunque," 758.

49 *palatium ... quod habebat in insula de Pilisio pro venationis requie*. Gergely Gyöngyösi, *Vitae Fratrum Eremitarium Ordinis Sancti Pauli Primi Eremitae*, ed. Ferenc Hervay. Bibliotheca Medii Recentisque Aevorum. Series Nova IX. (Budapest: Hungarian Academy of Sciences, 1988), Cap. 18. István Méri identified some walls and carved stones from a building earlier than the monastery, that might be the remains of an earlier monastery or a royal manor. At the same time, Júlia Kovalovszki warned that the relationship between the two buildings might not be straightforward. Kovalovszki (1992), "A pálos remeték Szent Kereszt-kolostora," 173–207. Further archaeological research is needed for advanced conclusions.

50 *domunculum lapidea venationi regum preparata*. Györffy (1956), "Adatok," 284.

Pilisszentlélek[51] (later the Pauline Monastery of Holy Spirit). The existence of most of these residences that would become monasteries is based on written sources, but in the case of Pilisszentkereszt and Pilisszentlélek, their use as hunting lodges can be demonstrated by archaeological data.[52] Most likely these royal houses were operating next to the *clausura* because they were a suitable space for the royal court (See Holy Spirit Monastery, Chapter 2.2).[53]

It is almost unnecessary to highlight the beneficial aspects of being close to the king and his court on behalf of the monastic communities. However, from the perspective of sustenance, one aspect should be raised: the king could donate lands and properties only from his own possessions, which all had a very stable supply system—clearly an exceptional advantage. Therefore, these donations stabilized the first monasteries. The daily life of a newly founded community became sustainable and it has created a solid basis for the creation of a new order, the Pauline Order.

The Pilis had been transformed into a forest county by the thirteenth century, at the same time as the end of itinerant kingship. The first appearance of the *comes* of County Pilis is from 1225 and there is data for royal servants.[54] In 1285 we also find forest guards dwelling in Bogud.[55] Other people in the service of the king also lived in the area, with specializations preserved in place-names. Kovácsi, the settlement of the smiths, was north of Pilis Mountain. Fedémes, which was named after the bee-keepers, was located southeast from here. Peszérd, southeast of Esztergom, was the home of the royal dog-keepers and Solymár, further to the southeast, was probably where the falconers lived.[56] Not much is known about the physical extent of the forest; a part of its boundary was mentioned only once,

---

[51] Gyöngyösi (1988), *Vitae Fratrum*, Cap. 21. Archaeological excavations here also confirmed the presence of earlier buildings, possibly connected with royal manor houses. Lázár (1997), "A pilisszentléleki volt pálos kolostortemplom kutatása 1985-86".

[52] There are two additional places located by archaeological survey that may also have been hunting lodges. Szabó (2005), *Woodland and Forests*, 94.

[53] Benkő (2015a), "Udvarházak és kolostorok a pilisi királyi erdőben," 728–729.

[54] Szabó (2005), *Woodland and Forests*, 94.

[55] Ferdinand Knauz, *Monumenta Ecclesiae Strigoniensis,* vol. 2, (Esztergom: Horák, 1882), 192, 207; Györffy (1998), *Az Árpád-kori Magyarország történeti földrajza*, 583.

[56] Szabó (2005), *Woodland and Forests*, 94.

at Csaba, today's Piliscsaba,[57] but other data supports the idea that today's Pomáz to the southeast was located right next to the boundary as well.[58]

There was a change in this system by the thirteenth century, in the development of the forest county the role of the Pilis had changed—in parallel with the degression of itinerant kingship. The hunting lodges were all transformed into monasteries; first Cistercian, then Pauline. The Cistercians and the Paulines had a somewhat similar relationship with the Pilis Forest: the geographical position of the forest made it possible for the two orders to achieve a status peculiar to this region, since the Pilis was isolated enough to be an ideal traditional location for monastic orders, but at the same time the monasteries were within walking distance of the most important lay and ecclesiastical centers of the kingdom. The fact that all four of the monasteries located within the Pilis were royal foundations, as Péter Szabó states, demonstrates the royal interest in maintaining control over the monastic orders in the forest. The king himself visited these monasteries with his retinue, but "these places were more 'hotels' than 'residences.'"[59]

By the middle of the thirteenth century, Pilis County was no longer simply an economic unit but had symbolic significance. Its *comites*, very far from being keepers and administrators, received their titles as a sign of the royal *honor* and cared little about the woods. The Pilis was managed, in ways that are unknown to us, by lesser officers appointed by the *comites*. This tendency was in connection with the decreasing importance and role of the temporary residences and also the stabilization of the royal residences and therefore royal power, mainly the construction of the castle of Visegrád[60] by the wife of King Béla IV, Queen Mary, in the mid-1200s.

In 1259 Béla donated "the castle with county and district of Pilis" to the queen, which might have been motivated by the weak income of the county.[61]

---

[57] As *ubi separate de syluavestra Pilis vocata*. Perambulation of Csaba. György Fejér, *Codex diplomaticus Hungariae ecclesiasticus ac civilis*. vol. 5/2. (Buda: Regiae Universitatis Hungariae, 1829), 159–161.

[58] In 1278, Ladislaus IV donated the village of Pomáz to his daughter; Pomáz was located below the Pilis Forest (*sub silva Pilis*) next to *castrum cum comitatu et district de Pelys*. Cod. Dipl. vol. 5/2, 160, 446; Szabó (2005), *Woodland and Forests*, 94–95.

[59] Szabó (2005), *Woodland and Forests*, 95, 117.

[60] Szabó (2005), *Woodland and Forests*, 95.

[61] In 1263–1264 it was stated that the income of the county was less than fifty golden marcs; compared with the income of the provostry of Dömös, which was estimated around sixty marcs, this was a poor income indeed. Szabó (2005), *Woodland and Forests*, 94–95.

After the death of the last Árpádian King (1301), a new era commenced in the life of Visegrád and the surrounding Pilis Forest. Until the 1320s, however, Charles Robert, the new king, had more important issues to handle than the forests. At the same time, the importance of the region is well demonstrated by the fact that one of the most important aristocrats of the period, Máté Csák, ruled his almost independent territory from the castle of Visegrád. In a similar way, one of the most important political negotiations of this internal war period took place in one of the Pauline monasteries in the Pilis forest near Visegrád.

In 1323 Charles Robert moved the royal court from Temes to Visegrád. From this time until 1366 the castellans of Visegrád used the title of *comes* of Pilis, then they became less and less interested in the county and the castellans ceased to call themselves *comes*. There was probably no need to demonstrate royal power in the county, because it was overwhelmingly present. Alongside this system, noble magistrates were present from 1333, which was a sign of the new "noble" counties, serving as a balance to overwhelming royal influence and disregarding the symbolic power of the Pilis as a Royal Forest. The territory of the county started to grow in the fourteenth century, acquiring extensive territories south of its core area. Interestingly, King Sigismund addressed a letter to his apparently non-existing officers, the *comites*, and talks about *silva* nostra *Pilisiensis*, which still reflects thirteenth-century royal attitudes. In 1468 something similar was repeated by King Matthias, but this mandate was dedicated to the castellan of Visegrád and one reads about the woods of Visegrád. By the end of the fifteenth century, the royal forests had disappeared; Pilis County was united with Pest County sometime in the fifteenth century.

In addition to the general history of the kingdom, the dynamics of the area are visible through the settlement system and road network of the area. Medieval people usually settled in the valleys and in general did not inhabit the depths of the Pilis Forest (*Figure 3*). Although this might seem obvious, as Péter Szabó points out, the reasons behind it may be very complex. The most influential of these reasons was probably the existence of the royal forest; to reveal other reasons, however, multidisciplinary research is crucial—not just to attain a wider view, but as the sources relating to the earlier centuries are poor, archaeological-topographical research and spatial patterns are the basic sources.

Based on these sources, it can be observed that the dynamics of inhabited areas change through the centuries: there are many settlements in the eleventh century, and then the number decreases. This area with its hills and woods was not an exception to the general patterns of change in the medieval Hungarian

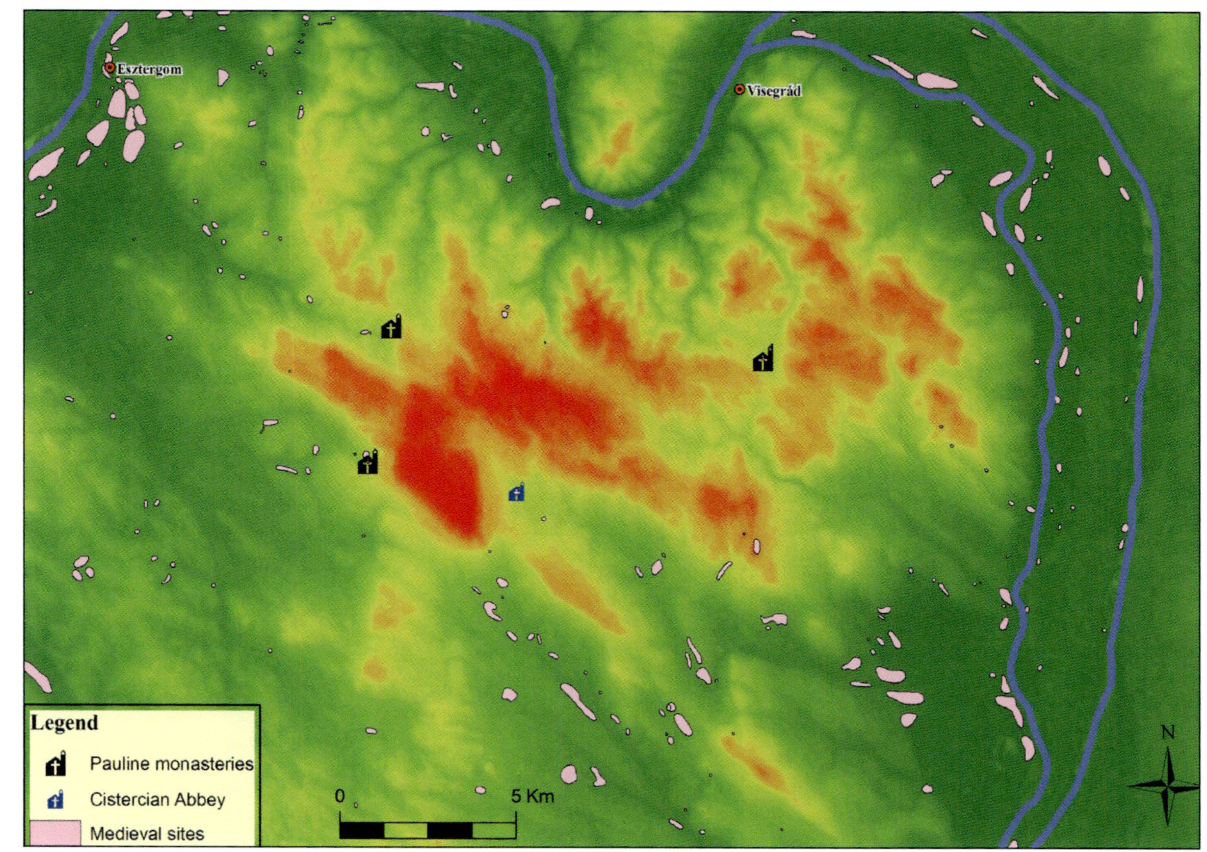

Figure 3. The known medieval sites from archaeological field surveys in the Pilis region. Map based on the digitization of all medieval sites from Torma, ed. (1979), Magyarország Régészeti Topográfiája 5, and Torma, ed. (1986), Magyarország Régészeti Topográfiája 7, based on an ASTER GDEM cut

settlement system. Many settlements disappeared in the thirteenth and fourteenth centuries—an overall trend in medieval Hungary—and also in Europe. However, there are two significant unique characteristics: contrary to other areas, where villages occupied hilly areas as well, here it cannot be demonstrated. Further, castles can typically be found on most peaks, as the hearts of private estates—such buildings were not erected on the peaks of the Pilis during the Middle Ages. Among the reasons for these attributes the most significant one is that originally the Pilis area was the king's royal forest, with a private royal function (that is hunting and representation).[62]

On the Danube bank some settlements were located where the Roman road had crossed the area. However, it is clear that the southern part of the Pilis Mountains was dotted with many more settlements that were close to the *via magna*, the geographically smooth main road between Óbuda (from the mid-1200s also Buda, which lies south of Óbuda) and Esztergom.[63] This spatial attribute is rarely associated with other features, like royal manor houses or monasteries.

Another piece of the medieval picture of the Pilis has been revealed, namely, data on the fauna. Generally, the Pilis, should have been covered with trees, although written evidence does not exist and quality maps are too late for present purposes. As archaeobotanical investigations and written sources suggest, walnut was probably well-represented and fruit trees were a specialty of the region. How intensive the management of orchards was is unknown, although there should have been many many types, from the gardens of the monasteries and royal residences to the presence of different fruit trees in the woods.

Spatial Approaches: Pauline Landscapes

After discussing various aspects of Pauline space and the unique background of the Pilis it is easier to address some previously proposed questions and develop

---

62 József Laszlovszky, "Agriculture in Medieval Hungary," in: *The Economy of Medieval Hungary* (Series: East Central and Eastern Europe in the Middle Ages, 450–1450, Volume: 49), ed. József Laszlovszky et al., (Leiden: Brill, 2018), 79–112. Hereby I would like to thank József Laszlovszky for his related suggestions and important notes.

63 Written sources mention 37 settlements. Many of them (18) existed long before their first appearance in written sources, as the archaeological evidence shows. There are many other sites containing household materials that can predominately be dated between the eleventh and thirteenth centuries. They were found by archaeological field surveys but cannot be dated precisely. The number of these unmentioned settlements decreases after the thirteenth century. Szabó (2005), *Woodland and Forests*, 106–107.

new ones concerning the correlation between Pauline landscape and the Pilis as historical region. The approach of the research will start from two points; first, the Pauline space itself has to be examined, then the known spatial developments and changes of the Pilis royal forest. Therefore, the framework has a minimum and maximum spatial resolution: from the entire Pilis to the smallest unit of a single monastery.

With this in mind, the main questions can be examined, namely: What was behind the Pauline foundations? What can their location inside the forest mean? In other words, what kinds of factors were taken into consideration in the site selection for individual monasteries, and in general, in the site selection process of the order? What is the correlation between site selection strategies and the known spatial features of the Pilis (settlements, roads, royal and ecclesiastical centers, other Pauline monasteries)? What other dynamic phenomena can be revealed by examining religious representation of royal power? Moreover, how did the regional role of each monastery change over time?

On the level of monasteries, their properties and spatial connections are discussed in this book, as well as their closest and direct features of supply. In connection with this, it is also a task of this study to record, list, and systematically analyze the spatial features around them. Thus, some of the features discussed here (archaeological, architectural, landscape, etc.) can reveal, how landscape and human-nature interaction have affected (in different time periods) the Pauline monasteries and influenced their particular monastic character? Which features of each historical period and spatial level of Pauline life are recognizable in the Pilis Forest? Finally, as a large and well-researched amount of background research is available for wider synthesis, accommodating the monasteries of the Pilis into known patterns will also result in the formulation of some general conclusions on the relationship between the order and the royal power. All of the questions and unclear areas within the Pauline research will be examined, and all available sources will be synthesized and combined; the results of these analyses will be presented in a time/space graph.

1.2 Sources and Methodology

Examining historical space means that all kinds of sources have relevance, but the organization of these sources requires a special methodological approach, which is affected by the research area. Probably the clearest way of studying Pauline monastic space is that the view point is generated by combining traditional sources (direct and indirect) and landscape archaeology, in which datasets are elaborated on a digital platform, on which the archaeological landscape analysis can be conducted.

The discipline of landscape archaeology uses a complex research method. It is based on both historical (written and pictorial) and environmental information (historical geography, climate history, geoarchaeology, etc.), utilizing direct (medieval) and indirect (early modern, modern) sources. This is a multidisciplinary approach, which—using archaeological survey techniques—also reveals information on past human-nature interaction. The following types of sources appear in the Catalogue, which focuses on the level of individual monasteries, collecting data for each of these communities separately.

One has to take into consideration that there is no well-founded protocol for spatial research in Hungary, applied to regional history and the environment; even the term landscape archaeology (Hungarian: *tájrégészet*) appeared after the millennium. Therefore, methodological solutions have to be imported at least occasionally from those areas of Europe where landscape archaeology has a long tradition. These solutions include both source types (environmental and historical) and the approach of spatial analysis as well. As was mentioned, research on the Pauline Order goes back for many centuries and a considerable amount of literature has been published on its history;[64] therefore, a critical selection and a strict ranking was essential during the working process, as using the most recent and critically evaluated material was the main intention. In the following chapter the different types of sources (written, pictorial, topographical, and archaeological) and methods will be summarized with an emphasis on those that are most helpful in the characterization of the Pauline monastic space in the Pilis.

Traditional Sources: Documents, Maps, and Archaeological Data

Traditionally, Pauline history has been assessed by economic, cultural, social, and political approaches, but less is known about the monastic space itself, although the basic sources are generally the same.[65] Contemporary charters contain chiefly legal data—perambulations, contracts, and other financial documents; therefore, the questions that scholarship posed were usually limited to estate and financial aspects until recently. However, the nature of this information also makes it the

[64] See Belényesy (2004), *Pálos kolostorok Abaúj-Hegyalján,* 88–91.

[65] Beatrix Romhányi was the last to highlight this, see her work Romhányi (2010), *Pálos gazdálkodás a középkorban,* 11.

basic source in landscape studies and among the several types of financial data one can find a considerable amount of thus far unassessed, direct and indirect spatial information (different types of properties, prices, locations of properties, and objects like mills, fishponds, roads, bridges, etc.). Moreover, it provides information about the daily routines of the friaries and monasteries of various orders, which, in turn, helps us to understand their roles and interactions in different situations.

Altogether about five thousand charters concerning the Pauline Order are available for research, but the chronological and geographical distribution as well as the quality of these documents are not balanced.[66] Additionally, not all of the data has been collected or interpreted, partly because there is no complete catalogue of the documents. Many of them were collected in the volumes of *Documenta Artis Paolinorum*,[67] but with special attention to art historical information, which has resulted in a lot of the data still being unknown. The data on economy has been gathered by Beatrix Romhányi in her articles and book (ca. 1000 charters[68]), but this also means that it is a selective collection.

Along with these documents three major sources help the research, all written in the sixteenth century.[69] The historical work of Prior General Gregorius Gyöngyösi,[70] called *Vitae Fratrum*,[71] is the best-known of these documents since his work was the first overall work on the history of the Pauline Order, based on original charters, legendaries, and breviaries. It is a typical work from the internal viewpoint of an order on its own history; besides important chronological data

---

66 Most of these documents are published, moreover, these source collections or the digital copies of the original charters are usually available online. See primary sources in the bibliography. Most of them are available online. *Digital Library of Medieval Hungary*. (Arcanum Hungaricana), https://archives.hungaricana.hu/en/charters/.

67 Gyéressy et al. (1975-1978), *Documenta Artis Paulinorum*.

68 Romhányi (2010), *Pálos gazdálkodás a középkorban*, 11.

69 The list is based predominately on the summary of Beatrix Romhányi, "Life in the Pauline Monasteries of Late Medieval Hungary," *Periodica Polytechnica* 43 (2012): 53–56.

70 For more on his life and activity see Gábor Sarbak, "Prior General Gregory Gyöngyösi and the History of the Pauline Fathers in the Early 16th Century," in: *Infima Aetas Pannonica: Studies in Late Medieval Hungarian History*, eds. Péter E. Kovács and Kornél Szovák (Budapest: Corvina Kiadó, 2009), 250–260.

71 Gyöngyösi (1988), *Vitae Fratrum.* The translation, published first Gregorius Gyöngyösi, *Arcok a magyar középkorból* [Faces from the Middle Ages], ed. Ferenc Hervay (Budapest: Szépirodalmi könyvkiadó, 1983).

and some anecdotes, the ancestors of the order (mainly prior generals) are the focus, whom Gyöngyösi marked as ideal monks for his contemporaries.[72]

This personal approach indicates two major problems with the source. First, the earlier biographies in the work are schematic and sometimes idealized, but even more problematic from the present perspective is that the solidity of the information decreases as Gyöngyösi describes earlier periods in the history of the Paulines.[73] Fortunately, there are other contemporary sources, both listed and not listed in the *Vitae Fratrum,* to confirm some of the information. In addition, it is important to note that some of the medieval charters and some other documents that Gyöngyösi used to compile his history of the order are only known from his text.

An inventory of the medieval charters (*Inventarium*), also compiled by Prior General Gyöngyösi, was partly published in the *Documenta Artis Paulinorum* series. In this collection, Gyöngyösi highlights only those aspects that are important from the Pauline Order's perspective and only mentioned information about already known properties. Therefore, he only listed charters that recorded real, existing properties of (both existing and abandoned) monasteries or the order in general in his time.[74] Comparing the surviving charters, the *Inventarium*, and *Vitae Fratrum*, historians have concluded that Gyöngyösi took many original documents in his hands, but that he also sometimes recorded false copies of charters, e.g., Slavsko Polje in Croatia.[75]

Another important early modern document, the *Formularium maius*—published recently by Beatrix Romhányi and Gábor Sarbak—was used from

---

72 Since there is no medieval evidence for the existence of Eusebius, at least not about his leading role in the foundation, except for in the *Vitae Fratrum*, Beatrix Romhányi argues that the character of Eusebius in the Pauline tradition is more likely a model of the ideal Pauline hermit. Romhányi (2008), "A pálos rendi hagyomány". The life of an ideal monk should be valued in terms of *devotio moderna*. Still, Eusebius, the canon of Esztergom, and his role is essential in the understanding of Pauline history.

73 Some historians (lay and cleric) have pointed this out. Elemér Mályusz, "A Pálos rend a középkor végén" [The Pauline Order at the end of the Middle Ages]. *Egyháztörténet* (1945): 1–53; also Elemér Mályusz, "Remeterendek" [Hermit Orders], in: *Egyházi társadalom a középkori Magyarországon*, [Ecclesial society in medieval Hungary] (Budapest: Akadémiai Kiadó, 1971), 254–274. Also see one of the most recent and detailed summaries of early modern Pauline sources: Beatrix Romhányi, "A pálos élet forrásai a középkorvégi Magyarországon" [Sources of the Pauline life in Hungary at the end of the Middle Ages], *Az Egyetemi Könyvtár Évkönyvei* 14–15 (2011): 323–330.

74 Romhányi (2011), "Pálos élet forrásai," 323.

75 Romhányi (2011), "Pálos élet forrásai," 324.

the 1530s by the secretary of the prior general, and also contains some specific information about the Pauline economy, hierarchy, and structure. During the office of Archbishop Péter Pázmány (1616–1637) the reprint of a fifteenth-century inventory of the Pauline monasteries and vicariates was printed (1629). The original of this edition, written at Marianka (present-day Slovakia; Hungarian: Máriavölgy, German: Mariathal) around 1470, lists 20 monasteries that were vicariate centers as well.[76] These sources also report the internal hierarchy and offices of the order, which follows the structure of the Austin order: the prior general is appointed every year on Pentecost, in the main cloister. The *diffinitor* or vicar is closest to the prior general and elected by a few monasteries. The *discretus* is elected by every cloister.

Most of these sources (from original charters to later summaries and catalogues) are well-researched,[77] so during the work it was possible to find reference points regarding sources and results on Pauline history and economy.

Besides written data, in a spatial topic it is definitely crucial to use modern (topographical) maps from the beginning of the twentieth century (for example the maps of the Unified National Map System[78]) and historical maps (especially the Habsburg Military Surveys of Hungary[79] and cadastral maps from the eighteenth and nineteenth centuries stored in the National Archives[80]) as basic

---

[76] Szentlőrinc, Nosztra, Diósgyőr, Gombaszeg, Lád, Újhely, Ungvár, Bereg, Kápolna, Szentmihályköve, Szentlászló (Baranya County), Told, Szentpéter, Garic, Remete (Zagreb County), Csáktornya, Gvozd, Örményes, Jenő, and Csatka. See the list in Péter Pázmány, *Acta et Décréta Synodi Diocesiana Strigoniensis* (Bratislava: 1629); the list is summarized in Ferenc Hervay, "Pálosok" [Paulines], in: *Magyar Katolikus Lexikon 10. kötet* [Hungarian Catholic Lexicon, Vol. 10], eds. István Diós and János Viczián (Budapest: Szent István Társulat, 2005), 484–489.

[77] Especially Romhányi (2010), *Pálos gazdálkodás a középkorban*, 2010.

[78] The so-called *Egységes Országos Térképrendszer* (EOTR), projection: 1: 10 000. Digitized map, 2010.

[79] *Első katonai felmérés: Magyar Királyság* [The First Military Survey: The Kingdom of Hungary], DVD, (Budapest: Arcanum, 2004); *Historical Maps of the Habsburg Empire – The Second Military Survey*. Österreichisches Staatsarchiv, Arcanum, Eötvös Loránd University, Metropolitan Archive, and Institute and Museum of Military History, 2014. http://mapire.eu/en/.

[80] During my research I used the online database of the Magyar Nemzeti Levéltár - Országos Levéltár, Térképtár [The National Archives of Hungary, Map Collection] (Arcanum Hungaricana) https://maps.hungaricana.hu/en/MOLTerkeptar/

sources. It is equally important to take into consideration the geological[81] and (historical/reconstructed) hydrological maps.[82] Sadly, other kinds of medieval pictorial sources are not available for the Paulines in the Kingdom of Hungary.[83]

However, contemporary visual sources of average hermits and the legend of St. Paul the First Hermit emphasize the image of the meditating men close to nature who live absolutely secluded from inhabited areas. This is true all around Europe, including Hungary. One such example, an important image of St. Paul, was found in the Abbey of Budaszentlőrinc on a fragment of a keystone.

Only one large-scale map depicting the whole country in the Middle Ages is available for my research. The scale of the Lazarus map (*Tabula Hungariae, Figure 4*) does not allow one to formulate a detailed image of the Pilis or Pauline monasteries, but it confirms the general landscape character of the area.[84]

Archaeological sources—the results of the excavations at the Monastery of the Holy Cross[85] and the Holy Spirit[86] and field surveys in connection with *The Archaeological Topography of Hungary* series[87]—partly revealed ruins of these monasteries. With the help of these volumes, the built structures, archaeological

---

[81] Digitized maps of the of the Magyar Állami Földtani és Geofizikai Intézet [Hungarian National Geological and Geophysical Institution], 2014 (Last accessed: May 5, 2018), https://map.mbfsz.gov.hu/.

[82] The reconstructed hydrological map of the Carpathian Basin is based on historical maps (eighteenth to nineteenth century), which were made before the river regulations, as well as on the plans of the regulations, (Budapest: Hungarian Royal Agricultural Ministry and Hydrological Institution, 1938). Available online in good resolution (Last accessed May 5, 2018), http://foldepites.files.wordpress.com/2009/12/5-karpat-medence-kesz-wo9.jpg.

[83] See Pic. 1, Archive of of Fővárosi Szabó Ervin Könyvtár [Metropolitan Ervin Szabó Library], online database of the *Exhibition on the Religious Life in Pest-Buda*, 2001. Organized by the Archive of the Metropolitan Ervin Szabó Library (Last accessed May 5, 2018), http://www.fszek.hu/kiallitas/webkiallitas/tablok/palos/palos.html.

[84] Lajos Stegena, ed., *Lazarus secretarius. The First Hungarian Mapmaker and His Work*, (Budapest: Akadémiai Kiadó, 1982). See the accepted application for UNESCO World Register (Last accessed: May 19, 2014), http://www.unesco.org/new/fileadmin/MULTIMEDIA/HQ/CI/CI/pdf/mow/nomination_forms/hungary_tabula_hungariae.pdf.

[85] See Chapter 3 (Catalogue), 3.2 Pauline monasteries in the Pilis, 1. Monastery of the Holy Cross.

[86] See Chapter 3 (Catalogue), 3.2 Pauline monasteries in the Pilis, 2. Monastery of the Holy Spirit.

[87] See István Torma, ed. *Magyarország Régészeti Topográfiája. Komárom megye régészeti topográfiája* [The archaeological topography of Hungary. The archaeological topography of Komárom County: Esztergom and Dorog districts], vol. 5, (Budapest: Magyar Tudományos Akadémia, 1979); Torma, ed. (1986), *Magyarország Régészeti Topográfiája* 7.

Figure 4. A cut from Tabula Hungariae by Lazarus. Online source, Arcanum – Hungaricana Database. Vas Megyei Levéltár [Vas County Archives] Reference code VAML T 541 (Last accessed: May 2, 2018) https://maps.hungaricana.hu/en/MegyeiTerkepek/5058/

material, and collected features in the landscape can be discussed and one can gather a lot of information on the daily life and spatial structure of monastic estates[88] Previous archaeological research was based on published and archival data,[89] the aim of this study is to follow up and verify the past results in the field, select new approaches, and find additional features of the landscape around the monasteries; therefore the catalogue summarizes both past and present data.

There are other types of sources and approaches that are important, but less relevant for this work; art historical and architectural information on the

---

[88] On the Monastery of the Holy Spirit see Lázár (1997), "A pilisszentléleki volt pálos kolostortemplom kutatása 1985-86," 493–518. On the Holy Cross see Kovalovszki (1992), "A pálos remeték Szent Kereszt-kolostora," 173–207.

[89] For instance, in the archive of the Hungarian National Museum some new essential data was found on the past landscape around the site of the Holy Cross Monastery. See István Méri (1959c). "Kesztölc-Klastrompuszta, pálos kolostor. Fotódokumentáció 1959" [Kesztölc-Kalstrompuszta, Pauline monastery. Photo documentation 1959]. Hungarian National Museum, Archive, II/1960/73.

monasteries are not represented in this book in a detailed way. There are two major reasons behind this decision. Published data from the Pilis area is only (and just partly) available for the Holy Spirit Monastery. At the Holy Cross Monastery some parts of the structure were revealed during excavations, but only a limited amount, and less detailed data is available for the ground-plan, building phases, and the internal structures of the buildings. In the case of the St. Ladislaus Monastery, the identification of its site is still problematic.

At the same time, a general picture of the architecture of Pauline monasteries has been formulated in a comparative study of the architectural heritage by Tamás Guzsik.[90] Since the posthumous publication of his work, much more new data has been published and modified—usually dramatically—the past viewpoint of the research.

The complex study of religious space demands a multi-disciplinary approach where historians, archaeologists, art historians, architectural historians, and other specialists have crucial roles. Isolated research and topics can produce an incomplete, or worse, a misleading picture.[91] Thus, there are several ways to summarize all of these approaches, and further, other forms of investigation (integrating monastic landscape studies, archaeological, and new archaeometrical data) can produce significant new results by re-summarizing ideas and revealing the different aspects of Pauline monastic tradition.

Monastic Landscape and Landscape Archaeology

Human-nature interaction has left marks and features on the landscape that are the basis for further historical investigation into politics, economy, and culture. The common denominator in this issue is space, where each type and detail has its own role. A spatial research approach can gather all the available information on human-nature interactions; for the present research topic, they are direct (medieval) and indirect (early modern, modern) sources investigated by historical (written and pictorial sources), archaeological, and environmental studies (historical geography, geology, historical climate, etc.). The spatial approach is an interpretational framework in this case. Some of the basic categories of this framework (site selection, distance, natural resources for monastic life, settlement network) were also important factors for the Pauline monastic community,

90 Guzsik (2003), *Pálos építészet.*

91 Bond (2004), *Monastic Landscapes*, 13.

therefore, the results of this perspective is closer to the perception of medieval people, and more can be understood about the features of the medieval world.

Almost all Pauline monasteries were founded in marginal areas of inhabited regions, in hidden, mid-hilly lands, close to streams and stream-heads; supposedly they were built on the remains of hermitages, close to the original dwellings of hermits, or at least in regions where early hermitages were documented in charters. However, the distance of the monasteries from habitation areas does not mean that they were secluded from the lay sphere and each other.[92]

This characteristic of the order was highlighted first by Tamás Guzsik, who not only contributed to the architectural research of the order but integrated a view in his studies that could be called a landscape archaeological perspective. Guzsik not only personally collected all available information about all the monasteries in present-day Hungary, but he usually had also drawn a sketch of the surrounding landscape. (*Figure 5*) His notes are highly appreciated in contemporary research since a lot of the monasteries had been unlocated until his survey or worse, had vanished since his documentation.

In the case of the Paulines in the Pilis forest, the landscape holds many important, though only partially revealed, historical features. Thus, in addition to gathering and visualizing the previous research, it is essential to find new spatial information concerning the potential and structure of the land. These existing elements are the physical remains and features of historical human-nature interactions in the medieval (and here monastic) space; most often they are so-called earthworks.

Around a monastery one can find typical spatial features: moats, dikes, fishponds, water supply leats and drains, wells and streams, remains of arable land, boundaries of woodlands and pastures, the remains of market gardening or the location of mills, other industrial buildings, and roads close to the monastery.[93] These earthworks are well-preserved on many sites in our research area; especially in the wooded, uninhabited areas of the Pilis many—until recently undiscovered—earthworks exist.

---

92 As Belényesy mentions concerning the Abaúj region, "all settlements can be reached within one-hour by walking, but generally the distance is not more than one to two kilometers. This is a symbolic separation from the secular environment, to which the community is linked in numerous ways." Belényesy (2004), *Pálos kolostorok Abaúj-Hegyalján*, 103.

93 On this topic see Bond (2004), *Monastic Landscapes*; and Bond (1989), *Water management*. On medieval fisheries and ponds see Aston (1988), *Medieval Fishponds*.

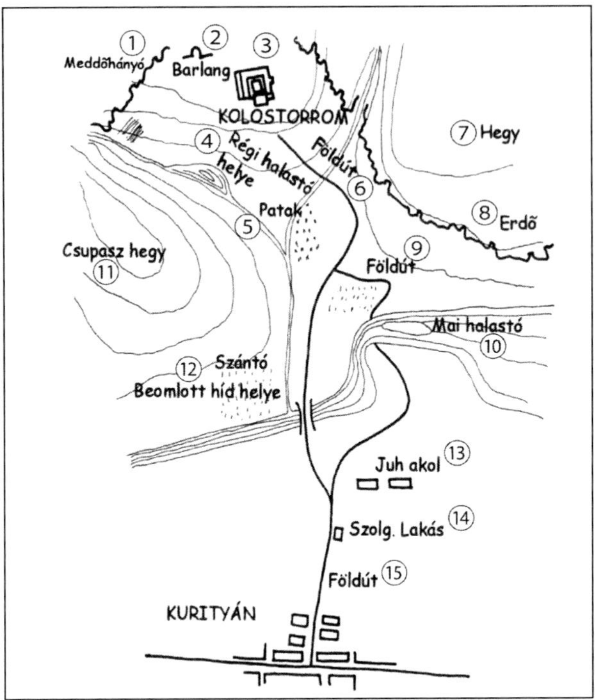

Figure 5. The remains of archeological and historical features in the landscape. 1.) Spoil heap 2.) Cave 3.) Monastery ruins 4.) Site of the old fishpond 5.) Stream 6.) Dirt road 7.) Hill 8.) Forest 9.) Dirt road 10.) Present-day fishpond 11.) Csupasz hill 12.) Plow land, site of the ruined bridge 13.) Pen 14.) Service accommodation 15.) Dirt road. Guzsik (2003), Pálos építészet, 129.

In England, for example, a great wealth of evidence related to spatial features survives from all kinds of sources. Landscape archaeological approaches and the concept of monastic landscape highly developed in scholarly studies in the United Kingdom are particularly important. The great wealth of evidence combined with other sources (pictorial, sites with earthwork features) can produce significant new results, particularly regarding spatial features. This richness of different types of sources has helped scholars to interpret complex elements and historical processes of monastic landscapes. Therefore, it is useful to give an overview of this research of the main elements of monastic space that survived there but that can also be correlated with features of the Pauline space in Hungary.

On the medieval monastic economy a few, mostly Western European, sources helped the research, especially in the use of ponds, fish species, or simply the ways of farming.[94] In this context, monastic landscape is one of the key issues. The basic concept of monastic landscape is built on the interaction of spiritual ideas and the material aspects of a monastic foundation, very much present in site selection and in landscape architecture. In other words, the creation of a monastic community in its natural setting and the transformation of the physical environment around it creates an interpretational framework for the landscape analysis. There are particular aspects that can be studied in this context with very good results. One of the most characteristic features of the monastic landscape is the complex use of water—the presence of varied forms of water management elements.[95] In his paper on water management James Bond summarizes that: "the basic requirements for the use of water were similar in all monastic establishments. In other respects, however, there are significant distinctions to be made."[96] The practice of water management was imported from the Cistercians at Clairvaux to the English landscape, where three main points should be highlighted as the framework of water supply systems.[97] At the same time, these particular features are relevant for different types of water systems in many other parts of medieval Europe.

As James Bond highlights, it was essential: (1) to bring water to areas where it was needed, (2) to make use of it for a variety of purposes, and (3) to remove water from places where it was not wanted. Also, the quality and volume of water were important, and sometimes it was necessary to draw water from more than one source.[98] Fishponds, dikes, streams, and springs formed a complex system

---

94 Bond (2004), *Monastic Landscapes*, 209, Figure 31, 32; Medieval Parks, Gardens, and Designed Landscapes. Article by Spencer Gavin Smith, posted (Last accessed November 17, 2013), http://medievalparksgardensanddesignedlandscapes.wordpress.com/2013/11/17/pond-life/; Article Old Babbling Carp. Carpiopedia, Last edited by Jerome Mois and 5 years ago, (Last accessed January 14, 2018), http://carpiopedia.pbworks.com/w/page/15277490/Article%20Old%20Babbling%20Carp%20-%20Part%202.

95 Bond (1989), "Water Management," 100–101; Csilla Zatykó, "People beyond landscapes: past, present and future of Hungarian landscape archaeology," *Antaeus* 33 (2015), 378.

96 The Cistercians developed a complex system of pond and leat; "their regulations recommended their monasteries to be built by streams which could be harnessed to provide power for mechanization." Bond (1989), "Water Management," 83–85.

97 Bond (2004), *Monastic Landscapes*, 198–199.

98 It could happen that although streams were adequate for filling fishponds, they were not always pure enough for drinking; in these cases wells and springs served as sources. Bond (1989), "Water Management," 85.

in the English landscape, which has been studied intensively since the 1950s.[99] "Natural watercourses had to be diverted out of the valley bottom, dams had to be built, sluice gates made and feeder and overflow leats constructed. Small ponds sometimes were constructed immediately above larger ones to serve as silt-traps."[100] Fish and fisheries throughout the medieval period were almost as important as forestry and more important than hunting. It was even more important for monastic communities, as fasting and other dietary restrictions were often related to fish. English research has made many efforts to reveal as many features of fresh-water fisheries as possible; the results are that the acquisition of a water supply could be achieved in a variety of ways.[101] Monastic water management was a typical practice in medieval Europe, thus, it can also be studied in the context of Hungary in the Middle Ages. Here just the types that are connected to the Pauline sites in the Pilis are mentioned.

The characteristics of valley ponds are also present in the area, such features are also typical in the hilly zones of the Pilis. In a steep-sided valley, a strong dam creates a classic reservoir pond, which demands careful provision for floodwater control (floods will produce a greater volume of water, which can result in a dangerously accelerated speed of water flow, which can then cause damages). Here the size, depth, and degree of the pond's exposure to shade or sun (therefore the average temperature of the water) basically modifies the usage and the particular function of these mane made structures.[102]

Much is known about the structure of these ponds as well (*Figure 6*); they were dug into the sub-soil and puddled, i.e., covered with layers of clay or sometimes wood (usually elm). Usually two types, surface or sub-surface, of water inlets and outlets were constructed, controlled by sub-surface sluices (made from wood). It was essential for all pond systems for rearing fish that the excess water be drawn off not from the depths of the pond, but from the surface, or if a pipe was used, that screens should be installed.[103] Regarding the water supply, pure fresh water(as from a spring) is best for incubation, but water rich in nutrients and washing

---

[99] B. K. Roberts, "The Re-discovery of fishponds," in: *Medieval Fish, Fisheries and Fishponds in England,* ed. Michael Aston (Oxford: British Archaeological Reports, 1988), 9.
[100] Bond (2004), *Monastic Landscapes*, 203.
[101] Bond (1989), "Water Management," 85.
[102] Roberts (1988), "The Re-discovery of fishponds," 10–11.
[103] Roberts (1988), "The Re-discovery of fishponds," 12–13.

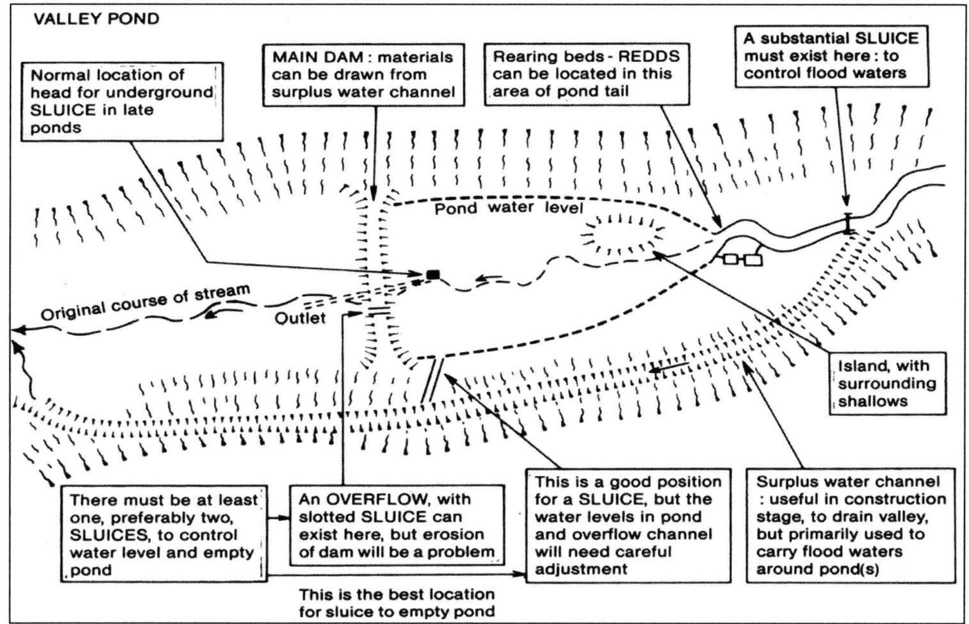

Figure 6. The valley pond. Roberts (1988), "The Re-discovery of fishponds," 11.

in from fields is the best for producing fish in larger quantity in these ponds.[104] Aeration is easily achieved by small falls, especially in hilly areas. Summarizing the background of such solutions, James Bond emphasizes that "the slope of the ground and the alignment of existing natural water channels or potential drain courses was one of the fundamental considerations in monastic planning," but it was also not unusual for artificial watercourses to lead off of natural streams.[105]

There are typical problems that have been recognized in the English scholarship, which are relevant in this region as well. As C. C. Taylor points out,[106] the cloudy origins and development (as well as construction and operational details) of water management systems create research problems, mostly attached to fishing.

[104] Roberts (1988), "The Re-discovery of fishponds," 13.

[105] Bond (1989), "Water Management," 91. On the use of canals and rivers see Bond (1989), "Water Management," 97–98.

[106] C. C. Taylor, "Problems and Possibilities," in: *Medieval Fish, Fisheries and Fishponds in England,* ed. Michael Aston (Oxford: British Archaeological Reports, 1988), 465–474. He also mentions a problem that might be interesting in the context of the Paulines in Croatia or Dalmatia, namely, the question of sea-fishing. In England, he argues, river fishing, ponds, and weirs tend to obscure the importance of sea fishing.

The typology should also be gathered and unified with special attention to form, siting, and complexity. Associated functions may also differ; in Hungary, mills were mostly attached to water management systems, but in England, individual millponds were often located beside fishponds.[107]

Detailed and complex analyses (on topics such as the construction of fishponds through artificial watercourses, the disposal of waste with historical and archaeological approaches, and specific fishes,[108] etc.[109]) are available from all over in England, as the last overall publication on the topic demonstrates, edited by one of the most active researchers in this field, Mick Aston.[110] Hungarian scholarship still stands far from this kind of complex research approaches, but there are already good signs in the publication of such approaches more and more regularly. Besides water management studies,"various other ways of landscape exploitation and the monks' impacts on the environment are among the subjects of monastic landscape studies that have been conducted only in the past decade in Hungary. Excavations, field surveys and GIS analyses have exposed several fishponds, agricultural terraces and roads, and remains of industrial activities such as evidence for glass production related to the grange of the Cistercian monastery at Pilis."[111]

In the case of the Paulines of the Pilis, the natural and often symbolic (ref. *desertum*) elements of hermitages (caves, stream-heads/wells) also play a unique role in the landscape, especially in the relevant archaeological findings that correlate with the timeframe of this study. These features defined not only the hermits' living-sphere, but also their symbolic meaning, as they were identified with hermits even in the late Middle Ages.

---

[107] Bond (2004), *Monastic Landscapes*, 203.

[108] Interestingly, carp reached England only in the 1460s, coming from the Danube basin. Bond (2004), *Monastic Landscapes,* 205.

[109] Bond (1989), "Water management," 101–102; Bond (2004), *Monastic Landscapes*, 204–210.

[110] Michael Aston, ed. (1988), *Medieval Fish, Fisheries and Fishponds;* also Michael Aston, *Monasteries in the Landscape*. (London: Tempus, 2000).

[111] Zatykó, "People beyond landscapes," 378. For further literature and references see: Laszlovszky (2004), "Középkori kolostorok a tájban"; also Laszlovszky et al. (2014) "The 'Glass Church'".

Collecting data from various sources is not an easy task, therefore gathering and properly documenting the monastic landscape features was the first crucial task of this work. As these spatial features are just starting to play an important role in the next level of interpretation in Hungarian scholarship,[112] there is no strict, well-prepared protocol for documentation. Thus, this work can also be regarded as an experimental method of recording such spatial features (see the Catalogue).[113]

All sites for which information is available are incorporated into this study. They are sites, which consist of the relevant data for different resolutions of the medieval space to be explored. This dataset operates with different spatial levels (scale of the site or of the archaeological feature) of information. Besides the spatial level of earthworks, the study area offers valid information in other spatial frameworks as well. They represent different scales, from the level of the artifacts to the entire Pilis forest itself (e.g., regarding the role of medieval road network and settlement structure).The monasteries and their surroundings represent only one part of the whole documentation. The main problem to solve is that this data represents various levels of everyday life, and also dates to different time periods. An important methodological question has to be posed: how can such a varied and manifold dataset, containing information on different spatial levels, be managed within a unified yet flexible model?

The different origins and scales of the research material make it essential to create a manageable framework of datasets. If the space is separated into various levels on the basis of a spatial approach, each level can represent a distinct chance for a historical examination of already revealed or new phenomena, problems, and questions.

The observable medieval space here has five spatial levels (*Figure 7*). The structure of the data—the background of the approach—starts with the smallest physical objects (archaeological material) and ends with the Pilis area, but the

---

[112] See on this Laszlovszky (2004), "Középkori kolostorok a tájban"; also Romhányi (2010), *Pálos gazdálkodás a középkorban,* 11.

[113] Moreover, these spatial earthworks in Hungary play only a minor role in cultural heritage, even though their validity as heritage sites is the same as other sites. The documentation and registration of these elements are important from this perspective as well.

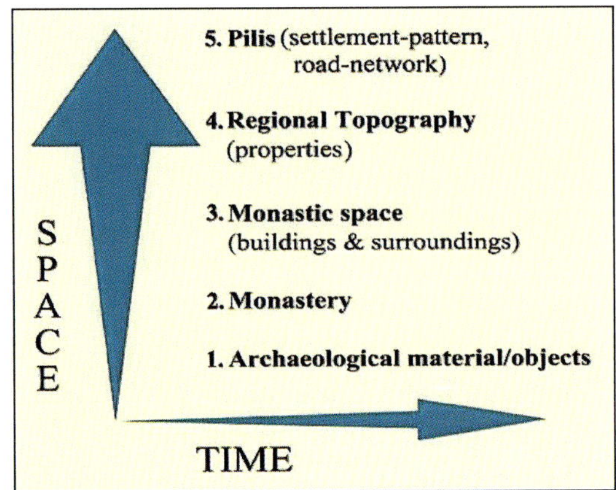

Figure 7. The structure of spatial levels, which is used in the study

focal point of this system is on the level of the monastic space (Level 3).[114] This system leads to viewing the results in two major ways: from a local (Level 1–3) and a regional perspective (Level 4). Regional topography (Level 4) contextualizes the framework of monastic space through the spatial location of a monastery or group of monasteries (with their surroundings or other properties) in the light of the contemporary topography.

The interpretation of the whole Pilis region (Level 5) is also possible. It can be seen as a geographical unit and also as a monastic cluster within the region.[115] In reference to the latter, Pauline monasteries can be handled as clusters, regional units, in which each monastery had its own status or role in the local hierarchy: according to the internal organization of the order (which is known from written sources) the most influential community of every four to six neighboring monasteries appointed a vicar who became the leader of the vicariate.[116] The monasteries in the Pilis were regulated by the vicar and prior general of St. Lawrence Monastery, near Buda.

[114] Archaeological and architectural sources (Level 1–2) are indirect sources for our work. It is essential to study the objects and finds from the monasteries, but further investigations and collection of new data are not the task of this work.

[115] The numbering of the levels from 1 to 5 represents that more spatial levels can be added to this system; e.g., 6 as a wider region, like the Pilis-Börzsöny area together, or the central part of modern Hungary. This study claims and will demonstrate that in the context of a microregion (a wider geographical unit), especially the mid-hilly areas, the introduced spatial system would work well.

[116] Belényesy (2004), *Pálos kolostorok Abaúj-Hegyalján,* 104–105; based on Mályusz (1971), "Remeterendek," 259.

This Pauline spatial unit of the Pilis is more likely to be regarded since the medieval historical and legal boundaries of the Pilis area changed through the centuries, sometimes encompassing the entire Pilis as a geographical unit, sometimes not—written sources do not define the physical framework of the Pilis royal forest. The details are also unclear because there is a lack of contemporary sources on the topic.[117]

How can one can apply these approaches to find all of the discoverable and relevant features of monastic space, collect them into an appropriate database, and synthetize the information? After gathering the available historical and pictorial sources—and particularly maps—archaeologists conducting a traditional archaeological field survey explore the territory using a photo machine and GPS (Global Positioning System) and record the status and location of archaeological features. Such targeted field surveys were made several times at the monasteries of the Holy Cross and Holy Spirit, and partially at Pilisszentlászló.

If there is an opportunity to use more precise methods in addition to the GPS-based survey of earthworks, optionally the local terrain may be digitized, or, in unique cases, other remote sensing techniques may be utilized (satellite images, LiDAR, etc.) in order to create a precise terrain model. In the Pilis, in addition to using a GPS unit on each survey, at one of the sites the digital surveying of the spatial features was done with total station (focusing on a fishpond and two dikes, as well as the eastern area of the ruins, where the downhill part of the terrain begins in the direction of the fishpond). Currently—as opposed to the first studies in this field in the 1970s[118]—the methodology is based on a digital platform, so all information is uploaded into a GIS (Geographical Information System) database. This process starts with recording the spatial data from primary sources (charters, descriptions, maps, and archaeological data) and ends with uploading information on the features surrounding the sites.[119]

---

[117] In these circumstances, Pilis means a geographical territory and for historical units the exact terms are used (e.g., Pilis County, Royal Forest, etc.); see previous discussion on the issue in Chapter 1.1.

[118] The definition of landscape archaeology (within which the monastic space is interpreted) was first used by Mick Aston and David Rowley in their principle book, *Landscape Archaeology* (Newton Abbot, London, Vancouver: David & Charles, 1974). In the work they dedicated individual chapters to field techniques and to the organization and application of fieldwork.

[119] The demo version of ArcGIS Software (ESRI) was used to develop the database and to do trials on the area.

A Digital Application of Sources

At this point it has to be underlined that the sources and methodology are closely related to each other. GIS not only serves as a database of the digitized and visualized spatial data, but it is possible to develop further analytical methods and models within this system.[120] Despite the fact that most of the valuable geostatistical methods are based on (digital) elevation/terrain maps and that the more detailed the available model is, the more successful the analysis will be, all other layers (spatial datasets, maps) also contain spatial information. With the help of different methods (digitizing, georeferencing, etc.) these layers can be overlapped with each other, helping to find new spatial connections between various maps on a digital desktop. Features, unknown earthworks, or simple spatial connections can be revealed in this way, which might also have correlating data in medieval written sources.

During this work, the spatial information was extracted from all the available modern and historical maps,[121] but only the following maps were georeferenced (i.e., invested with real geospatial data) with a selection of the listed data:

- tourist/hiker map from the beginning of the twentieth century[122] (concerning the whole Pilis area):
  - streams, lakes, springs (also the modern route of the Danube)
  - caves
  - mills (or names that contained the definition)
  - other names and objects of note
- map of the Unified National Map System (projection 1: 10 000, concerning the whole Pilis area):
  - streams, lakes, springs
  - caves
  - other names and objects of note
  - modern highways and pathways
- First and Second Ordnance Surveys of Hungary (concerning the monasteries and monastic space, *Figure 7,* Level 3):

[120] For further examples see Mark Gillings and David Wheatley, *Spatial Technology and Archaeology: the archaeological applications of GIS* (CRC Press: London and New York, 2002).

[121] See the precise references of the sources in the subchapter Traditional Sources.

[122] Digital version of a Reprint (1928) by Honvédelmi Minisztérium [Ministry of Defense] (Budapest: Zrínyi Carthographical Public Company, 2007).

  - roads
  - some types of land management: arable lands/vineyards
  - remains of water management: mills, ponds, streams
- maps from the *Archaeological Topography of Hungary* (all of the medieval sites in the Pilis region were digitized, which is the basis of the settlement structure)
- several historical maps were not drawn well enough for georeferencing, but information was extracted from some of them, e.g.:
  - cadastral map of Pilisszentlélek from 1788, stored in the National Archive[123]
  - cadastral maps of Pilisszentlászló from the eighteenth century, stored in the National Archive[124]

Additional spatial data that was integrated includes:[125]

- digitized terrain and features (total station and GPS unit) around the monastery at Kesztölc[126]
- digitized features (GPS unit) around Pilisszentlélek and the Holy Spirit monastery[127]

Based on these layers (see *Figure 8*), further (geostatistical) analyses and models can be developed, but for every analysis, a precise digital geographical and elevation map or model (DEM) is essential. The open source layers are quite accurate (accurate in 30 meters at best), which is sufficient for middle or large scale tests. With a DEM, slope inclination and slope aspect are measurable on the selected area, just as the landscape units and slope classes can be identified. The potential sources of water supply and past stream channels can be identified on the basis of a potential drain density model (pdd), which uses a combination of slope inclination with optimal flow direction, based on the terrain. As this model requires a precise terrain model as a basic layer, in this work this was used only for a control and as a test version for the Pilis region. Based on the author's previous observations, this model with the present accuracy of the terrain model

[123] S 12 Div IX No 0099.

[124] Reference numbers: S 11 No. 30; S 86 No. 1; S 86 No. 2; S 86 No. 4; S 86 No. 5; S 86 No. 6.

[125] See the details in Chapter 3 (Catalogue), 3.2 Pauline Monasteries in the Pilis.

[126] By Katalin Tolnai and András Harmath.

[127] By the author.

Spatial Level	Original Source	Digitized Features	Analysis (based on ASTER GDEM)
Pilis (Level 5) - Road-network* - Medieval settlement pattern** - Terrain - Hydrology	Archaeological Topography of Hungary***	• Archaeological features of the land (medieval settlements, cloisters, roads, boundary marks, etc.)	• *pdd* (potential drain density) • LCP (Least Cost Path)
	First Military Survey of Hungary	• Main roads • Control for hydrological features	
	Second Military Survey of Hungary	• [Main roads] • Control for hydrological features	
	ASTEG GDEM	• Digital Elevation Model (DEM)	
	EOV/ Unified National Map System	• Natural features (streams, caves, springs, mills) • Roads	
Regional Topography (Level 4)	Historical Maps and Maps by Unified National Map System	• Look for spatial features	
Monastic Landscape (Level 3)	ASTEG GDEM	• Digital Elevation Model (DEM) for modelling	• *pdd* (potential drain density)
	Digitized terrain	• Documentation, • Basis for further researches	
	First Military Survey of Hungary	• Main roads • Control for hydrological features	
	Second Military Survey of Hungary	• Main roads • Control for hydrological features	

* Torma, ed. (1979), *Magyarország Régészeti Topográfiája* 5 and Torma, ed. (1986), *Magyarország Régészeti Topográfiája* 7; Benkő (2011), *"Via regis,"* 115–119; Ferenczi et al. (2013), *"Történeti útvonalak kutatása a Pilisben."*

** The medieval (Árpádian Era, Late Medieval, Medieval) settlement pattern was reconstructed on the basis of the digitized result of *Archaeological Topography of Hungary*, where the scholars gathered all the available written evidence on each site; although this happened many decades ago, there is no significant change in the identification of the medieval settlement, which could modify this picture dramatically. I corrected the information only once, concerning the grange of the Cistercian Abbey at Pomáz-Nagykovácsipuszta site, where archaeological research identified the glass product workshop and a complex water management system around it, which served the Abbey.

*** Torma, ed. (1979), *Magyarország Régészeti Topográfiája* 5 and Torma, ed. (1986). *Magyarország Régészeti Topográfiája* 7.

Figure 8. Used sources on digital platform on each spatial level

can be used successfully in flat and hilly regions; the Pilis is not an ideal place for this.

In the mid-hilly area of the Pilis, a Least Cost Path (LCP) analysis, which measures the shortest and easiest way between two points, was used successfully. It is based on a cost distance analysis, on the basis of the distance and the energy that is needed to take the path (calculated on a digital elevation model by slope categories). The irregular terrain decreases the inaccuracy of the model, which is caused by the mid-/low resolution of the DEM.

Lastly, the digitization of the terrain has to be emphasized. This gives us a unique opportunity to examine some of the geographical conditions and circumstances of establishment, development, and approximate capacity of these fishponds and dikes. However, if this method stands alone it can mislead the results, because simply measuring and recording the condition of the earthworks in their present-day form cannot be valid for medieval times. Geodesy and digitization are just the first step to further research, mainly with geoarchaeological approaches, which are, moreover, essential regarding heritage preservation and management of these lands.[128]

All these new landscape approaches, which have a short-term tradition in Hungary,[129] can influence the image of the Pauline Order and can reveal many new elements concerning the connection between the Pauline political role, character, and economic traditions. As the most important spatial and landscape factor, the Pilis royal forest could have a strong effect on this whole medieval (economic, political, and evidently spatial) spatial organization system. With the help of a wider spatial approach, as described above, royal and Pauline relations can have a new or re-contextualized meaning, as well as a spatial framework. Moreover, new elements can be revealed of the medieval daily life of the Paulines by a better understanding of their perception and usage of space, and by a new interpretation of their monastic landscape and world.

---

[128] On the topic see József Laszlovszky, "Az Európai Táj Egyezmény és a hazai tájrégészet," [The European Landscape Convention and the national landscape archaeology] *Műemlékvédelmi és Építészettörténeti Szemle* 52/2 (2008): 101–104.

[129] See Laszlovszky (2004), "Középkori kolostorok a tájban."

2. Shaping Pauline Space

The aim of this study is to answer some key research questions and to summarize and visualize the evolution of the character of the Pauline Order at different levels of space in the Pilis: from the basic spatial organization of the smallest monastic estate to their role in the entire area of the main royal forest of the Kingdom of Hungary (see *Figure 1*) The location of the monasteries at the largest scale (Level 5) of the research is examined considering the supposed settlement pattern, road network, properties, and geographical (terrain and hydrology) sphere.[130]

The regional topography (Level 4) uses the same features of the historical space, but the focus is on a smaller picture: on the known estates and properties of the monasteries outside the basic monastic space—spatial research may highlight their unique or common relationship with the owner monastery. At this level a main point of the research is to examine the relationship between the monasteries in the Pilis, in order to learn more about the original idea behind their settlement. A spatial adaptation of local features (Level 3) informs us about the monasteries (individually), their closest sphere, and properties (buildings, workshops, features of the water management system, etc.). In the following, the spatial analysis is conducted according to the indicated structure of space and the geographical and historical spatial features in chronological order.

2.1 The Impact of Pauline Monasticism and Economy on the Landscape

The Core of the Early Eremitic Communities in the Pilis – Location and Land Management

The Order of St. Paul the First Hermit is the only order of Hungarian origin, and according to the order's tradition they first emerged in the Pilis forest. According to the tradition, Eusebius, a canon of Esztergom, gathered the hermits who lived in the Pilis and founded the first hermitage near the hidden caves at the later Holy Cross Monastery (present-day Kesztölc-Klastrompuszta),[131] which

[130] For more on the sources see *A Digital Application of Sources* in Chapter 1.2.

[131] The unification of the secluded clerics was not an unusual phenomenon in those times; in other regions, such as the Mecsek or Bakony regions, hermitages were founded even before the 1250s (when the hermits founded their first community in the Pilis). Belényesy (2004), *Pálos kolostorok Abaúj-Hegyalján,* 88.

was also constructed by his initiative around the 1250s.[132] In the Pilis (and in other regions as well) hermitages were founded in hidden, mid-hilly areas (the sources refer to these places as *desertum*[133]), as the Pauline tradition says, secluded from the lay sphere and closely connected to nature (near caves and springs, which were always crucial), with the difficult goal of "forgetting the world and by the world forgot."[134]

It is certain that the Pilis has many features that supported hermit life; e.g., many small caves are hidden in the region and at least three of them—just nearby the Holy Cross Monastery—can be associated with the Pauline order,[135] or more likely with the hermits who might have lived there unorganized, long before the foundation of the monastic communities. These features also reflect the Pauline tradition. The Holy Cross Monastery itself, near the caves, should have been founded a few years later than the early modern sources suggest, between 1263 and 1291 (though certainly closer to the earlier date).[136] According to the early

---

[132] Gyöngyösi (1988), *Vitae Fratrum,* Cap. 8.

[133] The concept of "desert-forest" was developed by Jacques Le Goff, see Belényesy (2004), *Pálos kolostorok Abaúj-Hegyalján,* 88; and Jacques Le Goff, "Le desert-forêt dans l'Occident medieval," *L'imaginaire medieval* (Paris: Édition Gallimard, 1985). For a summary on the earliest monasteries of the desert fathers and the English research, see Aston (2000), *Monasteries in the Landscape*, 29–42.

[134] It is also true that the location of monasteries is unpredictable, because human sanctity is spontaneous, it "erupts wherever the spiritual urge is felt." Butler (1989), "Archaeology of Rural Monasteries," 1.

[135] Szabó (2005), *Woodland and Forests*, 116.

[136] In 1263 Paul, the bishop of Veszprém, listed the existing hermit communities in his diocese (in which this part of the Pilis region was integrated). He does not mention the Holy Cross, not even other monasteries but the next inventory, written in 1291, does mention it (with the St. Ladislaus Monastery). There was a long debate in the scholarship about the reason for the Holy Cross Monastery being missing from the earlier inventory, while the tradition says that the monastery has been already founded by that time. Also, the precise identification (the contemporary name) of the monastery was questioned, but finally László Solymosi disproved many of these debates and articulated the date of foundation to 1263–1291. See László Solymosi, "Pilissziget,"vagy Fülöpsziget? A pálos remeteélet 13. századi kezdeteihez" [Island of Pilis or Philip Island? Additions to early Pauline hermit life in the thirteenth Century], in: *Emlékkönyv Orosz István 70. születésnapjára*, eds. János Angi and János Barta Jr. (Debrecen: Debrecen University Press, 2005), 11–23; also Laszlovszky (2009), "Ciszterci vagy pálos?" However, all this cannot exclude the inhabitance of caves or huts at the site before 1263, because hermits could live there unorganized until they were unified as an order.

modern tradition of the order, in 1270 the first general provost was elected in the Holy Cross Monastery,[137] which is a clear sign of the monastery's leadership over the hermit movements, which existed much earlier, since the beginning of the thirteenth century.

Besides the Holy Cross Monastery, the St. Ladislaus Monastery was founded by 1291 as well, as the second inventory of the Veszprém diocese mentions them.[138] More precisely, as József Laszlovszky argues—and with whom the author completely agrees—this could have been a foundation of King Ladislaus IV (1272–1290).[139] The Holy Spirit Monastery might have existed as a sub-cloister of the Holy Cross Monastery,[140] as it was founded in 1287,[141] but was not listed in 1291.

In addition to the hermit origins, one other feature is emphasized by scholars, namely that the monasteries in the Pilis were founded on the basis of royal "hunting lodges," as the secondary literature defines these royal properties, which were used, e.g., as *palatium* in the sources.[142] This is a key to understanding why the locations of the Pauline monasteries show that the traditional hermit schema cannot apply to the case in the Pilis; although they were situated in a wooded area, in the valleys between the mountains (and this phenomenon is a general

---

[137] Gyöngyösi (1988), *Vitae Fratrum*, Cap. 13.

[138] The monastery was listed in the second inventory of the Veszprém bishopric in 1291. Gyöngyösi (1988), *Vitae Fratrum,* Cap. 10, also 17. Charter evidence mentioned in Györffy (1956), "Adatok," 285; Györffy (1998), *Az Árpád-kori Magyarország történeti földrajza* 4, 700; Torma (1986), *Magyarország Régészeti Topográfiája* 7, 167.

[139] This is because the contemporary tradition was to give the founder's name, especially the king's name, to the monastery (e.g., the St. Andrew Monastery at Visegrád was founded by King Andreas I [1040–1062]). Also, as the sources report, King Ladislaus IV supported other eremitic communities in the Pilis by donating properties for the Holy Cross Monastery. This argument is crucial because here it is clearly visible (as was just discussed) that the traditional history by Gyöngyösi, which mentions King Charles Robert I as the founder, and the data from the original documents, also used by Gyöngyösi (the list of the *Inventarium*), do not correlate with each other. Therefore, in his *Vitae Fratrum* there is a significant paradox. Gyöngyösi (1988), *Vitae Fratrum*, Cap. 9, 23.

[140] As suggested by Beatrix Romhányi (2012a) see Romhányi (2012a) "Pálos kolostorok a Pilisben," 225–226.

[141] Gyöngyösi (1988), *Vitae Fratrum*, Cap. 15; Szabó (2005), *Woodland and Forests*, 116, ref. 75; Gyöngyösi (1988), *Vitae Fratrum*, 209.

[142] Gyöngyösi (1988), *Vitae Fratrum,* Cap. 15; Szabó (2005), *Woodland and Forests*, 116-117.

trend among all Pauline settlements up until the late Middle Ages),[143] the Pilis was not a typical *desertum*.[144] The Paulines were not very far from the lay sphere (on the contrary, small settlements were found around them), nor from roads (they typically lay along main trading routes, a few kilometers away),[145] and not even from each other (the hermits of the three hermitages in the Pilis could reach each other in a day).[146] Furthermore, there was another monastery nearby, the Cistercian abbey of Pilis, which was most probably also founded near a royal curia.

Another feature of the changing impact of the Pauline economy should be highlighted. In their beginnings, the hermit communities were recorded as being too poor to ask for papal allowance in 1263. The next inventory in 1291, however, finds the main communities in better conditions. Between the two dates at least two monasteries in the Pilis were founded, from these the Holy Cross Monastery took leadership over the hermitic movements and royal patronage had already shown its significant affect in the area by donating lands. This period marked the transition from a clearly hermitic life-style to a changing, more developed economy.

It should be noted that, as Beatrix Romhányi suggests, it is better to avoid the term "monastery" or "cloister" to define certain communities in the thirteenth century. It is better to use the terms "hermitages" and "hermits," or more precisely "Pauline hermitages" and "Pauline hermits," referring to their status in

---

143 Szabó (2005), *Woodland and Forests*, 117.

144 See on this Máté Urbán, "Puszta sivatag és Paradicsomkert – Táj és természet a remeterendek és a ciszterciták középkori felfogásában" [Abandoned desert and Paradise – Landscape and nature in the understanding of hermit orders and Cistercians], *Vigilia* 75 (2010): 2–9.

145 However, it is also true that relations with laymen were confined to economic and other mundane, daily interactions; there was no religious communication (mass, religious liturgy) between the peasants and the Paulines until the beginning of the fifteenth century, except the praises and masses that were for the salvation of the founders and donators. See more, e.g., Gábor Sarbak, "Pálosaink írásbelisége a középkor végén" [Pauline scripts at the end of the Middle Ages], *Vigilia* 66, no. 2. (2001): 112–119; and also Romhányi (2010), *Pálos gazdálkodás a középkorban*, 10–12. On the Pauline landscape see Laszlovszky (2004), "Középkori kolostorok a tájban," 348–349; and Guzsik (2003), *Pálos építészet*, 67–69, 162.

146 Károly Belényesy pointed this out it in the case of the Pauline monasteries in the Abaúj-hegyalja region. Belényesy (2004), *Pálos kolostorok Abaúj-Hegyalján*, 102. Péter Szabó also argued this in the context of the Pilis Forest. Szabó (2005), *Woodlands and Forests*, 111.

the thirteenth century, because (1) at this time, there were no Pauline monastic buildings (at most there were huts for the hermits), (2) the historiographical tradition also uses these terms, (3) and the brothers of the Holy Cross near Esztergom (*fratribus S. Crucis prope Strigonium*), according to references from the thirteenth and sometimes even the fourteenth centuries, were regarded as a community, the origin of the later Pauline Order. Only in 1309 the papal legate Gentilis referred to the hermits of the Holy Cross as the Order of St. Paul the First Hermit (*fratribus S. Crucis de Heremo, Ordo S. Pauli Primi Eremite*). This clearly states that the hermit communities, who legally followed the regulations of St. Augustine (not just the ones in the Pilis!), were called coincidentally both the brothers of the Holy Cross, and the Order of St. Paul the First Hermit.[147]

Some features, such as the ideal location of the monasteries were inherited through the centuries in the Pauline tradition, but many other elements changed significantly even in the early fourteenth century. These changes are mostly related to the Pauline economy and administrative system; partly because these types of written sources survived. The most recent and most detailed studies on the Pauline economy and character were published by Beatrix Romhányi. Based predominately on her research, the following complex pattern of Pauline estate management has been revealed.[148]

The beginnings of the order are not well known, but it is sure that at the turn of the thirteenth and fourteenth centuries the "hermit monasteries" were given small lands and properties. Vineyards had a main role since the very first donations,[149] but depending on local facilities/availability, arable lands, meadows and pasture-lands, woods, and fisheries also had primary importance in the local Pauline economy during the Middle Ages.[150]

This smaller, basically self-sufficient system started to lose its exclusivity and the Paulines broadened their facilities in the mid-1300s. In 1359 a charter

[147] Romhányi (2010), *Pálos gazdálkodás a középkorban*, 15–17.

[148] Based on Romhányi (2010), *Pálos gazdálkodás a középkorban*, 9–17, 130–142; and on an English summary on the late medieval period see Beatrix Romhányi, "Life in the Pauline Monasteries of Late Medieval Hungary," *Periodica Polytechnica* 43 (2012): 53–56.

[149] Solymosi (2005), "Pilissziget."

[150] It is clear from the charters that different holdings had different values depending on the territory, which modified the basic holdings of the monasteries to some degree. E.g., in Northeastern Hungary there were more vineyards, while in Slavonia woods had more value and therefore were preferred. Romhányi (2010), *Pálos gazdálkodás a középkorban*, 132.

on donation privileges to the monastery of Bereg summarized the basic features of Pauline subsistence: vineyards, fisheries (fishponds and channels built by the Paulines), pannage, and the usage or rent of mills.[151] What is crucial from this charter is that besides the features that usually—but not exclusively—served for direct supply of the monasteries, such as fisheries or pannage, there were others that produced regular financial income for the monks, mainly from vineyards and mills. Based on this extra income the Pauline monasteries started to systematically develop a monetary economy in the first half of the fourteenth century.

The new monetary economy allowed the Pauline Order to cultivate their lands with lease-work, or if they could manage, increase the number of their properties. From the end of the fourteenth century, there was a clear division in the Pauline economy. On one hand, there were well-to-do monasteries, which wanted to evolve their economy on the basis of a monastic system, had granges and manors, and urban houses with several privileges. For example, the main Monastery of St. Ladislaus could provide for thirty-forty monks. On the other hand, the small hermit-like monasteries, which had a self-sufficient, small economy and husbandry with six to ten monks, existed until the end of the Middle Ages.[152] Many examples fit in this category, most probably the monasteries at the Pilis as well.

Based on the charter of Pope Eugene IV to Dionysios, the Archbishop of Esztergom, in 1440 the contemporaries saw the evolution of the Pauline Order in this way:

> ...first the order was settled only in deserted, uninhabited, wooded places, far from populated areas and lived a monkish life in small cells and chapels, which can still be found at some places; but as time went by, through ones' donations the cells have been transformed to great monasteries, the chapels to splendid churches and around the monasteries several other necessary buildings were erected.[153]

---

[151] This charter confirmed and verified these opportunities and features for the Paulines. Gyéressy et al. (1975), *Documenta Artis Paolinorum* 1, 10.

[152] Altogether, almost 1,500 Pauline monks lived at the same time in the ca. seventy friaries in Hungary and the surrounding regions. Only the Franciscans had more monasteries in Hungary. The Paulines were present also in Dalmatia, Croatia, Silesia, Poland, Austria, and Germany (as well as in Rome) with an additional 25 friaries.

[153] Translated from Hungarian into English by the author. Hungarian text available in Romhányi (2010), *Pálos gazdálkodás a középkorban*, 17. Original charter: DL 13521.

In both cases, the basic features of properties, concerning farming and cultivating, were almost the same, but depending on the environment regional differences were recorded. Most of the larger monasteries evolved their economy by focusing on one property or product, which could have been vineyards, mills, or even crops. Supposedly, in some territories keeping animals could assure income for the monasteries, like pigs in Slavonia. Although the nature of the monetary economy was emphasized previously, it has to be highlighted again that the lands (arable, meadow, etc.), which represented the basic sources of income until the mid-1300s, even after their effacement were still kept, meaning that they were basic features even of larger monasteries as well until the end of the Middle Ages.

On the Road of Change[154]

In the thirteenth to fourteenth centuries the dominance of the monastic orders (Benedictines, Cistercians) gave way to the mendicant orders (Dominicans and Franciscans), which was followed—and later surpassed—by the Paulines. This is why the development of the Pauline network occurred during the fourteenth century, a movement that decreased by the fifteenth century. Their patrons donated complete villages and estates to them, thus their whole estate system reached its peak. This encouraged the reception of other estate management systems.

After the thirteenth century, a self-sufficient Pauline community focused on the strategies of survival, which is why the order can be described as a half-monastic, half-mendicant order with monetary-based estate management in the fifteenth century. This improvement has many stages. Around the time of the consolidation of the order—mainly after the official papal approval (1368)—the first flourishing period started in the last third of the fourteenth century, when the first Pauline monasteries appeared outside the borders of Hungary.[155] This popularity strongly affected the Pauline estate structure and character. High-ranking aristocrats also supported the order by establishing monasteries and donating houses in the towns,

---

[154] This section is based on the following sources: Gregorius Gyöngyösi, *Decalogus de beato Paulo primo heremita comportatus*, (Cracow: Florianum Unglerium, 1532); see Felícián Gondán, *A középkori Magyar pálos rend* és *nyelvemlékei (Festetich-* és *Czech-kódexek)* [The medieval Pauline Order and its monuments (The Festetich and the Czech codexes)] (Pécs: Printed by József Taizs, 1916), 37–38; Romhányi (2012b), "Life in the Pauline Monasteries," 55–56.

[155] In 1382, the first foreign Pauline monastery was founded in Częstochowa by Ladislaus, the Duke of Opole.

mostly in Buda, which were intended to be long-term properties and besides receiving regular rent, could serve for commercialization; the Paulines could sell their products, mainly their wine or salt in the cities and towns. A different attitude is connected to urban houses; donating these properties to Paulines became a practice after King Louis I (1342-1382) donated the *Kammerhof*, the old royal residence at Buda, to the Paulines,[156] when the translation of St. Paul's relics took place from Venice to Buda, and then to the Monastery of St. Laurence (*Figure 9*).

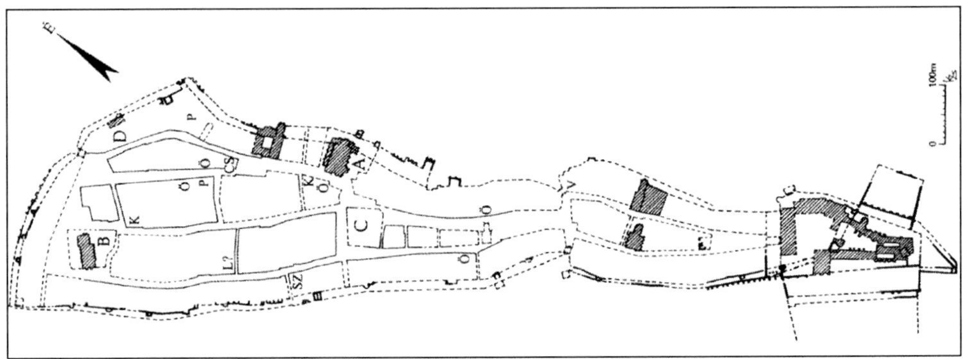

Figure 9. Buildings in Buda known to have belonged to Pauline monasteries: A. Parish Church of the Virign Mary; B. Parish Church of St. Mary Magdalene; C. Town Hall; D. Synagogue; Cs. Monastery of the Virgin Mary at Csatka; K. Monastery of St. Ladislaus at Kékes; L. Monastery of the Virgin Mary at Lád; Sz. Monastery of Holy Cross and Holy Spirit (Szentkereszt and Szentlélek) in the Pilis; Ö. Monastery of the Virgin Mary at Örményes; P. Monastery of St. Lawrence near Buda (Budaszentlőrinc); V. Monastery of St. Paul, St. Sixtus, and St. John at Veresmart (Pálosveresmart). Romhányi (2015b), "Ceperuntque," 761, 7. ábra (Figure 7)

Since this royal donation the number of Pauline urban houses (by donation or purchase) started to grow and soon they had the support of other members of the royal court (e.g., the high noble families of the era, such as the Cudar, Kanizsai, and Kont families). Several times these houses were allowed to run as tap-houses (Hungarian: *kocsmáltatási jog*), which meant extra income for the monasteries. It was also recorded that different monasteries owned and used urban houses together. Additionally, as part of the financial system and estate management,

[156] However, a bit later the Paulines exchanged this house for another one, which the sources mention as the "great Pauline house." For more on this see András Végh, *Buda város középkori helyrajza* [The Medieval map of Buda], vol. 1, (Budapest: Budapesti Történeti Múzeum, 2006–2008), 256–258.

landed estates and properties, such as vineyards and mills, were exploited through renting.[157]

The money that they received was then lent at rates to partners, from local nobles to cities, such as Buda or Vienna. Several general and individual privileges were given to the Paulines concerning first their basic provisions; they received immunity from paying tax to their lord (Hungarian *kilenced*) on wine (and occasionally on crops), which *they* produced on their lands.[158] Also, the Paulines received exemption from paying the ecclesial tax (Hungarian *tized*) on wine; first in 1329 just on the ones which they produced,[159] but in 1459 they received a general immunity from Pope Pius II (1458–1464).[160] The number of alms and donations as significant features of support increased in the sixteenth century, but the first donation can be connected to King Louis I, who gave the order a yearly rent of salt to the value of 300 florins.[161]

King Matthias I (1458–1490) was the most significant patron of the order.[162] During his reign the Paulines got more and more privileges in their second flourishing period; they received legal privileges (e.g., Paulines could execute guilty people), and even received a great number of monasteries, which were built and occupied previously by other orders. The strong relationship between the King (his sympathy and policy) and the order is apparent in many ways. For example, the Prior General Gregorius Gyöngyösi influenced the king politically in the 1470s and 1480s and it is clear from the sources that King Matthias regarded the Paulines as the sacral representation of the kingdom; also, the new monastic foundations can be seen as symbols of loyalty. Based on King Matthias' support, the patronage of the Paulines was continued after his death and as it seems like they served in the court of the Holy Roman Emperor as well.[163]

Fishponds, woods, meadows, and pasture-lands brought the Paulines only a small profit, while vineyards, mills, and urban houses, as well as tolls, the

---

[157] Romhányi (2010), *Pálos gazdálkodás a középkorban*, 131–132.

[158] The privilege of King Louis I in 1357. Romhányi (2010), *Pálos gazdálkodás a középkorban*, 55, 70. Gyöngyösi (1988), *Vitae Fratrum*, Cap. 32.

[159] The privilege of Pope John XXII (1316-1334). Romhányi (2010), *Pálos gazdálkodás a középkorban*, 113. Footnote 631.

[160] Romhányi (2010), *Pálos gazdálkodás a középkorban*, 70, 112-113. Source is a copy of the original charter from 1466: DL 25984.

[161] Romhányi (2010), *Pálos gazdálkodás a középkorban*, 120, 122–123, 131–132. Gyöngyösi (1988), *Vitae Fratrum*, Cap. 21.

[162] Romhányi (2012b), "Life in the Pauline Monasteries," 54.

[163] Romhányi (2010), *Pálos gazdálkodás a középkorban*, 134.

salt-trade, and other privileges meant more income for the Paulines. Vineyards were originally present as basic properties since the thirteenth century; mills—in greater number—show up in the fourteenth century; urban houses were mentioned from end of the fourteenth, but more often from the fifteenth century. As Beatrix Romhányi summarizes, the status and economy of the Paulines had changed considerably by the end of the fourteenth century, but the monks continued to live in small, sometimes hermitage-like communities. Additionally, "...the order had a clear concept of the ideal estates it needed, nevertheless, the sustention of the monasteries and the religious also necessitated alms."[164] She continues, "although the order had contacts to the towns and cities, its presence there was essentially of economic character; Pauline monasticism has never been an urban feature."[165]

All these features of the Pauline economy and structure clearly show that the character of the Pauline Order cannot be articulated by using the traditional categories of religious orders (monastic, mendicant, hermit).[166] They had transformed their economy, and therefore their impact on the landscape had also changed from the thirteenth century until the end of the Middle Ages. The German historian, Kaspar Elm, referred to the Paulines as an "unmade mendicant order"[167] (because, e.g., they received alms for pastoral work), while Beatrix Romhányi highlighted the other character of the order that was similar to other monastic orders. Her conclusions were based on a complex analysis, and it was clearly argued that the described features of Pauline economy became diverse as the monastic character of the order changed. The Paulines had landed estates from the beginning, but later they managed them in an innovative way as the incomes apparently did not cover their expenses.[168]

As a result of this general overview, the archaeological and historical data on the monasteries of the Pilis becomes valuable in a broader view. Those features, which are still recognizable in the landscape and were systematically researched

---

[164] These incomes were gathered from different testators, donators, and believers visiting the pilgrimage places run by the Paulines, as well as from high-ranking persons whom the Paulines addressed with supplications or gifts. Romhányi (2012b), "Life in the Pauline Monasteries," 55; Máté Urbán, "Pálos zarándokhelyek a késő középkori Magyarországon" [Pauline pilgrimage sites in late medieval Hungary], *Vallástudományi Szemle* 5, no. 1. (2009): 63–85.

[165] Romhányi (2012b), "Life in the Pauline Monasteries," 56.

[166] Laszlovszky (2004), "Középkori kolostorok a tájban," 348–349.

[167] Romhányi (2012b), "Life in the Pauline Monasteries," 54.

[168] Romhányi (2010), *Pálos gazdálkodás a középkorban*, 139.

in the royal forest, can be analyzed and evaluated with a historical approach by comparing them to the general trends. To examine these features in a meaningful, detailed way, a closer look is essential on the written, archaeological, and spatial aspects of the features of the Pauline monastic space, which was hidden in nature (but not secluded) and strongly connected to water. At the same time the Paulines had been managing a complex economy since the end of the thirteenth century.

Boundaries

In the valleys, under the hills, beside the monastery buildings themselves, the nucleus of the monastic space was separated from the world by walls. These features were destroyed first by the Ottoman army and then perished after the centuries, not only due to natural deterioration, but because these easily-reachable stone structures served as a quarry for local people. Around the St. Elisabeth Monastery at Tálod, the wall around the monastery, built by stone, fences an irregular 110 x 200 x 120 x 180 meters shaped area.[169] In the Pilis, the remains of the precinct wall were found around the Holy Cross Monastery and in better condition at the Holy Spirit.[170]

Manors and Lands (Arable Lands, Meadows, Woods, Truck Farms)[171]

Landed estates were acquired by the Paulines one-by-one from the thirteenth century. There are no records on the value of such lands, but this is because of a lack of surviving data (e.g., there is no data on the buying of lands).[172] It is clear from the *Vitae Fratrum* that an accurate record of possessions (size and structure) was generally kept in the Pauline monasteries.[173] This documentation was a part of the land management. The Paulines tried to unify and concentrate

[169] Kékedi (2008), *Nagyvázsony,* 73–75.

[170] See Chapter 3 (Catalogue), 3.2 Pauline monasteries in the Pilis. 1. Monastery of Holy Cross, 124, Figure 28; 127, Figure 29; Chapter 3 (Catalogue), 3.2 Pauline monasteries in the Pilis. 2. Monastery of Holy Spirit, 146, Figure 56; 152, Figure 57.

[171] This section is based on the summary of Romhányi (2010), *Pálos gazdálkodás a középkorban*, 18–41, 132.

[172] However, most of the legal cases concern the violation of ownership regarding properties, e.g., stealing crops, cutting woods, fishing in ponds, etc.

[173] In one such example, the provost of Nosztre declines the donation of King Louis I, because the monastery already owned too much land. Gyöngyösi (1988), *Vitae Fratrum*, Cap. 26.

their properties; those which were not close enough to their monastery they tried to sell or barter with other properties. This intention must have had an effect on the spatial distribution of their lands on the level of regional topography.

Donations of woods to the Paulines were usual in the first few decades of the order's history; soon after the Paulines usually cleared the woodlands, which they already owned or were newly acquired, and used the free lands as arable, vineyards, orchards, or meadows—it depended on local circumstances. A part of the woods was used for pannage, which was typical in the forests and woods. There is a lack of information on animals kept by the monasteries. There are examples when a monastery received valuable horses as donations, but of course they had workhorses as well. The monasteries also had cattle which gave milk, and some monasteries were involved in the cattle trade. A significant amount of the extant data concerns pigs (besides the fish, which lived in the ponds). Pork was the most common food in the monasteries; therefore, pannage was a regular activity, which also represents the most discussed topic in the sources concerning the usage of woods. The income from this part of the economy cannot be measured because there are no relevant sources on the matter.[174]

Usually a few peasants served at the monasteries by cutting trees, cultivating lands, and helping in household activities. This has been verified by archaeological field surveys as well; e.g., a medieval settlement might have existed next to the Holy Cross Monastery and also, near the Holy Spirit to the southwest, a settlement or a manor could have existed.[175] (It rarely happened that monasteries gained complete villages and if so, this happened rather in the late Middle Ages). These people helped in cultivating different types of cereals (wheat, rye, spelt, sty, millet) on arable lands, or in truck farming (here lentils, pea, parsnip, melon, carrot, poppy seed, cabbage, etc. could be found.) However, there is a large debate in the scholarship about when the Paulines were allowed to work with peasants. It was strictly forbidden in the thirteenth century, they worked by themselves, but after they had gained more money from their businesses, they could pay the peasants for their work. However, there are sources that mention the peasants working

[174] Romhányi (2010), *Pálos gazdálkodás a középkorban*, 90–96, 130–142.

[175] Torma, ed. (1979), *Magyarország Régészeti Topográfiája* 5, 236. There is no special regulation on this question concerning the Paulines; although it is sure that they were not secluded from the lay sphere. The monasteries were not far from settlements, which were—at least in the late Middle Ages—attached to monasteries. Several times in the late Middle Ages, the larger settlements, attached to the Paulines, had permission to hold fairs and markets.

with the monks, and archaeological field surveys have repeatedly determined that the sites next to the monasteries are the settlements of the servants from the Árpádian Age. [176]

The Paulines harvested several types of fruits in their fruit gardens (*pomarium*), such as apple, peach, pear, cherry, plum, almond, walnut, medlar, blackthorn, etc., and wild fruits—like dogwood, elderberry, etc.—also had an important role. Although there is a lack of evidence for the use special herbs in the monastic space, it should have existed in the Middle Ages.[177] The archaeobotanical research revealed that developed horticulture existed in the area close to the Cistercian monastery in the Pilis. The studies revealed that there was a general lack of tree pollens; instead, the research identified specified pigweeds and mugwort, in addition to walnut, in the study area.[178] The wild fruit trees also still exist around the monastery.

In only a few cases could the research specify and reconstruct the land-use system of a monastery, and in even fewer cases the structure of the fields and forms of cultivation. For example, in Nagyvázsony (Veszprém County), after the basic studies of *The Archaeological Topography of Hungary* series,[179] Andrea Kékedi could identify on the basis of written sources and historical maps the following categories of land *terras autem, pratafaenilia, campos, silvas, rubeta, nemorasedet dictam, piscinam.*[180] As later historical maps showed, this system existed until modern times.[181] Also, there were still wild fruit trees at the monastery, which were fenced in with a 1.5-meter high stone wall, which can still be seen at the site. Some fields of land cultivation (on terraces or lynchets) were detected at the Pauline

[176] Romhányi (2010), *Pálos gazdálkodás a középkorban*, 11, 18.

[177] A codex survived in which indirect information discusses the usage of comifrey, cocklebur, etc. See Tamás Grynaeus, "A pálosok orvosló tevékenységének egy elfeledett emlékéről" [On the forgotten memories of Pauline medical care], in: *Varia Paulina. Pálos Rendtörténeti Tanulmányok*, ed. Gábor Sarbak (Csorna: Árva, Vince, 1994), 234–236, 294–298.

[178] Bálint Zólyomi and István Précsényi, "Pollenstatistische Analyse der Teichablagerungen des mittelalterlichen Klosters bei Pilisszentkereszt," *Acta Archaeologica Academiae Scientiarum Hungaricae* 37 (1985): 153–158.

[179] For this region see region see Éri, ed. (1969), *Magyarország Régészeti Topográfiája* 2.

[180] Meadows, fields, woods, blackberries, parklands, and fishpond. Source charter: DL 19562. Translated into English by the author. Kékedi (2008), *Nagyvázsony*, 43.

[181] Kékedi (2008), *Nagyvázsony*, 43–47.

monastery of Tálod (Veszprém County).[182] Another interesting preliminary report analyzed grain finds at the monastery of Pogányszentpéter, where the specialists suggested that the complex cultivation and harvest of wheat with barley occurred. Evidence of pear and plum trees were also documented from the very same excavation pit, which dates back to the beginning of the sixteenth century.[183]

Vineyards[184]

Vineyards played a leading role since the beginnings of the Pauline economy. The reasons behind this are more or less clear: at first the work with peasants was prohibited in the order, so vineyards could be cultivated by the Pauline monks themselves. Later, they received money or grapevines from the tenants; therefore, almost every single Pauline monastery had at least one vineyard among its properties, even the smallest ones.

Usually, the charters mention the tools that were used at vineyards, such as barrels, cellars, rams, etc. Most of the charters localize the vineyards precisely, but their localization is a bit easier in any case since cultivating grapes for fine wine is geographically (and therefore spatially) conditioned; the Paulines, like anyone else, tried to own the best properties, where the soil was good and the

[182] Kékedi (2008), *Nagyvázsony*, 68. In other parts of Hungary traces of medieval farming have been documented since the 1980s. The most well-known sitesare in Veszprém County, the medieval village of Sümeg-Sarvaly, and Tamási in Tolna County. See Gyula Nováki, "Szántóföldek maradványai a XIV–XVI. századból a Sümeg-Sarvalyi erdőben" [Remains of arable lands from the fourteenth–sixteenth century in the woods of Sümeg-Sarvaly], *Magyar Mezőgazdasági Múzeum Közleményei* (1985): 19–32; István Torma, "Mittelalterliche Ackerfeld-Spurenim Wald von Tamási (Komitat Tolna)," *Acta Archaeologica Academiae Scientiarum Hungaricae* 33 (1981): 245–256. On land-use patterns and traces of medieval fields in general see: József Laszlovszky, "Field systems in medieval Hungary," in: *The man of many devices, who wandered full many ways...: Festschrift in honor of János M. Bak,* eds. Balázs Nagy and Marcell Sebők (Budapest: CEU Press, 1999), 432–444.

[183] Miklós Füzes, "Előzetes jelentés az 1967. évi pogányszentpéteri kolostor-ásatás XVI. század eleji gabonaleletéről" [Preliminary report on the sixteenth-century grain find from the 1967 excavation of Pogányszentpéter cloister], in: *A Thúry György Múzeum jubileumi emlékkönyve* (1919-1969) [The Jubilee Volume of the Thúry György Museum (1919-1969)], ed. Gyula Kiss (Nagykanizsa: Thúry György Múzeum, 1972), 285–290.

[184] This section based primarily on Romhányi (2010), *Pálos gazdálkodás a középkorban*, 55–72, 130–142.

terrain's inclination was adequate. Furthermore, the cultivation of such lands meant that the Paulines had to invest a large amount of money, and until the first return of their financial and physical efforts, many years would pass. Therefore, vineyards were stable properties of the Pauline economy, and thus a stable spatial feature as well. This was expressed by contemporaries, when they mentioned large areas of vineyards (*promontorium*).[185] In the Pilis region, the Holy Cross and St. Ladislaus Monasteries owned vineyards.

Fishponds, Dikes, and Springs

The closeness of water was always crucial for daily life, thus it was also essential for the Pauline monasteries. The valleys in between hills are usually the ideal places for water mills using the permanent streams, which were also important elements of the Pauline monastic landscapes. Fishponds as part of water management systems were usually developed with the help of geographical conditions, close to the monasteries. This means that they were part of the daily routine (in regard to the importance of fish in the monastic diet, as well as the multiple uses of reeds). Although not much is known on their value and the ideal size that produced income for the monks, three or four ponds should have been enough for a stable, or more, a rich subsistence.[186]

In some cases the name of the ponds is known.[187] Several charters on donations mention the name of fishponds in the late Middle Ages, but the oldest known name of a fishpond, called Swan/Swany-pond (Hungarian: *Hattyas-tó*) at the Danube was recorded in 1282.[188] Their value is not known, only that they were mostly donated to the Paulines (of course, sometimes it is impossible to determine whether the Paulines constructed the pond or not; it can be just supposed in the case of those ponds that were the closest to the monasteries). Sometimes the charters mention the price of their repair (supposedly the construction of moats and dikes, cleaning the bend, etc.), as in the case of the St. Ladislaus Monastery in the Pilis.

An interesting spatial character of the fishponds is that mills were usually attached to them. Both written and archaeological investigations have pointed

---

[185] E.g., the monasteries of Budaszentlőrinc, Fehéregyháza, Garics, Ruszka, Zágráb. Romhányi (2010), *Pálos gazdálkodás a középkorban*, 55.

[186] Romhányi (2010), *Pálos gazdálkodás a középkorban*, 84–89, 130–142.

[187] In a few cases the charters record lay people violating the law by secretly fishing in the monks' ponds or cutting reeds (!).

[188] DL 6292; manuscript cited in Romhányi (2010), *Pálos gazdálkodás a középkorban*, 84.

out this characteristic. Károly Belényesy verified that this phenomenon occurred around Budaszentlőric[189] (the St. Laurence Monastery), as well as in the Zemplén region (Gönc,[190] Regéc[191]); this feature was clear in other places as well.[192] Around Nagyvázsony (Veszprém County), Andrea Kékedi also recorded the correlation between mills and fishponds[193] (*Figure 10*).

After examining several monastic spaces, Belényesy and Kékedi highlighted and verified some further, general characteristics concerning fishponds. The ponds and the monasteries were located together in a relatively small area, forming an integral unit. Local features also defined the location and the form; for example, in the Zemplén region, where the climate is relatively dry, the ponds were constructed just under a spring. There were different types of ponds and their sizes were also diverse; the width of these ponds depended on the runoff of the supplying stream and the definition of the shore had to be managed with special attention.[194] Belényesy examined the function of the small ponds, which usually existed right under a spring, and highlighted the existence of a special type of pond, called *vivarium*, which served for the temporary storage of fish that had been selected for cooking. (This feature possibly exists at the Monastery of St. Ladislaus as well.) But of course, small ponds close to the monasteries (especially with stone beds) might serve as reservoirs—water storage lakes[195] —

---

[189] Gyöngyösi (1988), *Vitae Fratrum*, Cap. 57; Romhányi (2010), *Pálos gazdálkodás a középkorban*, 87.

[190] Gyéressy et al. (1975), *Documenta Artis Paolinorum* 1, 167–170; Belényesy (2004), *Pálos kolostorok Abaúj-Hegyalján,*, 27–28. manuscript cited in Romhányi (2010), *Pálos gazdálkodás a középkorban*, 87.

[191] Gyéressy et al. (1976), *Documenta Artis Paolinorum* 2, 309–311; Belényesy (2004), *Pálos kolostorok Abaúj-Hegyalján,* 13–14. Manuscript cited in Romhányi (2010), *Pálos gazdálkodás a középkorban*, 87.

[192] In Hangony, Jenő, and Örményes the same observations were recorded. Manuscript cited in Romhányi (2010), *Pálos gazdálkodás a középkorban*, 87. Medieval written sources mention ponds and mills together in several legal cases, e.g., in 1382, 1486, and in 1496. manuscript cited in Romhányi (2010), *Pálos gazdálkodás a középkorban*, 87.

[193] This is clear from the surveys around the monastery, where two fishponds, two dikes, and two mills were recorded. Kékedi (2008), *Nagyvázsony*, 61–66. The mills and fishponds were mentioned together in the perambulation of the Nagyvázsony Pauline monastery (1489). Kékedi (2008), *Nagyvázsony*, 42.

[194] Kékedi (2008), *Nagyvázsony*, 48.

[195] Belényesy (2004), *Pálos kolostorok Abaúj-Hegyalján,* 102–103.

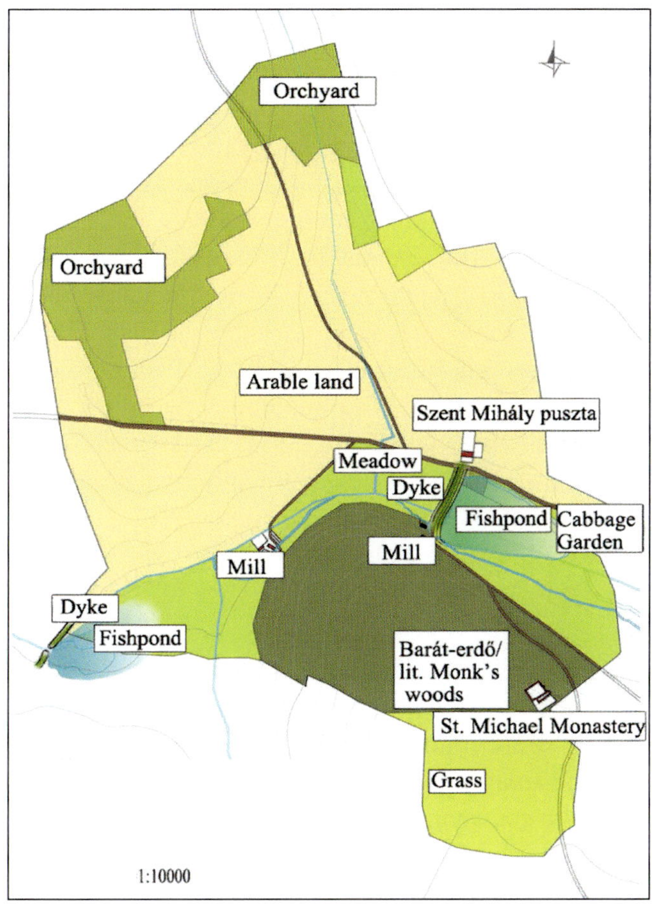

Figure 10. The reconstruction of the surrounding estates of the Monastery of St. Michael in Nagyvázsony. Kékedi (2008), Nagyvázsony, 46, Figure 3.

like the one next to the monastery of Tálod.[196] Springs and wells, which supplied these lakes and ponds, may appear inside the monastery, in the middle of the cloister garden, or at one side of the *clausura*. They could also be situated outside the monastery at nearby springs or streams, e.g. at Nagyvázsony.[197]

Several times dikes were used as roads, which doubled their usefulness. An 80–100-meter long dike, which contained Roman ceramics, was constructed close

[196] This was first mentioned by Flóris Rómer, the "Father of Hungarian Archaeology," in the mid-1800s. Kékedi (2008), *Nagyvázsony*, 68, 70, 75.

[197] Kékedi (2008), *Nagyvázsony*, 60–61.

to the Pauline monastery at Tálod.[198] Near the Pauline St. Michael monastery at Nagyvázsony, one of two large dikes was built by stone and was mentioned in a charter as serving as a road over a stream.[199] Another type of dike (supposedly medieval) was detected in Nagyvázsony (Hungarian *Határvölgyi-gát*, Boundary valley dike); it sheds lights on some of the constructions and reconstructions at the site, which were mentioned in the charters, namely, that the embankment was supported with a wooden structure made of panels.[200] All this data supports the idea that the features of past water management systems are usually detectable in the present-day landscape; it is more clear in the case of a recent study, in which a LiDAR survey detected the area of the Pauline monastery at Pécs-Jakabhegy (Baranya County). Here the relation between the monastery and the fishponds, as well as the roads leading to the ponds, is precisely visualized based on the produced terrain model.[201] As there are only a small number of sources on fishponds, the value of other types of data increases.[202]

Mills[203]

Charter evidence confirms that mills served as rental properties from their very first appearance among the Pauline possessions; half of the monasteries had at least one mill. It was an optional property, because a regular income mainly coming from milling soke could stabilize the financial livelihood of the monks. Other financial privileges connected to mills increased the stability, regularity, and amount of income for the monks. It is telling that the Pauline monasteries usually owned mills for 100–150 years; this shows how important a regular income was for them. Furthermore, donating mills was a good way of developing small and poor monasteries—this was recognized by royalty; therefore, since the reign of King Louis I, mills were donated to several monasteries— including the Monastery of St. Ladislaus in the Pilis.

---

198 Éri, ed. (1969), *Magyarország Régészeti Topográfiája* 2, 181.

199 Kékedi (2008), *Nagyvázsony*, 60.

200 Kékedi (2008), *Nagyvázsony*, 64.

201 Gábor Bertók and Csilla Gáti, *Old Times – New Methods. Non Invasive Archaeology in Baranya County (Hungary)* 2005-2013 (Budapest: Archaeolingua, 2014), Figure IV.2.

202 Even the researchers involved in *The Archaeological Topography of Hungary* project from the 1970s realized the need to document at least these basic features, which (in the case of the Paulines) was carried out in today's Komárom-Esztergom, Pest, and Veszprém Counties.

203 This section is based on Romhányi (2010), *Pálos gazdálkodás a középkorban*, 73–83.

It should be noted that although the number of donations in money was growing from the fifteenth century, based on charter evidence, there was supposed to be a general decrease in the number and size of lands. Begging was also strictly prohibited; therefore, the only stable resource for the Paulines were mills, which tended to be more and more significant from the mid-1300s, as the estate management tendencies show an order to develop a monetary economy for their needs.[204]

A spatial characteristic of mills is alluded to in a charter that verifies and summarizes the needs of the Paulines at Bereg in 1359.[205] The charter points out that mills could not be built near the mills of Paulines. This is because, on the one hand, the original mill might not function well after connecting another mill to the system (depending on local circumstances), but on the other hand, the existence of another, competing mill near the Paulines' mill would endanger the Paulines' revenue from rent.

Usually one or two mills served a monastery, but they might have more than one wheel, as was verified by several sources.[206] Regular maintenance was essential for the mills, just as in the case of the ponds, because the wooden part of the wheels should be changed regularly. Mills were used in daily life mostly for milling corn, but there is evidence for the existence of a woolen mill, a sawmill, and a mill that was milling leguminous crops. One of the two mills that were identified near the monastery at Nagyvázsony produced flour and had an individual channel (!) from the supply stream, which was also preserved.[207]

Other buildings were attached to these mills, which served the farmyard as well. If the mill was located near a fishpond, these attendant structures were sometimes located there. In other cases, there were also structures inside or next to the walls of the monasteries, which might have had similar functions, or as they are usually interpreted, functioned as workshops. This has been suggested at Nagyvázsony by the topographical surveys[208] and at the Holy Spirit Monastery in the Pilis as well.[209]

---

[204] Romhányi (2010), *Pálos gazdálkodás a középkorban*, 73.
[205] Gyéressy et al. (1975), *Documenta Artis Paulinorum* 1, 10.
[206] Romhányi (2010), *Pálos gazdálkodás a középkorban,* 78.
[207] Kékedi (2008), *Nagyvázsony*, 60.
[208] Kékedi (2008), *Nagyvázsony*, 60.
[209] See Lázár (2012) "Pilisszentlélek műhelyház," 219.

Inside a Monastery – The Pauline Community and the Built Space

Architecture and the arrangement of built space is another important factor in the study of the Pauline Order. It also helps the understanding of the Pauline character from a spatial approach. Generally, three main eras can be identified:

1. The time of the "requisite" architecture in the thirteenth century. This is regarded as the horizon of pre-Pauline buildings, mostly religious sites (hermitages, chapels, parish churches), which were sometimes abandoned. Secular spaces (hunting lodges) were also re-used by the Pauline communities.
2. The demand for representative architecture, or more likely, functionally appropriate space, which might have been present from the first decade of the fourteenth century. Supposedly the construction of the new central monastery of the order at Budaszentlőrinc might have been the first representation of Pauline individualism. In the time of King Louis the Great (1342–1382) a somewhat "classic" arrangement of monasteries became conventional; namely, that the church was erected south to the *quadrum* and usually there was at least one cellar constructed under one wing (see *Figure 11*). There are traces of some workshops at the Transdanubian region, as well as in the northeastern territory of the Pauline network.[210]
3. Construction at originally non-Pauline sites appears in the late fifteenth century, in the time of King Matthias I (1458–1490). Unfortunately, these modifications or reconstructions can be barely detected or researched. Among the originally non-Pauline sites, an exception is the Premonstratensian monastery at Zsámbék, where analysis of the excavation brought some information to light.[211] However, there are some remains suggesting that Pauline monasteries were rebuilt or modified in late Gothic style.

Generally, the Gothic Pauline church had a simple arrangement with one nave and a long apse, with space for the stalls for the monks. Interestingly, despite the secluded location of the monasteries, the entrance of the church on the western side was accessible from outside the *quadrum*. However, the *clausura* was sometimes

---

[210] For more on this see the list of literature in Guzsik (2003), *Pálos építészet.*

[211] Torma, ed. (1986), *Magyarország Régészeti Topográfiája* 7, 389.

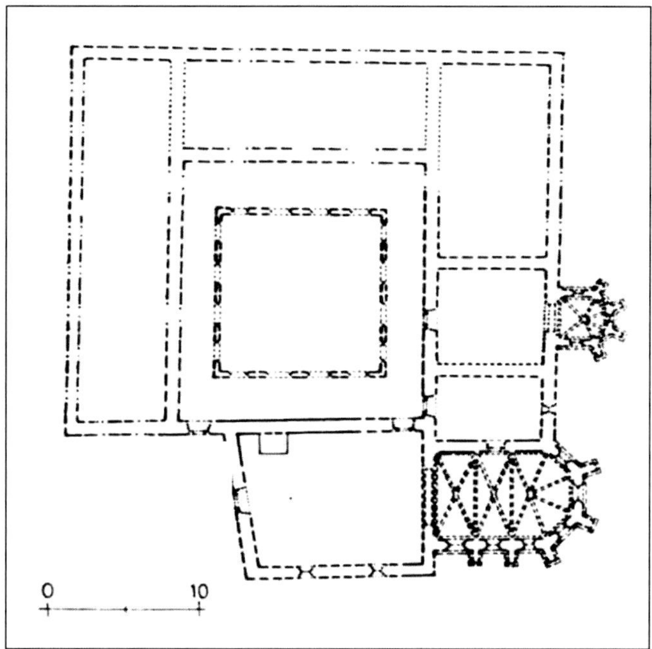

Figure 11. The plan of the St. Lawrence Monastery, first phase. Bencze –Szekér (1993), Budaszentlőrinc, 63, Figure 27.

not totally quadrate-shaped, it was sometimes just L- or partially U-shaped, thus the plan of the monastery should not necessarily immediately reflect the "openness" of the community. However, at least by the fifteenth century, pastoral care was one of the duties of the Paulines, so the church became the meeting point of the monastic and secular worlds.

Right next to the church, to the north usually the sacristy was built, and further to the north the chapter house was settled. There is no information on how and in which order these parts of the monastery were built, only a few data on the archeological research at the monastery of Martonyi (Northeastern Hungary) suggests that chronologically the sacristy might have been built first with the chapter house and the construction of the church and the *clausura* supposed to take more time, even a few years to finish. There some fragmented architectural remains exist, that show that from the sacristy a stair led to the upper area of the quadrate.[212]

---

[212] Cabello et al. (2008), "Háromhegy," 166–167.

Unfortunately information about the details of the daily life of the monks is lacking because, as of yet, no *clausura* of the Paulines has been excavated. Additionally, the written sources are quiet on this subject except for the Rule of St. Augustine and the *Vitae Fratrum*; the former mentions the existence of a pantry and that the monks were storing their clothes in one place. The place of books was also regulated.[213]

In our case, the *Vitae Fratrum* is more relevant. Cap. 11 mentions a *dormitorium* where all the brothers would have slept. A further caput (16) highlights the *refectorium* and some *cella*, which suggests that after a certain length of time or in some monasteries (supposedly in the late Middle Ages) a brother could have their individual space. The work of Prior General Gyöngyösi reveals that there was a separate room for sick brothers (a kind of *infirmarium*).

There are only small hints about the other areas and functions inside the monastery. A recent study by Krisztina Orosz summarized the history of the kitchen in castles and monasteries. She studied the character of the Pauline kitchen as well[214]: while in the case of other monastic orders, like the Cistercians, the kitchen had a fixed location in the architectural plan, there is not even a small piece of evidence of such a rule in the case of the Paulines. Orosz proves this with some examples: at Salföld the kitchen was located in the western wing of the monastery, north of the *refectorium*. The kitchen (size: 6.1 x 8.3 meters) was accessible from the western ambulatory. A pillar (0.95 x 1.30 meters) was also excavated here in the southwestern corner, which supported the chimneystack of the kitchen. Beside it was the place of cooking, which also heated the stove of the neighboring *refectorium*. From the same corner of the kitchen, next to the chimneystack, an entrance led to another room (1.8 x 3.4 meters), which could have been an oven.

The *refectorium* is located in the same area (next to the kitchen, at the southern end of the western wing, with a stove in the northwestern corner) in the Pauline monastery at Nagyvázsony (Veszprém Co., Transdanubian area) and Toronyalja (in the Börzsöny hills) as well. Quite the reverse was present

---

[213] The Latin Library,"Regula Sancti Augustini," (Cap. 5/30) *...et sicut pascimini ex uno cellario, sic induimini ex uno vestiario* (Cap. 5/38)*...qui codicibus praeponuntur,...* (Last accessed: March 25, 2018), http://www.thelatinlibrary.com/augustine/reg.shtml

[214] Krisztina Orosz, "Várak és kolostorok konyhái a középkori Magyarországon" [Kitchens of Castles and Monasteries in Medieval Hungary], in: *A középkor és a kora újkor régészete Magyarországon* 2. [The archaeology of the Middle Ages and the Post Middle Ages in Hungary], vol. 2, eds. Elek Benkő and Gyöngyi Kovács (Budapest: MTA Régészettudományi Intézet, 2010), 583–585.

in Northeastern Hungary at Felnémet, the kitchen was not part of the buildings around the ambulatory, but was located in a separate building connected to the northeastern side of the quadrate; however, this was built only in the sixteenth century. Only fragments of information suggest that the earlier medieval kitchen might have been attached to the *refectorium* here as well with the same cooking-heating solution like in the previous cases.

Water supply is closely connected to cooking and daily life; the needs of the kitchen were supported usually by wells in the courtyard of the monastery or piped fountains, or sometimes drinking fountains on the walls. However, it seems that in Nagyvázsony only one well, located in the farmyard, supplied the monastery.

Since a room that functioned as a kind of *infirmarium* can be identified in written documents, another type of kitchen should be mentioned as a supposed part of Pauline monasteries. However, this separate sickroom and supporting structures was typical only in larger monasteries and communities and has little relevance in the Pauline communities that had usually twelve to fifteen monks. Other activities, such as smithing, were revealed only at a few monasteries, for example, at the Monastery of the Holy Cross, the St. Michael Monastery in Nagyvázsony, and the Holy Spirit Monastery.

The people who lived in monasteries are also part of the space. Thus, it is reasonable to give a quick overview on those members of the community who are hidden behind the features and tasks of monastic life; besides, this is usually not well-articulated in the studies on the medieval Pauline Order. It is known and well-emphasized that Pauline monks were originally themselves working on their lands and around their houses, but after the hierarchy of the order became more defined (after the first general chapter in 1309), different types of tasks were clearly separated. Farming and cultivating the lands was the task of the lay brothers (*frater laicus*), but they are referenced very rarely in the charters. The only source mentioning them in a larger number is Gyöngyösi himself, and even he spoke only about the most notable *fraters conversi*, who ran the workshops or completed slightly more honorable (but not intellectual) tasks. The *Vitae Fratrum* remembers, for example, *frater* Jacob, who made window glasses, *frater* John, who constructed organs, and *magister* Dionysius the sculptor, who contributed to the decoration of St. Lawrence's monastery near Buda. These members of the Pauline community could become a noviciate (*novicius*), but it was rare; usually they could not do (and supposedly did not have time to do) other things besides their mandatory tasks.

On the education of the community members one can find only a few sources. The whole history of the order suggests that it basically represented an anachronistic way of religious life, closely and strictly connected to the *horae regulares*. The *trivium* was the maximum amount of knowledge that was supposed to be acquired by the prior general. Despite this, there are sources, mostly from the fifteenth and sixteenth centuries, in which educated monks appear, but they were educated before they entered the order. For the novices a basic knowledge of the *regula* was necessary, as well as to learn to read and sing (because of the hymns), but it was almost useless to know how to write. There were unsuccessful attempts to change this situation, such as the time a monk named Brother Michael made an attempt in the time of King Matthias I. Prior General Gyöngyösi was the one who broke this heritage, advanced the idea of *devotio moderna* in the community, and formulated a picture of the pious role model for the monks, who needed to absorb more knowledge in order to meditate and better understand their mission.

2.2 Shaping a Pauline Space in the Pilis – Shifting the Emphasis

The Emergence of Pauline Monasteries in the Pilis region. Foundations and the Tradition of the Order – Site Selection

The unique role of the Pilis royal forest is indisputable, as it was scattered with royal residences and surrounded by the most important royal and ecclesial centers. To understand some traits of the location of the Pauline monasteries on this spatial level (Level 5), the research has to go back as far as the circumstances of their foundations. The Paulines were the only Hungarian order established in the thirteenth century, as the later tradition of the order says,[215] in the Pilis. Eusebius, a canon of Esztergom, founded the first Pauline hermit community[216] in the 1250s next to Esztergom, near three caves and a spring close to the later Holy Cross Monastery,[217] present-day Kesztölc-Klastrompuszta.[218]

---

[215] Gyöngyösi (1988), *Vitae Fratrum*, Cap. 6–7.

[216] As was discussed in the Introduction, despite the fact that the community was first referred to as the Order of Saint Paul the First Hermit only in the fourteenth century (1308/1310, see Chapter 3 (Catalogue), 3.1 Overview of the significant medieval historical events regarding the Pauline Order and the Pilis region), it is not inaccurate to call the first hermit communities in the Pilis Paulines as well.

[217] *prope Strigonium ... prope speluncam triplicem, quam ipse alias in coluerat, iuxta aquam vivam.* Gyöngyösi (1988), *Vitae Fratrum,* Cap. 6–7.

[218] See Chapter 3 (Catalogue), 3.2 Pauline monasteries in the Pilis. 1. Monastery of Holy Cross, 124, Figure 28.

This traditional viewpoint of the order defined the historical interpretation until recent times; another history of the order has started to evolve in the past few years based on the critical examination of the thirteenth-century documents. This evolution of the research was instigated by Tamás Guzsik, who collected the architectural remains of the Paulines,[219] but *The Archaeological Topography of Hungary* also had an important role by surveying a significant part of those areas where the first hermitages and Pauline monasteries were founded.[220] Partly based on these directions, recent studies—mostly by Beatrix Romhányi, László Solymosi, and József Laszlovszky[221]—proposed the necessity for a reconsolidation of the research mainly concerning the chronology and circumstances of foundations. It is also worth mentioning that original historical documents were used by Gyöngyösi and preserved in his *Vitae Fratrum.* Because of these characteristics it is crucial to summarize briefly the two, partly contradictory perspectives of Pauline history concerning its foundation.

As the Pauline hermitage founded by Eusebius is located almost halfway between Esztergom, the seat of the archbishop,[222] and the Cistercian abbey at Pilis[223] (present-day Pilisszentkereszt), it suggests (in accordance with the tradition of the order) that this heavy ecclesiastical influence organized or at least spawned the first Pauline hermit communities, which seems plausible, given the strong influence of the Church in the Árpádian Period and the weakness of new religious communities.[224] The archbishop of Esztergom would not have allowed any other religious groups to settle close to his seat without his support or at least his permission.[225] If one accepts that the distance between Esztergom and the

[219] Guzsik (2003), *Pálos építészet.*

[220] I.e., in Veszprém, Pest, and Komárom-Esztergom Counties.

[221] See their publications on the topic listed in the bibliography.

[222] By this time royal presence was rare in Esztergom, see more in Györffy (1987), *Az Árpád-kori Magyarország történeti földrajza* 2, 246–247.

[223] The Cistercian abbey was founded by King Béla III (1162–1196) and Queen Gertrude, the wife of King Andrew II (1205–1235), was buried there. Torma, ed. (1986), *Magyarország Régészeti Topográfiája* 7, 159–164. For further data see Remig Békefi, *A pilisi apátság története* 1184-1814 [A history of the Pilis monastery 1184-1814], (Pécs: s.n. 1891–1892).

[224] In other parts of the country small communities sometimes decided to found monasteries with their own support, but it is impossible to believe that this could have happened so close to the religious center of Hungary. Romhányi (2012a), "Pálos kolostorok a Pilisben," 224.

[225] Romhányi (2012a), "Pálos kolostorok a Pilisben," 224.

Holy Cross Monastery[226]—calculated by a Least Cost Path (LCP) analysis—is not more than 13 km over low terrain, the seat was easily accessible[227] (*Figure 12*).

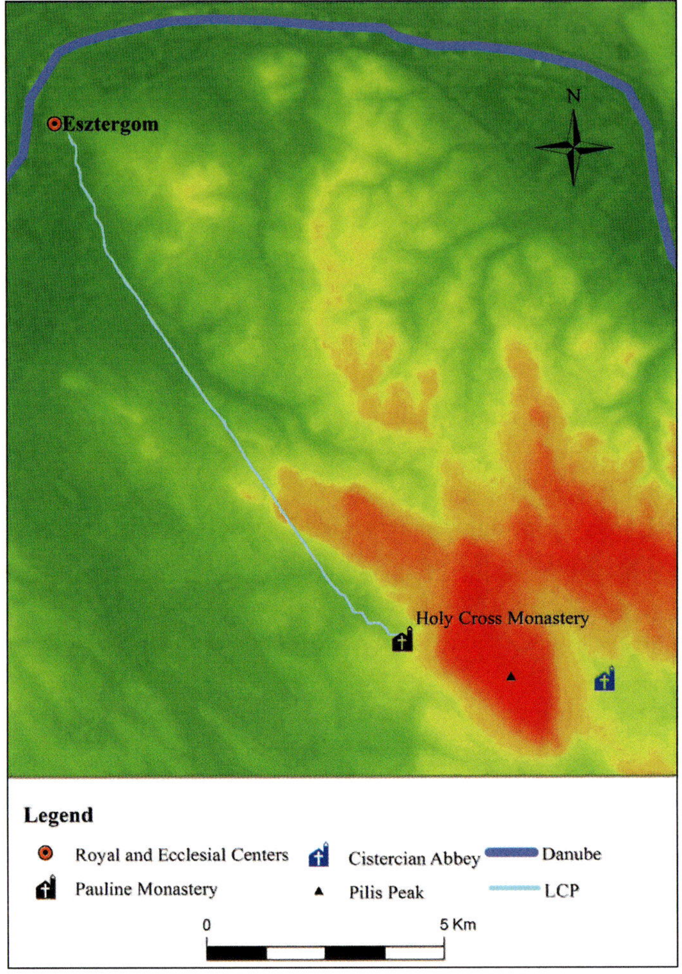

Figure 12. An LCP analysis between Esztergom and Kesztölc on ASTER GDEM

---

[226] It is believed that the Holy Cross Monastery was erected near the place where the first hermits, the hermits of Eusebius, were living in caves. This is the reason why the monastery is relevant as a fixed point for the hermit period of the Paulines.

[227] The path from the settlement of Kesztölc (even from the modern-day village) led to the *via magna*, the main road between Esztergom and Buda.

As Péter Szabó has pointed out, it seems that the king simply fostered a spontaneous process,[228] so the hermits in the Pilis seemed to be in the right place at the right time, and thus the Holy Cross Monastery could become the leading community of the Pauline movement by 1291. It is not misleading to regard the Holy Cross Monastery as the birthplace of the Pauline Order, if it is evaluated as an important step in the context of thirteenth-century eremitic movements. The desire of such communities in Hungary to become a regular ecclesial community, more likely an order, was supported by European events, namely the wish of the Holy See to join and regulate isolated hermits and eremitic brotherhoods. This is the century when the Augustine Order was founded and the eremitic Williamites appeared.[229] Maybe the *Vitae Fratrum* references this event as well, when Eusebius asks the Pope himself in Rome to allow the community of the Holy Cross to live by the Rule of St. Augustine.[230]

The next level of development started when the first religious community of the Paulines in the Pilis—just as in other regions of the kingdom[231]—became a (pseudo-) monastery some time between the 1260s and 1270s. The tradition says that Eusebius erected the buildings of the monastery near the caves; thus, based on the Pauline tradition, this site was more than a simple hermit community. They must have had at least some huts and a church, where—as the tradition of the order describes—Eusebius was buried.[232]

Although the steps of the evolution of the Pauline Order during this time are hardly known (and therefore cannot be described or even defined precisely),

---

228 Romhányi (2012a), "Pálos kolostorok a Pilisben," 224.

229 Kaspar Elm, *Die Bulle "Ea quae iudicio" Clemens' IV.30.VIII.1266. Vorgeschichte, Überlieferung, Text, und Bedeutung* (Heverlee-Louvain: Institut Historique Augustinien, 1966); Kaspar Elm, "Eremiten und Eremitenorden des 13. Jahrhunderts," in: *Beiträge zur Geschichte des Paulinerordens. Berliner Historische Studien, vol. 32, Ordensstudien 14*, eds. Kaspar Elm et al. (Berlin: Duncker und Humblot, 2000), 11–22. See also a posthumous collection of Kaspar Elm's essays: Kaspar Elm and James D. Mixson, *Religious life between Jerusalem, the desert, and the world* (Leiden: Brill, 2016).

230 Gyöngyösi (1988), *Vitae Fratrum,* Cap. 10.

231 The origins of the Pauline Order in other regions of the kingdom raise several questions. The process of becoming a unified order was a complex issue and had many steps. The only chance to get closer to the details of these steps is by a large and complex synthesis and summary of several regions where the Paulines were detected. The nature of the topic signals the future direction of monastic studies concerning the Pauline Order.

232 Gyöngyösi (1988), *Vitae Fratrum,* Cap. 12.

some assumptions can be drawn based on the small number of direct and indirect sources. This new interpretation focuses on the early phase of the hermitages and communities, as well as on the emergence of the Holy Cross Monastery. The site itself, its location, and the quick development of the community all suggest that the Holy Cross Monastery and the Paulines underwent a relatively radical transformation due to the change in their support.[233] Beyond religious influence, royal patronage was crucial for the hermits to live and for their community to evolve.[234] Therefore, the first and most important direction of the research is to articulate the presence of this support in early Pauline history.

King Béla IV (1235–1270) moved his royal residence to Esztergom again, next to the archbishop, in the mid-1260s, since he was in a dispute with his son, Stephen (who later became king as Stephen V [1270–1272]), the *rex iunior* of Hungary; therefore, the king was more aware of the events taking place in the area of Esztergom. The conflict between the king and his son began in the early 1260s; the first battle took place in 1264. Based on this data, the king would have spent more time in the archbishop's seat, Esztergom, at this time, rather than in the newly founded Buda, which was occupied by his son.[235] Additionally, it might be a sign of Esztergom's strong connection with the royal court that King Béla and his closest family members were buried there in 1270.

The king was obviously aware of and permitted or supported events like the foundation of hermitages/pseudo-monasteries near or in the royal forest close to Esztergom. As Beatrix Romhányi discusses in her short summary on the Pauline monasteries in the Pilis, the exact nature of this support is known from later written sources:[236] King Béla assured free territories for the hermits in the mid-1260s near the site that later became the Holy Cross Monastery.[237] This was less

---

[233] Belényesy (2004), *Pálos kolostorok Abaúj-Hegyalján*, 87–88; also Romhányi (2010), *Pálos gazdálkodás a középkorban*, 15–16.

[234] On the debates, see Romhányi (2008), "Pálos rendi hagyomány," 289–312. This is discussed in Chapter 1.1, see the subchapter on Pauline monasteries.

[235] Romhányi (2012a), "Pálos kolostorok a Pilisben," 224–225.

[236] Romhányi (2012a), "Pálos kolostorok a Pilisben," 224–225.

[237] Gyöngyösi (1988), *Vitae Fratrum*, Cap. 14, 15. See the event listed in Chapter 3 (Catalogue), 3.2 Pauline monasteries in the Pilis. 1. Monastery of Holy Cross, 131. This donation was recorded in a later charter, when some buildings were already erected, i.e., the monks had already settled down. It is also possible that King Ladislaus IV took back the donated lands by force from the Paulines (the royal army burnt down the monastery two years earlier), but then changed his mind, as Beatrix Romhányi suggests. See Romhányi (2012a), "Pálos kolostorok a Pilisben," 224.

than recognition, but more than simple permission, and fulfilled the need of such hermit-like communities: their own free and cultivatable territories. Besides this, he also donated a hunting lodge to the Holy Cross community, supposedly for founding a new monastery on the site. This was surely unsuccessful—as it was probably renewed by King Ladislaus IV (1272–1290)—but it shows that the king respected and personally supported the hermits.

The significance of such royal support becomes stronger if other events are considered in the synthesis. By this time, the first inventory of Pauline monasteries in the bishopric of Veszprém had been compiled, as the hermits living there had asked for formal papal permission to live by the regulations of St. Augustine,[238] that is, to be recognized as a legitimate monastic order. Bishop Paul came to the conclusion that these hermitages were too poor to become a legal order and a unified community; therefore, he prohibited the foundation of new monasteries in his territory, but at the same time he gave them a *regula*.[239] All this might have been completely disregarded in the Pilis Forest. Paul did not visit the Holy Cross Monastery, even though the area was still under the regulation of the Veszprém Bishopric.[240] As László Solymosi has pointed out, it seems unlikely that such an important monastery as the Holy Cross was omitted from the inventory and then, three decades later (1291), be listed as a monastery governed by the Veszprém Bishopric. There were some suggestions about its exemption from the Bishopric's regulations during the compilation of the first inventory, but those do not explain why the Bishopric had jurisdiction over the monastery again in 1291. This order of the ecclesial evolution contradicts any previously known medieval conventions.

---

[238] On this the text states: *provinciali setalii priores ac fratres heremitae diversorum locorum nostrae diaecesis*. Gyöngyösi (1988), *Vitae Fratrum,* Cap. 11.

[239] Gyöngyösi (1988), *Vitae Fratrum*, Cap. 9.

[240] Gyéressy et al. (1976), *Documenta Artis Paulinorum* 1, 400. Also Beatrix Romhányi, *Kolostorok és társaskáptalanok a középkori Magyarországon* [Monasteries and collegiate chapters in Medieval Hungary] (Budapest: Pytheas, 2000), 48. Although there have been debates on the regulation of the monastery, scholars more or less agree with the authority of the Veszprém Bishopric over this territory. Finally, in the next inventory, written in 1291, the Holy Cross Monastery and the St. Ladislaus Monastery are listed as parts of the bishopric. See Solymosi (2005), "Pilissziget," 14–15. Considering that each bishop who had such hermits under his control (like in Eger or Pécs) regulated them individually—but of course with similar conditions—the Holy Cross Monastery still occupied a place of higher importance among the communities; nevertheless, the written sources report about this outstanding role, see Gyöngyösi (1988), *Vitae Fratrum*, Cap. 7–9.

In any case, the royal presence and support clearly affected the further history of the order, since after the second inventory the Paulines appeared to not be too poor to found new communities and request estates to supply their monasteries.

All of the inventories (from 1263 and 1291) were preserved in Gyöngyösi's *Vitae Fratrum*, where the traditional history of the order's foundation is also described. On this, it should be highlighted that the traditional history and the original documents contradict each other. The traditional history emphasizes the Holy Cross Monastery and the Pilis area, though it also mentions earlier hermit movements, mostly in Baranya County (*Pécs-Jakabhegy*). These were founded a few decades earlier than the Holy Cross Monastery, sometime before the 1250s. Even so, the later tradition commemorates the Holy Cross Monastery as the first and earliest site of the Paulines. This ambiguity has greatly affected the historians and archaeologists as well. Summarizing the debates and pointing out the contentious data, László Solymosi came to the conclusion that the Monastery of the Holy Cross may not have existed at the time of the compilation of the first inventory (in 1263), otherwise there could be no reason to omit it. As it was listed in 1291 as the first monastery, it must have been founded between 1263 and 1291.[241]

The settling of the hermits may support this given time period. The lands (deserted lands, the village of Üllőkő, and *Bendwelgye*/Bendek valley) and even the hunting lodge, a property donated by King Béla to the Paulines of the Holy Cross Monastery (obviously donated after 1263),[242] may indicate that the foundation of a somewhat coherent community could have happened between 1263/64[243] (when the king stayed mostly at Esztergom) and 1270, the death of King Béla. The first donations supposedly led to the emergence of the Holy Cross Monastery within the hermit movements, which could have been the result of their geographical location as well.

The donations of King Béla seem to have taken place around the time of (or more likely after[244]) the visitation of Bishop Paul;[245] therefore, establishing

---

[241] Solymosi (2005), "Pilissziget," 18–23.

[242] See Chapter 3 (Catalogue), 3.2 Pauline monasteries in the Pilis. 1. Monastery of Holy Cross, 131–132.

[243] Note that the king had spent these years in Esztergom. Györffy (1987), *Az Árpád-kori Magyarország történeti földrajza* 2, 246.

[244] This should have been just after the *visitatio*, if it is accepted that the emergence of the Holy Cross Monastery, the royal land donation, and the presence of King Béla in Esztergom in 1264, one year after the *visitatio*, all correlate strongly.

[245] See more in Chapter 2.1.

exclusive royal support for the monastery. Although the exact date of the donation is unknown, the Paulines' legal status was complicated and unstable, which may be why Bishop Paul did not list the Holy Cross Monastery in the first inventory.[246] It seems that the first Paulines at the Holy Cross Monastery acquired the basis of their estates at times when they emphasized their separation from the hermitic community of the bishopric, at least from the 1260s. Although the whole character of the community was not well specified at the time, the Paulines seem to have had good (self) management.

This successful beginning and the emergence of the Holy Cross Monastery was followed by two more monastery foundations (the Holy Spirit and St. Ladislaus monasteries), probably by King Ladislaus IV around the 1280s.[247] In the case of the St. Ladislaus monastery, as József Laszlovszky argues, King Ladislaus IV could have been the founder, as the monastery was named after his patron saint.[248] It is also interesting that the last two, or perhaps originally all three Pauline monasteries,[249] were founded on the sites of royal hunting lodges[250] by the end of the thirteenth century (before 1291) during the reign of King Ladislaus IV.

---

[246] If we consider that King Béla knew about the result of the visit and that the donations to the Holy Cross Monastery happened afterwards, then there might be a connection between the two events. The Paulines may have asked for the land or the king may have realized the needs of the hermits and, therefore, supported them with his donations. If the Paulines had received the lands and the hunting lodge earlier than the visit of Bishop Paul, they might have had a different status in the hierarchy (which is poorly emphasized in the historical research) in that period.

[247] Romhányi (2012a), "Pálos kolostorok a Pilisben," 225.

[248] This kind of denomination has great relevance, as there are previous examples where the religious institution was named after the royal founder, e.g., the St. Andrew Monastery at Visegrád was named after King Andrew I (1046–1060). Hereby I would like to thank József Laszlovszky for his related suggestions.

[249] Evidence of earlier buildings was found during the excavations at the Monastery of the Holy Spirit and apparently at the Monastery of the Holy Cross as well. In both cases there is unfortunately very scarce archaeological evidence. The circumstances of the foundation of the St. Ladislaus Monastery is quite obscure: scholars have supposed that the charter on the donation of King Béla, verified by King Ladislaus IV for a hunting lodge, does not refer to the Holy Spirit, but to the St. Ladislaus Monastery. See the written sources for each monastery in Chapter 3 (Catalogue), 3.2 Pauline monasteries in the Pilis, 131–133, 154–155, 164–166.

[250] To the southeast the Cistercian abbey was also founded on royal lands. However, these might not have been just simple hunting lodges connected with the itinerant court, which had started to disappear around the end of the thirteenth century.

Besides the Holy Cross, Holy Spirit, and St. Ladislaus monasteries, there were small communities (with a maximum of six monks each), seemingly hidden in the wild, wooded areas of the Pilis; however, they existed on royal property, which in itself is particularly important.[251]

In parallel with the positive results of founding monasteries in the royal forest, the donation of royal lodges was also a sign of the decline of the physical royal presence in the Pilis.[252] This suggests that the role of the Royal Forest was changing and that the kings had started to prefer larger permanent residences over the small ones in the Pilis. Regarding the fact that these were all royal foundations, it should be highlighted that the kings aimed to keep their spiritual control over the region through these monasteries.[253] Maybe this change of perception was the original reason why King Béla IV donated his hunting lodge to the Holy Cross Monastery in the Pilis, which was repeated by his successor, Ladislaus IV, in 1287 in order to allow some monks from the former monastery to establish a new monastery.[254] The relavant sources (surviving in the *Vitae Fratrum*) refer to a small number of related events. Scholars suppose that King Béla's first attempt was unsuccessful,[255] which is why King Ladislaus repeated the donation and thereafter the Holy Spirit Monastery was established. This monastery may have operated alongside the Holy Cross friary for a few years or even decades, because it is not mentioned in the second inventory of Pauline monasteries in the Veszprém Bishopric from 1291.

---

[251] Romhányi (2012a), "Pálos kolostorok a Pilisben," 225.

[252] Even so, there is indeed some evidence of royal support behind this religious development: although the first ecclesial institutions (monasteries, chapters) were founded in the eleventh century, the increasing domination of monasteries in parallel with the declination of royal presence was actually the result of royal decision. See more in Romhányi (2012a), "Pálos kolostorok a Pilisben," 223. For more on the change, see the section "The Pilis Forest: Natural and Historical Environment" in Chapter 1.1, based on the ideas of Szabó (2005), *Woodland and Forests*, 97.

[253] As Péter Szabó points out, "these places were more 'hotels' than 'residences.'" Szabó (2005), *Woodland and Forests,* 95. The itinerant court, the kings during their travels (or hunting), could easily run into hermits in the Pilis Forest.

[254] Charters and sources cited in Chapter 3 (Catalogue), 3.2 Pauline Monasteries in the Pilis, 131–133, 154–155, 164–166.

[255] This is based on the commentary of Ferenc Hervay, see Gyöngyösi (1988), *Vitae Fratrum,* 209.

The plan of the church at the Holy Spirit Monastery clearly shows that it originally was not erected to serve religious purposes.[256] The excavations at the site revealed some unusual parts of the building, which are usually regarded by scholars as signs of the early royal hunting lodge, which was later donated and refurbished as a church.[257] Additionally, the physical royal presence was documented only here among the Pauline monasteries in the Pilis; therefore, as excavations have revealed, some structures served as living quarters for visitors, especially for the kings and members of the royal court.[258] Of course, different documented events and various architectural structures could represent time periods but they offer a hint for the researchers as to the general framework of the Paulines' function and character.

Although the foundation and early phase of the third monastery, dedicated to St. Ladislaus, are poorly documented and no archaeological remains of the monastery are known, it is sure that the foundation took place before 1291.[259] In this year Lodomér, the archbishop of Esztergom, verified the existence of the Paulines; therefore, by this time these monasteries—the whole community—were clearly ecclesiastical subjects. Moreover, the St. Ladislaus Monastery also had strong royal support; therefore, its foundation was substantiated for recordable reasons.

It is clear that the monasteries were founded on royal estates (hunting lodges), which were supposedly elements of a special administrative system of the Árpádian Period. Accordingly, the continuity of strong royal support is clear in the thirteenth century as well, but there are other features of the land that may help to explain the contemporary status of the Pauline monasteries in the Pilis more accurately.

---

[256] See the plan and data in Chapter 3 (Catalogue), 3.2 Pauline Monasteries in the Pilis. 2. Monastery of Holy Spirit, 158, Figure 57.

[257] These unusual features are: the asymmetry of the church and the unusual plan of the nave, additionally, there were earlier structures and traces of modifications recorded on the southern wall of the nave. See the listed works in the bibliography of Sarolta Lázár, who was leading the excavations at the site.

[258] See the data on the presence of King Charles Robert I (1308–1342) and, a few decades later, his son, King Louis I (1342–1382) in Chapter 3 (Catalogue), 3.2 Pauline Monasteries in the Pilis. 2. Monastery of Holy Spirit, 154–155.

[259] This is due to the fact that it is listed in the second catalogue of Pauline monasteries in the Veszprém Bishopric, see details in Chapter 3 (Catalogue), 3.2 Pauline Monasteries in the Pilis. 3. Monastery of St. Ladislaus, 164.

Integrating the Natural Environment, Medieval Pathways, and Known Settlements

It is clear that the locations of the royal hunting lodges—uninhabited, wooded areas of the Pilis—corresponded more or less with the environment preferred by hermits. It is generally supposed that this preferred territory can be described by clear geographical factors. The *desertum* nature of the mid-hilly area refers to a hidden territory; the Pauline monasteries—at first sight—lie in the wild area of the forest, in closed valleys, near springs and caves, distant from the eyes of laymen (*Figure 13*). But were the Paulines totally secluded from the outside world?

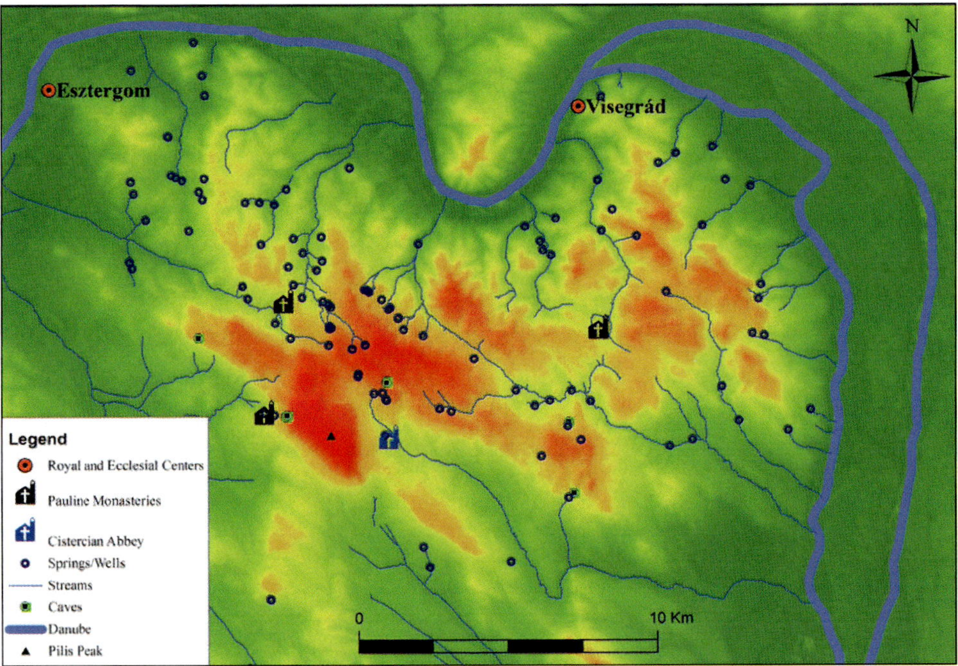

Figure 13. The natural features around the Pauline monasteries in the Pilis on ASTER GDEM, based on present-day environmental data

In the case of the Holy Cross Monastery, if the hermits sought an ideal space, the answer is more or less yes. Adding that the hunting lodges were supposed to preserve the privacy of the kings, the answer is, again, yes. But taking into consideration that the royals would have had servants living at the lodges and reachable residences (even another lodge) close to them, the Pilis does not seem particularly uninhabited.[260] Also, as partial regional studies have concluded,[261] in the mid-hilly region the maximum distance between Pauline monasteries was not more than a few kilometers (a few hours of walking) from settlements and main roads.[262] Thus, this area was not totally secluded from the secular sphere; the monasteries were accessible from the main roads and inhabited areas of the *medium regni* (*Figure 14*). A closer view of these landscape features, which is only partially visible in the secondary literature, helps us to understand the spatial structure of the area.

Research on the road network in the area has to deal with many problems, mostly related to chronology. The Romans left many traces of roads in the landscape, which were used in the Middle Ages as well. Research on the detailed documentation, separation (in time, space, and role), and analysis of these pathways is still a major task of the historical investigations in Hungary. Not much is known on the topic, but enough to emphasize some points about the monasteries and residences, and the question of royal power, the lay sphere, and religious centers.

The best-known route, the *via magna* (VM, *Figure 14*), was the main road for the settlements between Esztergom and Buda, crossing the settlement of Csaba; even the modern road follows the path of this medieval road.[263] A subsidiary trail was reconstructed by Elek Benkő based on written sources;[264] the exact route

---

[260] As Péter Szabó describes, "wherever the king and his retinue stayed in the Pilis, they had a lodge within a few hours' ride and the archbishop, the queen, St. Stephen's tomb, and their own residence within one day's journey." Szabó (2005), *Woodland and Forests*, 93–94.

[261] Belényesy (2004), *Pálos kolostorok Abaúj-Hegyalján*, 87–88.

[262] Note that the distance between the Pauline monasteries was no more than what they could cover in a day. See Belényesy, (2004), *Pálos kolostorok Abaúj-Hegyalján*, 87–88.

[263] *Magnam viam per quamitur de Strigonio Budam* is mentioned first in the thirteenth century and then in later periods as well. It was recorded in 1411 that it crossed Csaba, DL 1798, cited in Györffy (1998), *Az Árpád-kori Magyarország történeti földrajza* 4, 591. See also Benkő (2011), "Via regis," 116. It also crosses, e.g., the boundary between the monastery and the medieval village of Kesztölc. *...in quondam magnam viam de Strigonio versus Budam transeuntem saliendo,* DL 236647. The track of *via magna* is based on the presumably archaic road structure documented on the First Military Survey.

[264] The *viae magnae*, the main roads, led to Esztergom, Buda [!], and Dorog [!], and the *via antiqua*, the old road, is mentioned in the perambulation of the Nyír settlement, a neighbour of

is an ideal reconstruction and follows a modern motorway. Another important route known in the area was originally the main Roman road between Brigetio (present-day Komárom-Szőny) and Aquincum (present-day Budapest-Óbuda), through present-day Szántó. The track of this road led north to the medieval *via magna* from Óbuda to Szántó, crossing Üröm and Borosjenő, but turning west at some point to reach Szőny (R1, *Figure 14*). The remains of this ballast-road were recorded archaeologically.[265] It is visible on modern topographical maps and there is evidence for its use in the Middle Ages.[266] A group of settlements is known in this part of the Pilis foothills[267] (*Figure 14*).

Based on this information it became clear that the important medieval monasteries, (which had strong royal support and sometimes enjoyed the king's presence) did not follow these routes; they were apparently secluded. Scholars have started to integrate more information; it is clear that there are other parts of the Roman road network that can all be crucial for the research.[268] A route was detected from Szántó to Üröm, going the same direction as the previous road, but slightly more to the north (R2, *Figure 14*), on the southern side of a hill (Hosszú-hegy), which was probably mentioned as *via magna* in a medieval perambulation of Boron.[269] Another part of the route was found around Pilisszentkereszt and

Keszölc. Torma, ed. (1979), *Magyarország Régészeti Topográfiája* 5, 194–195, (Esztergom site 8/41). The *via antiqua* might be the main Roman road to Brigetio as it was found south of the settlement. The reconstruction by Elek Benkő is not supported by the sources. See Judit Majorossy, ed., *"A királynét megölni nem kell félnetek jó lesz" Merániai Gertrúd emlékezete, 1213-2013. Történeti vándorkiállítás, kiállításvezető* [The queen to kill you must not fear will be good ... Commemorating Gertrude of Merania, 1213-2013. Historical Touring Exhibition, Museum Booklet] (Szentendre: Ferenczy Museum, 2013), 10, Figure 31.

265 For the archaeological evidence see: Torma, ed. (1979), *Magyarország Régészeti Topográfiája* 5, 278–279 (Piliscsév site 16/5.); Torma, ed. (1986), *Magyarország Régészeti Topográfiája* 7, 156 (Pilisszántó site 17/12); 173–174 (Pilisvörösvár site 21/21).

266 E.g., an administrative map of Pilis County, S 12 Div XI. No. 89; or Benkő (2011), "*Via regis*," 116, ref. 1.

267 Benkő (2011), "*Via regis*," 116. At some point modern secondary roads might follow its route.

268 According to the summary of László Ferenczi et al., *"Történeti útvonalak kutatása a Pilisben: tájrégészeti-tájtörténeti vizsgálatok térinformatikai háttérrel"* [Research of historical pathways in the Pilis: landscape archaeological and landscape historical examinations with GIS], Manuscript, (Budapest: 2013).

269 The route was recorded by Dezső Simonyi, see Torma, ed. (1986), *Magyarország Régészeti Topográfiája* 7, 156 (Pilisszántó site 17/12a); 76–77 (Csobánka site 6/28); 143–144 (Pilisborosjenő site 15/8); 353 (Üröm site 37/11). See also Ferenczi et al. (2013), "Történeti útvonalak kutatása a Pilisben."

Dobogókő (R3, *Figure 14*),[270] which—as Elek Benkő argues—should have been the continuation of the road at Szántó (R2), crossing the Cistercian abbey. He is convinced that these roads (R2 and R3) were medieval; therefore, he identifies another road, a *via regis*, which was shorter and crossed a relatively uninhabited area in the Pilis (VR, *Figure 14*). As Benkő points out, kings might have used this "royal express road" to get to the hunting lodges or curia, later monasteries, and then continue on to Esztergom or Óbuda.[271]

Based on this idea, the latest research on the *via regis* using geographical and topographical evidence has revealed another option.[272] A Roman/medieval road (R2) passing through the medieval settlement of Boron (*Figure 14*, zoomed) may have also run on the north side of the hill Hosszú-hegy (maybe in two tracks) and connected the Cistercian monastery with the southern road system, skipping Szántó (VR, *Figure 14*). This path would have been practical for several reasons, which are still clear to modern tourists.[273] The slope was more balanced along the whole path and avoided the steep part of the road from Szántó to the Cistercian monastery. A side path also led to the Cistercian grange to the northeast.

---

[270] Recorded by Lajos Zambra, in Torma, ed. (1986), *Magyarország Régészeti Topográfiája* 7, 164–165 (Pilisszentkereszt site 19/2). Research indicates that this is part of the internal Roman road of the Pilis until Esztergom, but the question is still open. Benkő (2011), "*Via regis*," 115–119; Ferenczi et al. (2013), "Történeti útvonalak kutatása a Pilisben."

[271] The idea of this *via regia* was unknown in the scholarship until it was posed recently. The problems in the research of historical roads were caused by the complex history of the area. The ideal routes between different points may be identified, but in many cases the time period of their use is problematic. The function and route of the *via regia* between Üröm and Pilis have been researched recently by József Laszlovszky and László Ferenczi. I am grateful for their personal communications. Based on their idea and with their participation, ongoing research is revealing the route of the complete path. Further participants: Balázs Kohán, Zsolt Petkes, Márton Deák, Tamás Lantos, and the author. For the latest summary on the research status see: Ferenczi et al. (2013), "Történeti útvonalak kutatása a Pilisben." For research on historical roads see the following selected literature: Torma, ed. (1979), *Magyarország Régészeti Topográfiája* 5, Torma, ed. (1986), *Magyarország Régészeti Topográfiája* 7; Benkő (2011), "*Via regis*," 115–119. Also see the map reconstructed by Elek Benkő in Majorossy (2013), *Gertrudis*, 10, Figure 31.

[272] Sources include historical and modern maps, and a field survey from Üröm to Dobogókő. Ferenczi et al. (2013), "Történeti útvonalak kutatása a Pilisben."

[273] During the field survey it was discovered that at several points this pathway is still used as a secondary road or simple hiking trail. Ferenczi et al. (2013), "Történeti útvonalak kutatása a Pilisben."

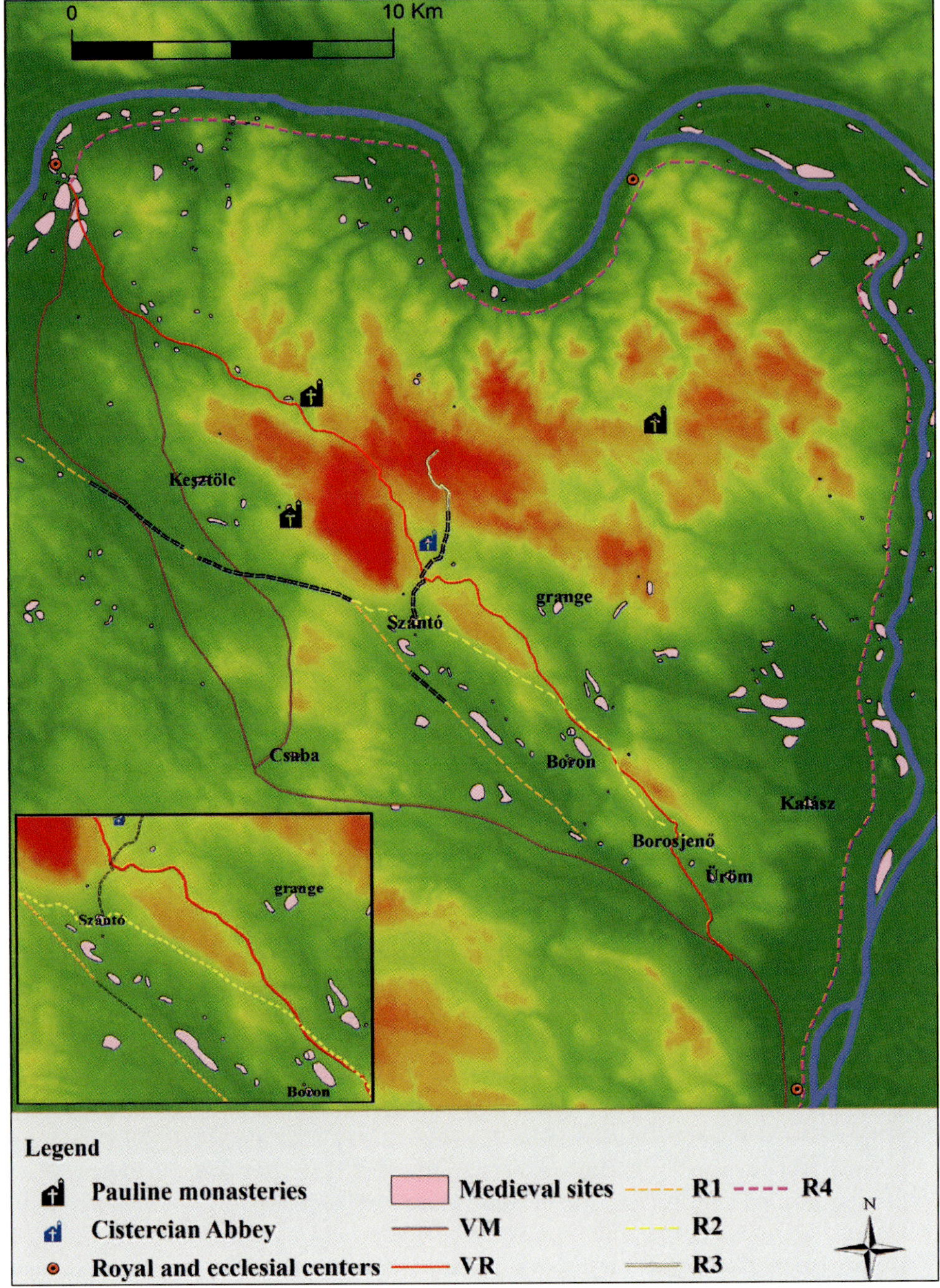

Figure 14. The main roads, centers, and monasteries in the Pilis on ASTER GDEM

The last known main historical road runs along the Danube bank, which is substantiated by visible landscape evidence; it was also part of the Roman road next to the *limes* of Pannonia (R4, *Figure 14*). In the Middle Ages there were several settlements there, due to the traditionally favorable circumstances for settling and the important role of the Danube as a transport route and a source for fishing.

This short summary of the known elements of the historical road network in the Pilis area indicates that a spatial approach—the use of GIS—can lead to the discovery of additional features. Some investigations were made to reconstruct the ideal pathways of the region based on the elevation of the area and compare the results with known information. First, by a Least Cost Path Analysis the shortest route between Esztergom and Óbuda[274] (LCP 1, *Figure 15*) was calculated, which resulted in the addition of new details to the research. It runs closest to the original main Roman road to Szőny (R1) at the beginning of its route and—oddly—it crosses an Árpádian Period settlement that stood near a Roman watchtower and the reconstructed path of the main Roman road (R1, *Figure 15*, zoomed).[275] The remains of this road—at some point—were probably used by medieval people as well.

This LCP 1 path goes near the Holy Cross Monastery, but here uncertainty grows, because the written evidence has not yet been identified and analyzed for this area.[276] The only sure thing is that more than one *via magna* is mentioned in this area. Remarkably, the archaic track of *via magna* goes near to the LCP

[274] Óbuda, as an early royal residence (see *Figure 1*), is a good reference point for all periods, considering that the road from Buda to the north or northeast should cross it. Indicating Esztergom as a starting point in this model raises some questions that may be the topic of studies on GIS techniques and cognitive sciences. Interestingly, the control analysis differs from the ideal path if the starting point is Óbuda. Of course, the difference is not so significant (a few hundred meters) or typical, but considering features of human behavior, could highlight some natural patterns on the question of road reconstructions and GIS techniques. It is remarkable that taking the same path between two points from different directions generates different sensations and experiences for the human mind. It should be noted here that during our LCP analyses the selection of the starting points was a subjective decision.

[275] Torma, ed. (1979), *Magyarország Régészeti Topográfiája* 5, 277–278. (Piliscsév site 16/1).

[276] However, it is clear from the collection of archaeological sources published in *The Archaeological Topography of Hungary* that a systematic analysis could result in further fixed points on the question of the road network. This could be a noteworthy topic for further research. Torma, ed. (1979), *Magyarország Régészeti Topográfiája* 5, e.g. 277–278.

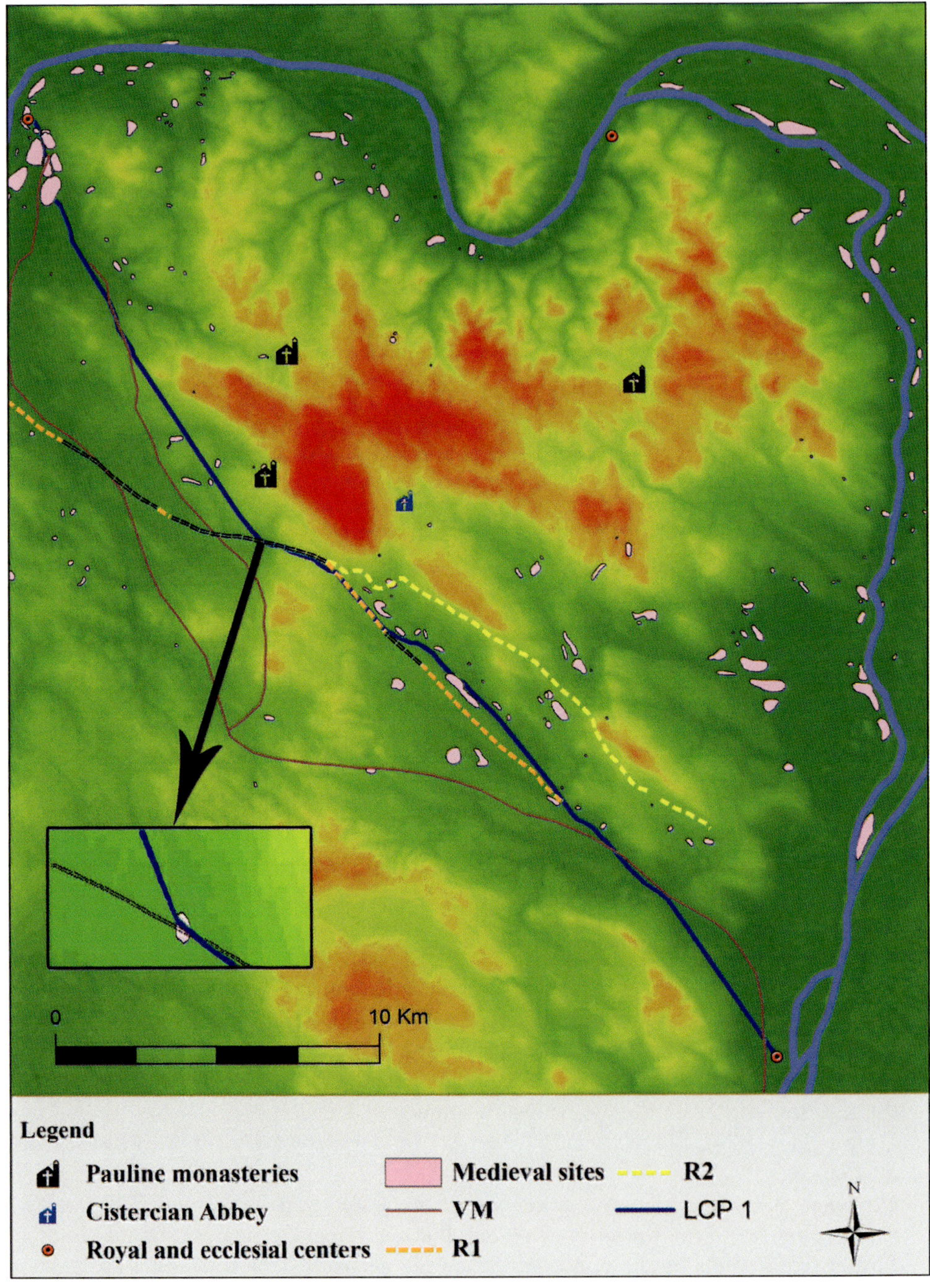

Figure 15. An LCP analysis between Esztergom and Óbuda (LCP 1) on ASTER GDEM

track, which also suggests parallel roads that could lead to Esztergom in the area. It is also noteworthy that the medieval village of Kesztölc and other anonymous settlements lie next to the reconstructed shortest and easiest path to Esztergom.

The LCP analysis has already made a determination in reconstructing the shortest and easiest path of the *via regis* from Óbuda to Esztergom. Additional features can be used to change the area examined. The main idea behind the *via regis* is the need for a connection between the royal and ecclesial centers and the monasteries in the Pilis, essentially in the Árpádian Period. On a straight line between the two main centers, Óbuda and Esztergom, the Cistercian abbey and the Holy Spirit Monastery seem to be ideal stops (LCP 2, *Figure 16*).[277] The route from Óbuda to Esztergom (LCP 2) followed the route of the main Roman road (R1), but on the south side of Hosszú Hill (Hosszú-hegy) it ran between the main and the supposed other (secondary?) Roman roads (R1 and R2). The track then turns north, crossing the northern Roman road (R2) and the probable route to Dobogókő (R3). After this, it joins (on the track of a modern hiking trail) the reconstructed route of the *via regia* (VR) and further follows it to Esztergom. Summarizing the results, this geographically generated model firmly demonstrates the validity of such roads in the Pilis.

Going to northern areas by searching for other options in LCP analyses, the location of the third Pauline monastery, dedicated to St. Ladislaus, implies a distinctive concept on the geographic area. First, a general geographical phenomenon is revealed: a spatial division is clear among the three monasteries in the Pilis. The geographical location separates a southwestern-western religious sphere (Holy Cross and Holy Spirit monasteries as well as the Cistercian abbey) and a northeastern-eastern section (the St. Ladislaus Monastery) in the Pilis.

Looking at the map, the status of the St. Ladislaus Monastery becomes clear by its location; it lies between Buda/Óbuda and the newly constructed royal castle of Visegrád.[278] The importance of this location is supported by a historical event, that is, the monastery hosted an important political meeting in 1308 between Cardinal Gentilis (as a papal legate) and oligarch Máté Csák in order to stabilize and verify

[277] For more on the idea and reconstruction of the *via regia*, see the recent study of László Ferenczi and József Laszlovszky, "Középkori utak és határhasználat a pilisi apátság területén" [Medieval roads and landscape management on the estate of the Pilis Abbey], *Studia Comitatensia* 1 (2014): 104–106.

[278] The construction of the castle of Visegrád, built by Queen Mary, wife of King Béla IV, to protect the nuns of Margaret Island (Margitsziget) from the Tatars, also strengthened royal control of the Pilis. Szabó (2005), *Woodland and Forests*, 95.

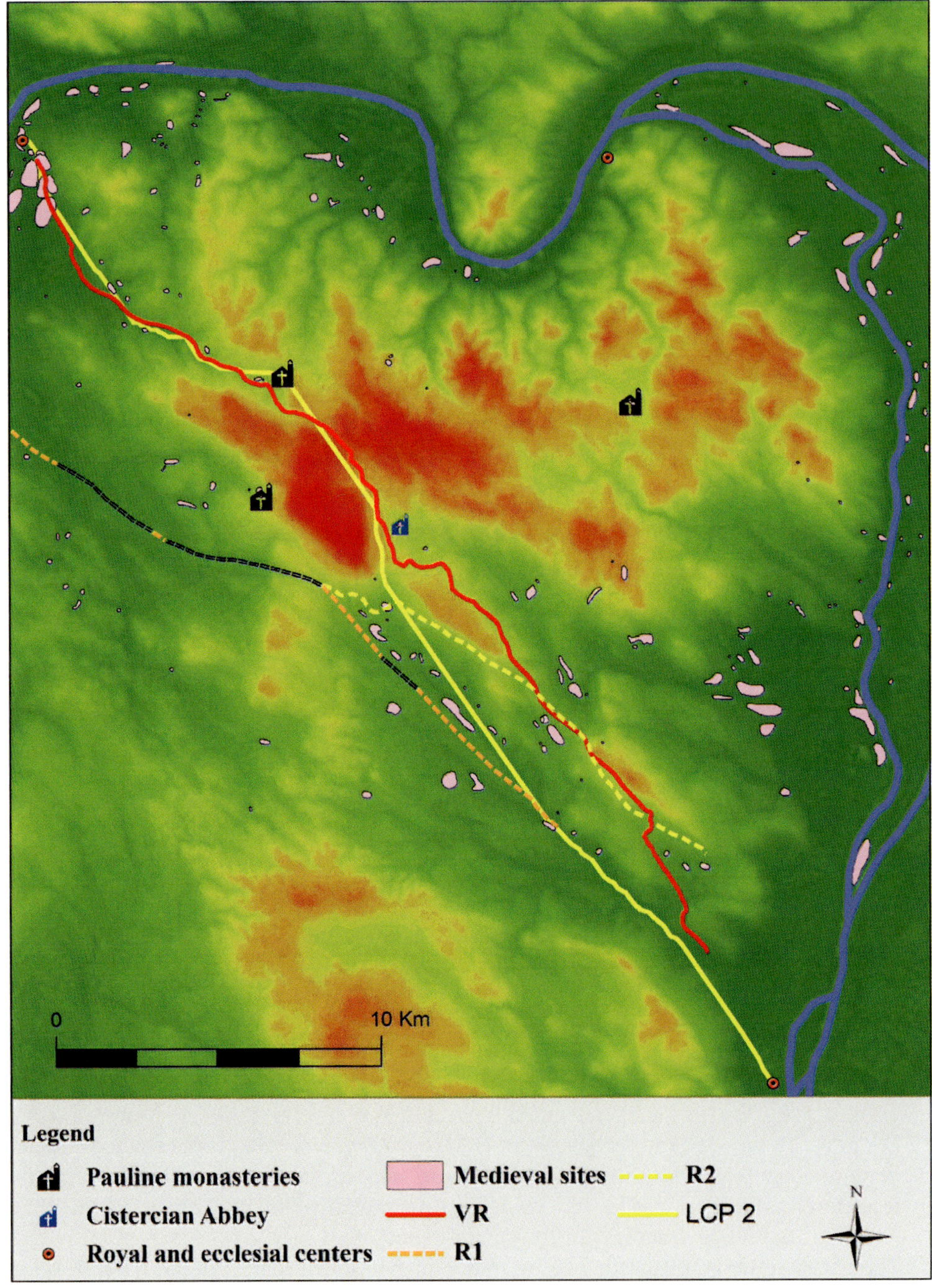

Figure 16. An LCP analysis between Esztergom and Óbuda (LCP 2) on ASTER GDEM

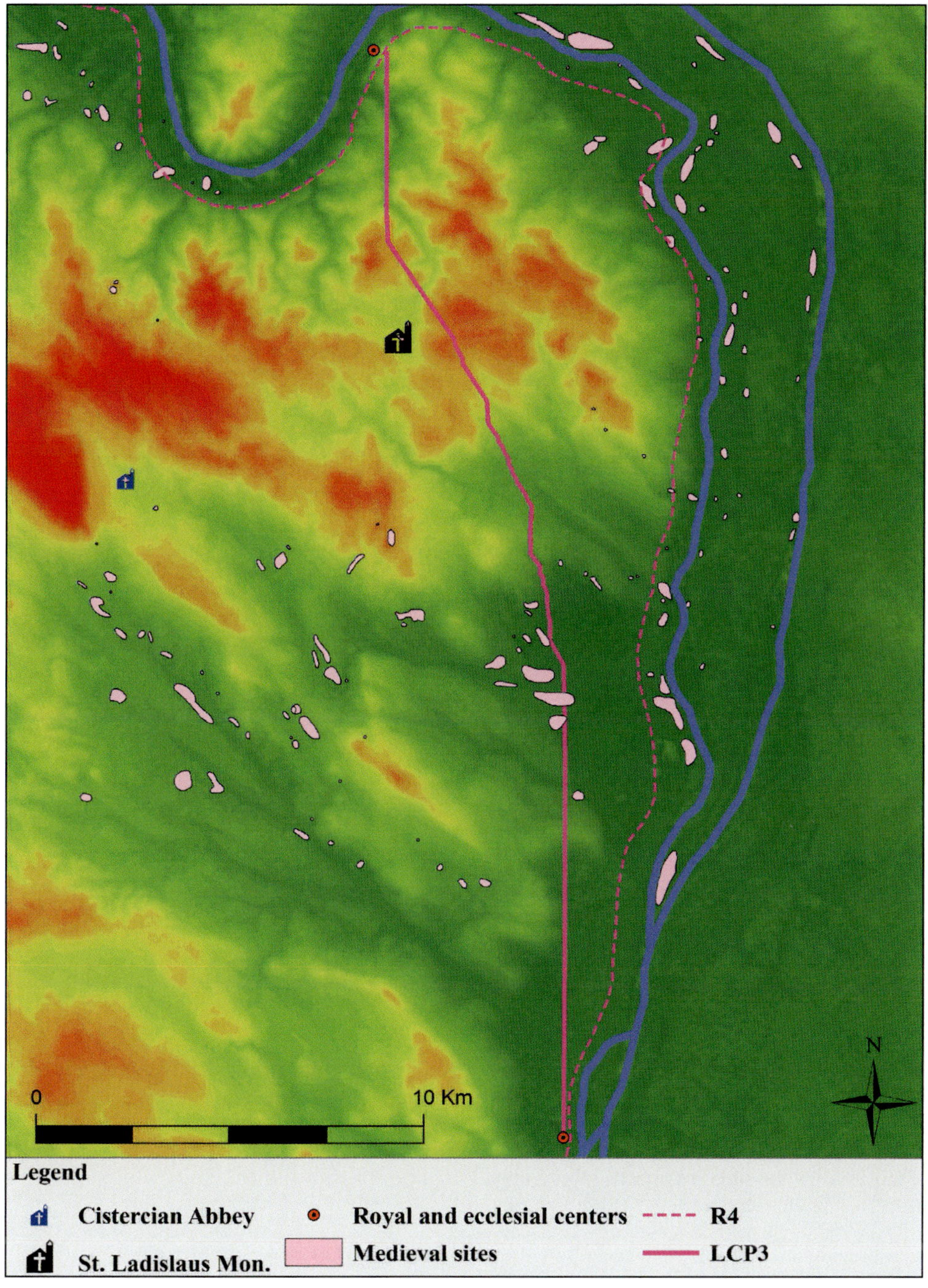

Figure 17. An LCP analysis between Visegrád and Óbuda (LCP 3) on ASTER GDEM

the reign of Charles Robert. The importance of this meeting (and therefore the important role of the monastery) is also emphasized by another event; a month after this meeting the papal legate officially confirmed the Rule of St. Augustine for the Pauline Order. As Beatrix Romhányi argues, the St. Ladislaus Monastery was an ideal location for discussing political and legal questions because it was hidden in the forest and political enemies were far from its premises.[279]

Through the modeling process, the start and the end points of the LCP analysis were certain. From Óbuda to Visegrád (LCP 3, *Figure 17*) there are both well-articulated and less clear areas on the DEM; therefore, in some areas the generated route is very informative,[280] but in other areas—mostly in the north—it is more of an outline than a precise track. The main and key result of the analysis is clear, however, the Monastery of St. Ladislaus was not simply hidden from settled parts of the region, but also offered an opportunity for rest between royal residences. From the mid-thirteenth century these stops became quite important. The close geographical relationship between the main royal residences and the St. Ladislaus Monastery could represent a spiritual connection between royal power and the Pauline Order in the Pilis royal forest.

A Long-term and Fruitful Relationship with the Angevin Kings

Around the time when the last Árpádian king died (Andrew III in 1301) and Charles Robert finally overcame political difficulties, a significant change is revealed in the spatial structure of Pauline monasteries. Side-by-side with the new concept behind the location of the St. Ladislaus Monastery, the center of the Pauline system moved from the Holy Cross Monastery closer to Buda, which was a growing royal center in addition to Visegrád and Óbuda. Written sources report that the Monastery of St. Laurence (at Budaszentlőrinc), built by the prior of the Holy Cross Monastery (*Figure 18*), became the most important center in the Pauline Order's hierarchy; the first prior general was elected there in 1309. Although it lay outside the Pilis, it had a great influence on the monasteries in the Pilis. Their decreasing importance and the changing concept of the Holy Cross Monastery as the paramount cloister can only be understood by examining the changes in the geographical periphery.

---

[279] Romhányi (2012a), "Pálos kolostorok a Pilisben," 225.

[280] The generated route follows the modern motorway.

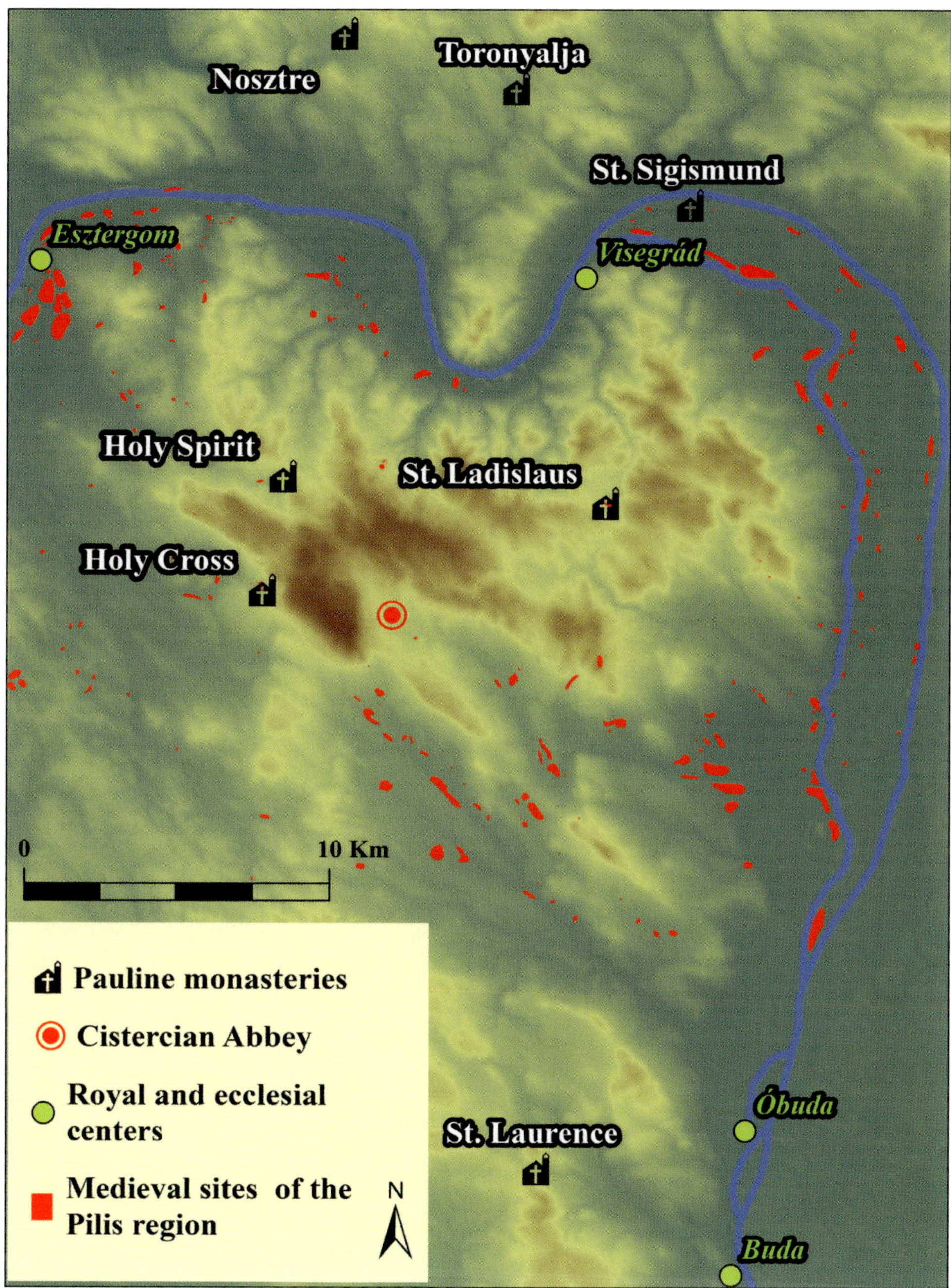

Figure 18. The Pauline monasteries in the Pilis and Börzsöny region, besides the medieval settlements and ecclesial/royal centers on ASTER GDEM

As the royal court moved from Esztergom and the royal centers were strengthened along the Danube, the newly founded Pauline Order had to re-contextualize its role and background. The Monastery of the Holy Cross was the perfect example of hermitic life, partly connected with the royal presence, but the decreasing importance of royal hunting lodges, the functional change of the Pilis Forest,[281] and the stabilization of the royal centers meant that the Paulines also had to move their center closer to royal power and presence.[282] They realized this need and managed to adapt to the new conditions.

The Pauline hierarchy was influenced by the primary royal centers, Buda and Visegrád, but dominance varied between the two. Pauline research and shows that the dominance of the St. Laurence Monastery was greater than any other monastery's during the Middle Ages. Its representation constantly developed, but the historical context and the spatial picture of the fourteenth and early fifteenth centuries highlight some basic questions and phenomena.

The Angevin kings, Charles I (1308–1342) and Louis I (1342–1382), reorganized the Kingdom of Hungary into a stable, developing, and flourishing country. They took every opportunity, in many respects, to build up their kingdom; supporting the Pauline Order was one element for them that was connected with imperial and foreign policy. But how exactly did they support the order?

After the royal court moved to Visegrád, the Angevin kings developed a royal seat and residence there. Their local policy also affected the Börzsöny area, which lies opposite Visegrád on the northern bank of the Danube. Here, King Louis I founded two Pauline monasteries at Nosztre[283] and Toronyalja[284] (*Figure 18*). The importance of this territory peaked during the translation of the relics of St. Paul the First Hermit from Venice to Hungary, and finally to the central royal territory of the country, the Monastery of St. Laurence, in 1381, after the victory of King Louis I over Venice.

This event was the emblematic verification of the order, as well as the St. Laurence Monastery, in a prosperous and successful period of Hungarian

---

[281] See more in Chapter 1. The decreasing importance of the Pilis went hand in hand with the changing administrative system of the country.

[282] Romhányi (2012a), "Pálos kolostorok a Pilisben," 225–226.

[283] The monastery at Nosztre was founded in 1352. Its significance is clear from the fact that Nosztre was the mother monastery of Częstochowa, the first foreign monastery of the order in Poland (1382), Romhányi (2000), *Kolostorok*, 64.

[284] It was founded between 1352 and 1381. Romhányi (2000), *Kolostorok,* 99–100.

history.[285] The significance of the relic translation was clear for the Paulines as well. The event was documented in several sources,[286] including the best-known and only medieval work on Hungarian Pauline history, the *Vitae Fratrum* (1523). It gives a short report on the translation of the relics to Buda and an explanation of the circumstances, emphasizing that King Louis I the Great promised the clerics and monks at the monastery of Nosztra (!) that if he was victorious over the Venetians he would translate the relics of St. Paul to the Paulines.[287] Gyöngyösi refers (in the introductory poem of the chapter) to the monastery in Buda as the final shelter of the relics in the future,[288] after the battle with Venice, but the same chapter also mentions Nosztra, founded by the king.

The text is remarkable because it is not clear why Gyöngyösi pointed out the place of the king's promise and attached many symbolic acts and events to this story: "[Rex] ... promiserat ... in *Nozthre* protunc constitutes audiente toto conventu, quod si omnipotens Deus meritis beati Pauli triumphare posse super Venetos donaret, extunc corpus eiusdem sancti eisdem donaret." To commemorate this oath, the king, "ante monasterium plantavit arborem tiliae, quae ... vocatur arbor regis Ludovici," which was still known many years later.[289] The text is not clear about what *totus conventus* means here: simply all the Paulines or the

---

[285] In 1308, Cardinal Gentilis, the papal legate, was the first to allow the Paulines to live under the Rule of St. Augustine. It was permitted again by Pope John XXII in 1328 and he also gave many large-scale privileges to the monks. In 1368 Pope Urban V approved and ratified the order. Belényesy (2004), *Pálos kolostorok Abaúj-Hegyalján,* 88–89.

[286] The Pauline Valentinus Hadnagy and an anonymous author focused on the life of St. Paul and the journey of his relics from the beginning of the relics' history to their arrival in Buda. Hadnagy also focused on the miracles of St. Paul in his *Vita Divi Pauli*, published in 1511. It is believed that all these sources report on a more or less detailed picture of the ceremonial translation from Venice to Buda and to the St. Laurence Monastery. This information—concerning events, places, and actors—can mediate a closer look at the connections between the relics of St. Paul and its respect, the representation, power, and politics within external and internal policy and the Pauline hierarchy. Gyöngyösi (1988), *Vitae Fratrum,* Cap. 80; Gábor Sarbak, *Miracula Sancti Pauli Primi Heremite. Hadnagy Bálint pálos rendi kézikönyve*, 1511 [The Pauline Handbook of Valentinus Hadnagy, 1511] (Debrecen: Debreceni Egyetem, 2003).

[287] Gyöngyösi (1988), *Vitae Fratrum,* Cap. 35.

[288] Gyöngyösi (1988), *Vitae Fratrum*, Cap. 34.

[289] "[The King] promised in front of the whole convent that if the omnipotent God grants him to be victorious over the Venetians by the merits of the blessed Paul, he will donate the body [i. e., relics] of this same saint to them." Gyöngyösi (1988), *Vitae Fratrum*, Cap. 34.

community of Nosztra in particular? If the latter presumption is correct, Nosztra can be regarded as the pre-selected place for the relics.[290]

The historical context and the Pauline strategy show that these two monasteries could have had enough power and impact at the court (in and close to the territory of the *medium regni*) to represent their own communities; moreover, they had outstanding support from the king himself, so they both could lay claim on becoming the keeper of the relics. Perhaps, finally, the Monastery of St. Laurence had a stronger impact[291] than Nosztra.[292]

---

[290] These events suggests (whether they are true or not) that the king had a special relation with the monastery at Nosztra and also that he himself promised the relics to his beloved monks at Nosztra. Finally, however, he betrayed them and gave the relics to the St. Laurence Monastery.

[291] Following the translation of the relics from Venice to Hungary, it is strange that the body was placed in Buda, in the king's chapel (St. John Chapel) at first, but one month later was translated formally (*...pulchro stilo scripta est in Breviario nostro...*) to its final resting place, the Pauline church of the St. Laurence Monastery on 14 November. At this point one could raise the question: Why did they keep the relics in the royal chapel for a month? Why did they not take them directly to the St. Laurence Monastery or somewhere else? Referring to the problem of the Monastery of St. Laurence and Nosztra, it can be supposed that the arrangements were not ready for the final location of the relics. It may also be a sign of royal mediation or, more likely, royal priority in religious (and ecclesiastical-political) questions. However, it should be noted that King Louis was busy to ratify the Treaty of Turin, which happened almost two weeks after the translation, on November 26 in the Castle of Diósgyőr–almost 200 km from Buda. Besides, there is no evidence that King Louis attended the translational ceremony. The ceremony from Buda to the monastery was also unique; the translation was led by Archbishop Demetrius and the papal legate, not by the general provost or the prior of the monastery, which absolutely represents the importance of royal and ecclesiastical power concerning the relics and the recognition of its value. Gyöngyösi (1988), *Vitae Fratrum*, Cap. 34; Ottó Kelényi, "A Buda melletti Szent Lőrinc pálos kolostor történetének első irodalmi forrása (1511)" [The first literary source (1511) on the history of the St. Laurence Pauline Monastery near Buda], *Tanulmányok Budapest Múltjából* 4 (1936): 94.

[292] It is strange that Nosztra had an important role in the early modern and modern history of the Paulines, even to today; history has struck a balance at least. Note that no other sources mention any previously declared place for the relics, nor was Nosztra mentioned. Gábor Sarbak, "Hadnagy Bálint: Remete Szent Pál gyógyító csodái" [Bálint Hadnagy: The healing miracles of Saint Paul the First Hermit], in: *Medicina renata*, ed. László András Magyar (Budapest: Semmelweis Orvostörténeti Múzeum, Könyvtár és Levéltár, 2009) (Last accessed: December 5, 2013), http://www.orvostortenet.hu/tankonyvek/tk-05/Green/author.php?name=Cs&begin=c-d.

Nevertheless, the location of Nosztra includes another layer of its role that helps us understand broader tendencies. King Louis treated this monastery as a special one on his lands, not just because he had personally founded it, but also because he had chosen its location quite meticulously. Referring to the idea of József Laszlovszky,[293] this monastery was also a feature of royal representation; it was, in fact, attached to the royal residence at Visegrád. This perspective emphasizes more clearly why the St. Ladislaus Monastery was founded so close to Visegrád.

From the mid-1200s the growing importance of royal representation generated the disappearance of the itinerant court and the establishment and development of royal residences. The Pilis, as the Royal Forest and the focal point of the *medium regni*, was surely a territory where other features of human-nature interactions could have a physical presence. Following the trends of other European countries, the religious orders in Hungary were seeking the highest support and the Hungarian kings likewise were searching for religious phenomenon that could increase their royal representation, broaden their influence, and, of course, ensure their salvation.

Attached to the importance of royal representation, obtaining St. Paul's relics had a more important meaning in a wider context than a simple spiritual union. Under the rule of King Louis I the Great, the Kingdom of Hungary reached the highest point of its political power. The economy and cultural life saw a "golden age" and his power and the factors behind his power were imported into the regions where he ruled;[294] thus, the Paulines also moved outside the kingdom, but first just into Central Europe.[295]

In this context, the impact of St. Paul's relics could have helped the monks at the Monastery of St. Laurence to become the verified leaders, not only amongst the group of neighboring monasteries, but on a country-wide scale. After the translation, they became the absolute religious center of the order and also had

[293] Hereby I would like to thank József Laszlovszky for this information.

[294] The first university was founded in 1367 and the *Chronicon Pictum*, one of Hungary's most important medieval chronicles, was finished. King Louis ruled most of Central Europe, including Poland (after the death of Casimir III the Great) and Croatia.

[295] In 1382, the first foreign Pauline monastery was founded in Częstochowa by Ladislaus, the Duke of Opole, who received Pauline monks from the monastery of Nosztre—maybe this gesture just after the translation of St. Paul's relics was a compensation for the unsuccessful application for the relics.

political impact and access to financial resources.[296] However, remnants of the importance of the monasteries in the Pilis are still tangible by the fact that the Monastery of St. Laurence was founded by the prior and monks of the first Pauline community in the Pilis, the Holy Cross Monastery. This was a spiritual and religious continuity, which is strongly evident from the name of the community: *fratrea sancta crucis de eremo*,[297] even though the southern part of the Pilis area had lost its historical privileges. But did they also lose their donors and therefore the chance to develop their monastic space? Some historical events surrounding yet another change in royal policy indicate that the answer is more or less yes.

King Sigismund and a Mysterious Monastery

In contrast to the Angevin rulers' perception of the Pilis, King Sigismund (1387–1437) practiced an attitude more similar to that of the Árpádian kings towards the forest county. He addressed the territory as the Royal Forest, so financial and political control over the area was still focused in the king's hands; therefore, the financial acts of the existing monasteries in the area were also affected by royal power, even at times when most of the counties were governed by nobles.[298] Although the royal seat moved to Buda in 1408, Sigismund respected and regularly visited Visegrád and the baths of Hévkút close to the Pauline monasteries in the Börzsöny. Therefore, in this area another royal road, the *via regia*, appeared, which connected the royal center with Hévkút through the northern part of Szentendre Island, passing the ferry at Kisoroszi, and another Pauline monastery that was founded by Sigismund and has only recently been partly researched[299] (*Figure 18*).

This event shows that the memory of the hermitic Pauline system in the Pilis had absolutely collapsed by the first half of the fifteenth century. After the reign of

---

[296] ... *inipsa Ecclesia venerandum, cum summa reverential deposuit*. From the work of the anonymous author and Valentinus Hadnagy, source cited in: Urbán (2009), "Pálos zarándokhelyek," 72.

[297] The brothers of the Holy Cross were changed officially in 1309 to the Order of Saint Paul the First Hermit—*ordo fratrum Sancti Pauli primi eremitae*. Mályusz (1971), "Remeterendek," 258.

[298] Szabó (2005), *Woodland and Forests,* 118.

[299] On this royal pathway, the foundation of the St. Sigismund Monastery, and the connections between royal power and religious houses see József Laszlovszky, "The Royal Palace in the Sigismund Period and the Franciscan Friary at Visegrád. Royal Residence and the Foundation of Religious Houses," in: *The Medieval Royal Palace at Visegrád,* eds. Gergely Buzás and József Laszlovszky (Budapest: Archaeolingua, 2013), 207–218.

King Sigismund, from the first half of the fifteenth century, the Pauline hierarchy did not change much, and furthermore, they received many monasteries that had been run by other orders mostly unsuccessfully.

The career and impact of the Pauline Order reached its highest point under the reign of King Matthias I. This period has much more extant historical data that tells us about Pauline life—which was now directed from St. Laurence Monastery—than ever before. Until the Battle of Mohács (1526), which led to the fall of the Kingdom of Hungary, Pauline dominance in the royal court is undoubted. Changing the resolution of the research and concentrating on the sources with a more spatial approach leads us to finding more regional and local data on the Pauline monasteries in the Pilis that were hidden behind the scenes of historical events almost from the time of their foundations.

2.3 Pauline Monastic Space in the Pilis

Focusing on the lower spatial levels, further features can be revealed concerning all kinds of properties of Pauline monasteries. Regarding general trends, it has been proven by written sources that the Paulines wanted to unify their lands (mostly arable lands, vineyards, and mills) close to their monasteries. In regards to the Paulines in the Pilis, this referred to the preference for intraregional properties, whereas a one or two day journey—to a more productive property—should not have been a cause of problems for the monks. This seems to be the case of the St. Ladislaus Monastery,[300] which had a parcel in Visegrád, a vineyard at Borosjenő[301] and Vác, and a mill with a parcel at Sződ,[302] in this case more to the south on the other side of the Danube (*Figure 19*).

On this spatial level other questions could be researched concerning the Paulines' relations with the lay sphere, like the connection between the monasteries and settlements, but there is no complete database for these examinations yet.[303]

---

[300] See data on the properties of the monastery in Chapter 3 (Catalogue), 3.2 Pauline monasteries in the Pilis. 3. Monastery of St. Ladislaus, 164–166.

[301] DL 4230, also DL 4231. These medieval sources are cited in Romhányi (2010), *Pálos gazdálkodás a középkorban*, 56. The name of the settlement may refer to the vineyards there.

[302] The Paulines sold a vineyard at Szentendre to purchase the mill.

[303] Note that GIS analysis of the medieval archaeological sites is already in progress by the author as part of the research on this problem. The archaeological evidence of the settlements of the Pilis have been summarized by Péter Szabó recently. See Szabó (2005), *Woodland and Forests*, 105–110.

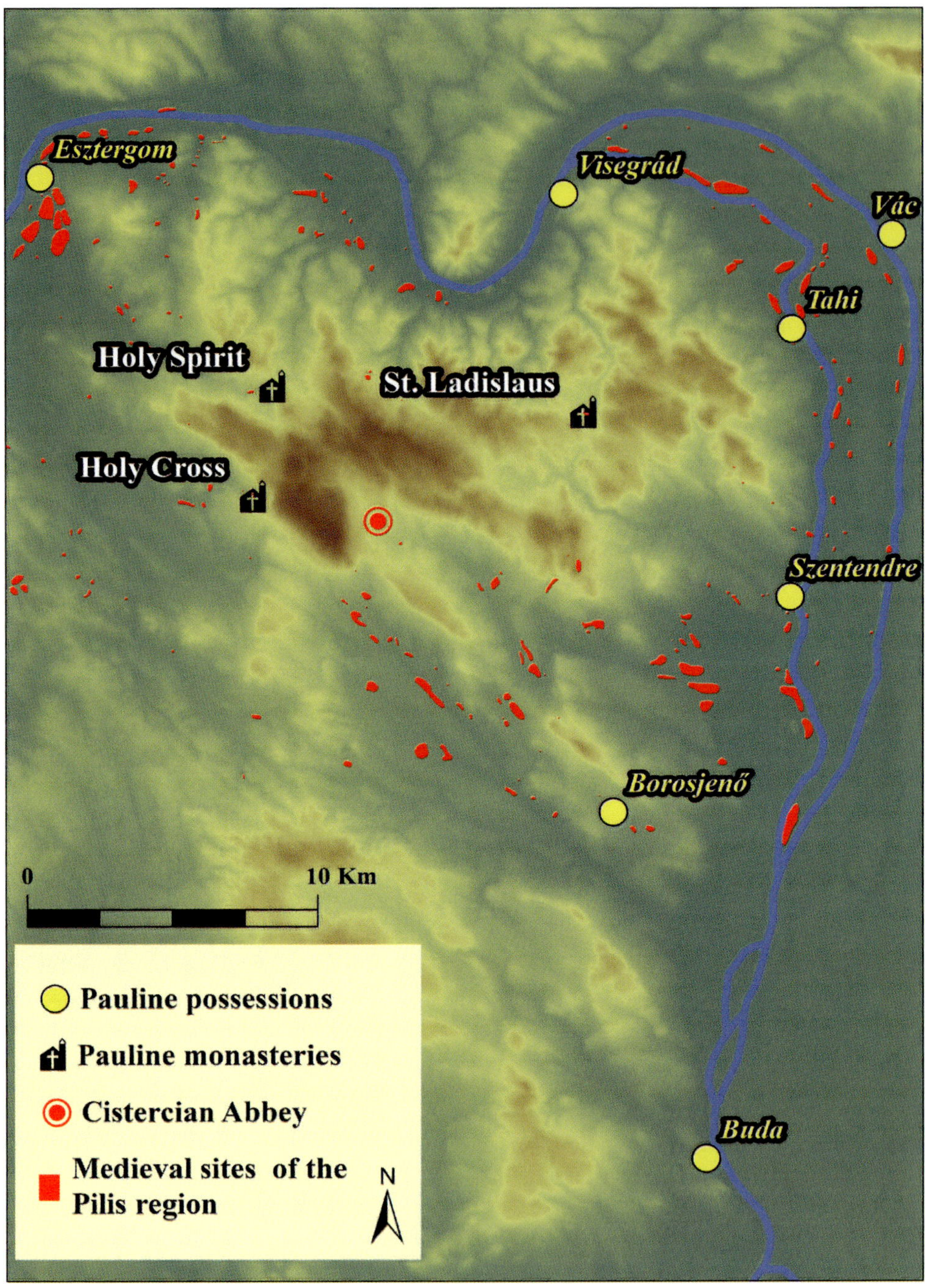

Figure 19. The region of Pauline properties on ASTER GDEM

At the same time, what can be studied is the connection between the monasteries. As previous investigation on the roads has revealed, most of the monasteries could easily reach each other. The *via regis*, connecting the Cistercian Pilis Abbey and the Pauline Holy Spirit Monastery, also offered a northern branch towards the Holy Cross Monastery; although the two Pauline monasteries were close to each other. Monks living in the latter monastery could use the *via magna* as well. The St. Ladislaus Monastery was part of a different spatial microregion. Besides the royal centers, the Danube to the east was also easily reachable by the monks. This is why the written sources mention people from Szentendre or Tahi. In addition to generalities, a closer look at the monasteries' closest space, and the recorded spatial features, is necessary.

Monastery of the Holy Cross (Kesztölc-Klastrompuszta)

The Holy Cross Monastery was of crucial importance in the early history of the order: the Paulines were called *fratres sancte cruces de heremo* even in the early fourteenth century. These monastic buildings were situated halfway between the Cistercian monastery and Esztergom, close to the *via magna* (or *viae magnae*) and to the supposed *via regis*. The western boundaries of the monastery were described in a perambulation, which was recorded 1393.[304] Here, based on the mentioned features, the route could be more or less reconstructed (*Figure 20*).

It is clear that the starting point was somewhere between the village of Kesztölc and the monastery, since the route from Kesztölc to the Holy Cross Monastery is mentioned just after the start of the perambulation route. Then, after several valleys and hilly areas, the *via magna* running from Esztergom to Buda appears, which was located on the most southern part of the area.

Unfortunately, no other names are recognizable on historical or modern topographical maps of the area, but in some cases the sites might be identified. I.e. *vallum Zeketarla* can probably be identified with a Roman watchtower, which—based on archaeological evidence—was also used in the Árpádian Period.[305] However, as the directions from the charter lead in the opposite direction, this

304 See the text of the perambulation in Chapter 3 (Catalogue), 3.2 Pauline Monasteries in the Pilis. 1. Monastery of Holy Cross, 134–135. DL 236647 (original from 1393); DL 8014 (copy, 1696).

305 Torma, ed. (1979), *Magyarország Régészeti Topográfiája* 5, 278 (Piliscsév site: 16/1).

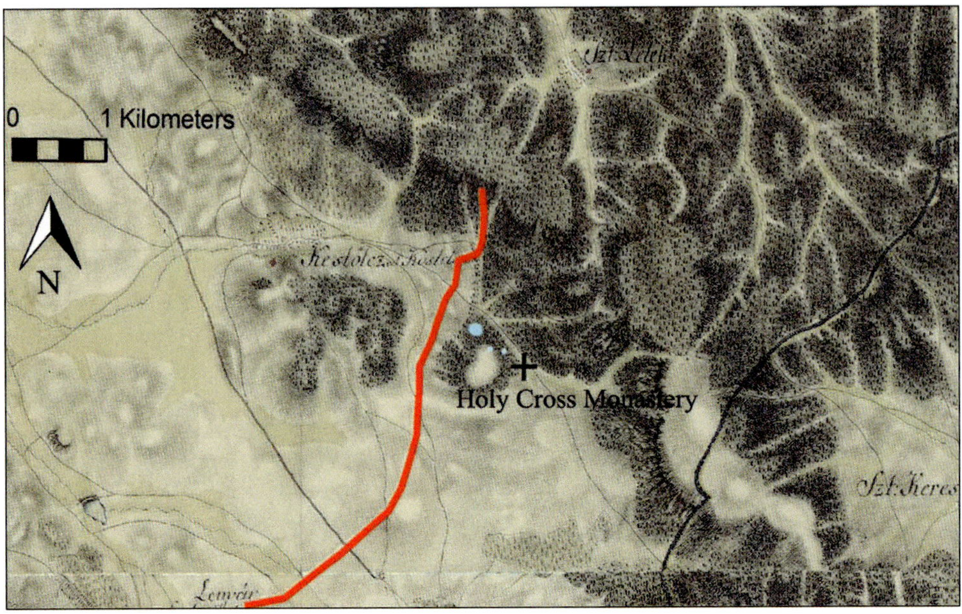

Figure 20. The reconstruction of the track of the medieval perambulation (1393), based on the First Military Survey

seems questionable. The reconstruction can be made more precise through the research of settlements and the articulation of regional topography.

Around the ruins of the monastery, which were partly excavated, several features indicate the existence of a complex water management system (*Figure 21*) in the valley, which runs from the southeast to the northwest. One kilometer west of the caves, which might have been used by the hermits, ran several springs (2.a-c) that could have possibly supplied the streams, but this can be reconstructed only indirectly. The Bence Well (2.a) might have supplied the monastery (1) directly with fresh water, being likely located in the cloister garden/courtyard, but the monks could also have led the water further to supply the ponds. As the spatial features had been destroyed between the monastery and the first detected pond (3.a), which was dug 200 meters from the ruins, it is not possible to make further conclusions on the starting point of the system. Nevertheless, it still seems relevant that the northern stream may have had a role in this system as well; we can suppose that the drainage channels could have emerged from the second pond (3.b), if we accept earlier reports on the existence of a vaulted stone drainage

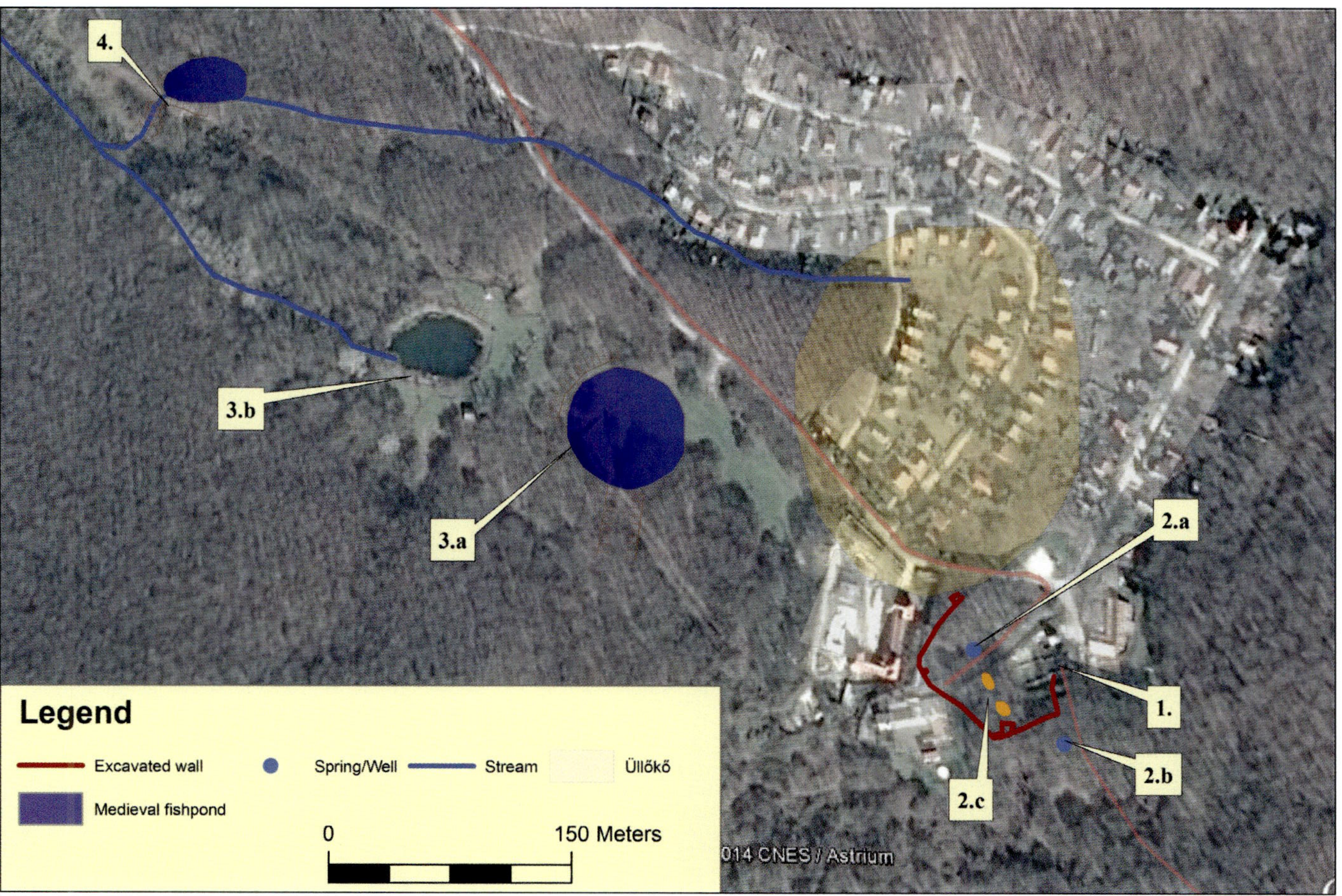

Figure 21. The recorded features around the Holy Cross Monastery. Based on a Google Map

outlet.[306] The earlier pond was destroyed by erosion, while the later one was destroyed by strong anthropogenic activities since the 1950s. Nothing can be said about the development and dating of the ponds; the only thing that must be true is that they have medieval origins.

Just as in the previous case, there is no written data reflecting on mills or other spatial features connected to the economy or land usage around the monastery, but according to the structure of a newly recorded dike (4), there might have been a mill at the end of the steep slope, where this earthwork is located. Archaeological evidence supports the existence of a medieval settlement just south of the monastery and the remains of workshops were also revealed by excavations. Slag that was found next to the walls (outside the buildings) of the monastery suggests the existence of metal workshops, for which water supply must also have been important. As the written sources suggest, the monastery had most of its properties (arable lands and vineyards) nearby.[307] The Monastery of the Holy Cross, following late medieval trends, focused on the development of a monetary economy; beside their estates, they owned at least two houses, including one at Buda with the Holy Spirit Monastery—which meant a mid-level regular income for them—and another at Esztergom.

Regarding the archaeological findings, three noteworthy artifacts were found during excavations of the Holy Cross that may reveal some details about the everyday life of the monks. The first is a collection of fragments from a clay sculpture portraying St. Christopher,[308] which served an important role in religious representation. The second is a group of fragments from a baptismal font, which must have been built after the Paulines were allowed to perform pastoral tasks, that is, after 1417. Thirdly, painted window glass fragments were also found here, which was a unique find of Hungarian medieval archaeology until 2012, when similar motifs were revealed on small glass fragments at the excavation of the church of a medieval village (Budakalász), near Óbuda.[309]

---

[306] For more information see Chapter 3 (Catalogue), 3.2 Pauline Monasteries in the Pilis. 1. Monastery of Holy Cross, 130, 3.b.

[307] For more information see Chapter 3 (Catalogue), 3.2 Pauline Monasteries in the Pilis. 1. Monastery of Holy Cross, 131–133.

[308] On the topic see Gerald Volker Grimm, ed., *Kleine Meisterwerke des Bilddrucks. Ungeliebte Kinder der Kunstgeschichte Handbuch und Katalog der Pfeifentonfiguren, Model und Reliefdrucke* (Aachen: Suermondt-Ludwig-Museum, 2011).

[309] The excavation was conducted by Gábor Tomka (Hungarian National Museum). Fortunately, the author was lucky enough to be present at the site.

Monastery of the Holy Spirit (Pilisszentlélek)

King Ladislaus IV donated the land of *Bendwelgye* or *Benedekvölgye* (again, which lies in the Pilis) with a *palatio* to the Paulines, namely Father Peter of Hévíz (*Petro de Calidis Aquis*) and his fellows. At the same time the king mandated that Prior Benedek, the prior of the Holy Cross Monastery, send some monks to settle the new monastery (supposedly the Holy Spirit Monastery). Ferenc Hervay argued that this donation refers to the Holy Spirit Monastery and recent research also agrees with this, it is also the closest to Dömös from all three monasteries, which localization is stated in the medieval charter.[310] It has been emphasized recently that Benedek might have had such a good relationship with the king that the name of the land that was donated to the Paulines, *Benedekvölgye*, may refer to the prior himself.[311]

The boundaries around the late medieval Holy Spirit Monastery and its landed estate are well known to scholars. The monastic building complex is located near the supposed *via regis* (see *Figure 14*). King Louis I confirmed the donations of his ancestors, donated further lands to the Paulines, and ordered a new perambulation. It states that a hill to the north called *Kyrállese/Királylese* (lit. "King's Peek") is the starting point, then turning east, the boundary crosses the road to Marót (today's Pilismarót on the bank of the river Danube).[312] From here it arrives at *ÓhRemete-hely* (lit. Old Hermit's Site, which may refer to the hermits who lived here before the foundation of the Pauline Order[313]), where it follows the Örümes stream (unfortunately its meaning is not known). It then turns to the south and west, where it crosses the *Soklós* hill (probably named after the grass snake, *sikló* in Hungarian), *Fekete-kő* (lit. "Black Rock"), *Fejér/Fehér-kő* (lit. "White Rock"), *Vodnyíló/Vadnyaló/Vadnyíló* valley (lit. "Wild Blooming," probably referring to the wild flora or wild animals that may have gone there for the salt), and then reaches again the Királylese hill.

A cadastral map of Pilisszentlélek from 1788, stored in the National Archive, covers some points of this perambulation (*Figure 22*). As a significant feature in

---

310 Gyöngyösi (1988), *Vitae Fratrum*, Cap. 15; Szabó (2005), *Woodland and Forests*, 116, ref. 75.

311 Benkő (2016), "A Szent Kereszt remetéinek korai kolostorai a Pilisben," 32.

312 See the Latin text transcribed by a later copy in Chapter 3 (Catalogue), 3.2 Pauline Monasteries in the Pilis. 2. Monastery of Holy Spirit, 155–156.

313 Torma, ed. (1979), *Magyarország Régészeti Topográfiája* 5, 299; Benkő (2015a), "Udvarházak és kolostorok a pilisi királyi erdőben," 743; the same is stated in Benkő (2016), "A Szent Kereszt remetéinek korai kolostorai a Pilisben," 26.

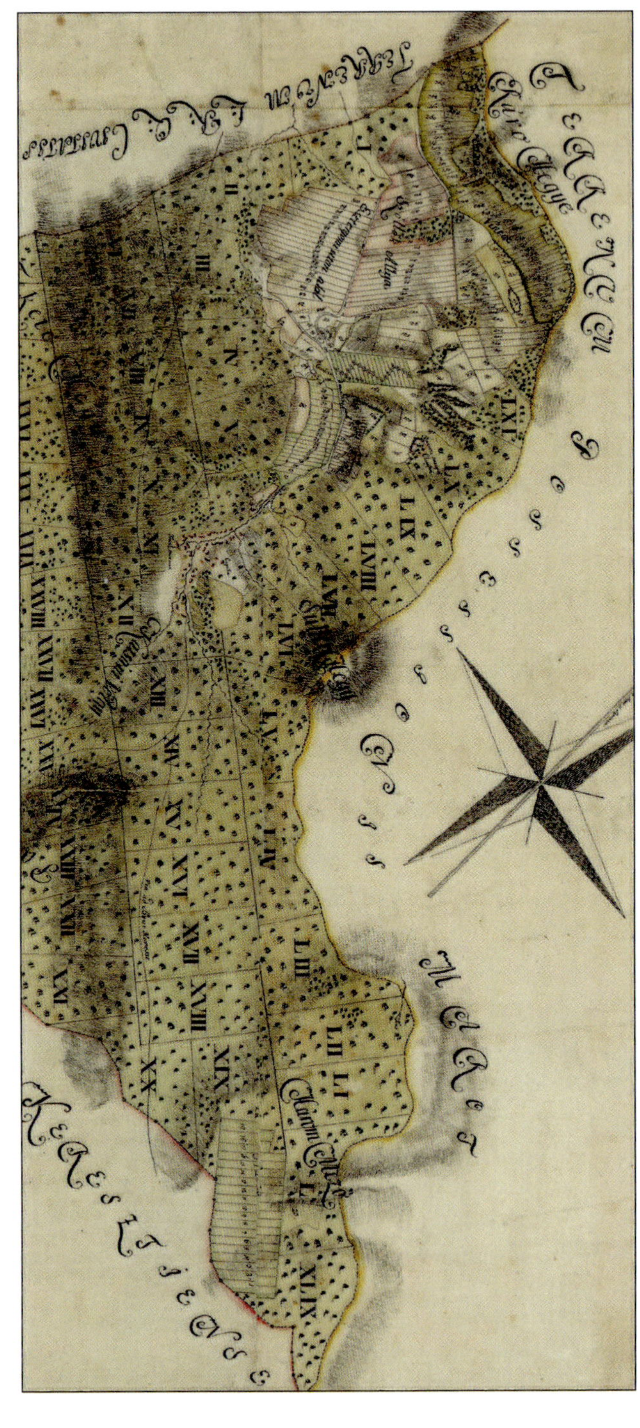

Figure 22. Cut from a cadastral map on the territory of Szentlélek (1788). National Archive, Catalogue No. S 12 Div IX No. 99.

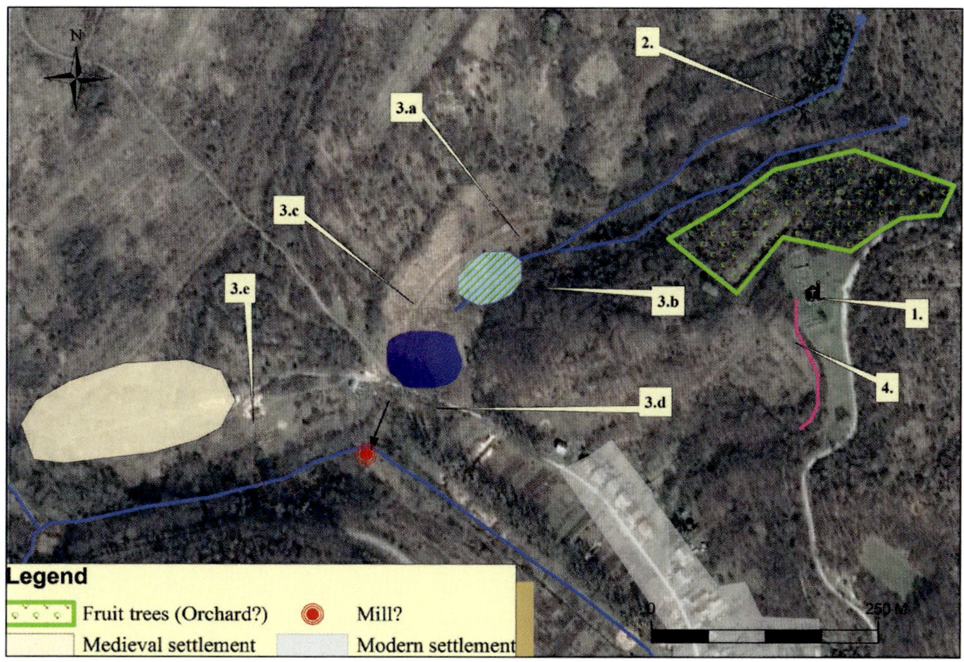

Figure 23. The results of the field surveys around the Holy Spirit Monastery (1), where near the orchard, streams and springs (2), fishponds and dikes (3.a-e) were detected with a supposed mill with its channel. Based on a Google Map

the landscape, the *Süllér* hill might be the medieval Királylese hill. This place name may refer to the memory of the royal hunting grounds or even to the era before the monastic presence, the time of the itinerant kingship when a royal house and domain existed here.[314] Unfortunately, only one further correlation can be suggested on the medieval boundary: in the southwestern area, the name *Fekete-kő* has been preserved until today.

A bit more is known on the environment around the monastery that was enclosed by a wall (*Figure 23*). First, among the Pauline monasteries in the Pilis, here the archaeological research revealed the ruins of a building, north of the monastery (see the plan in the Catalogue[315]), that might have been the *palatium* of the king; it should be noted that the very strange plan of the monastery is possibly

[314] On the *palatium* see: Torma, ed. (1979), *Magyarország Régészeti Topográfiája* 5, 298–299; Benkő (2015a), "Udvarházak és kolostorok a pilisi királyi erdőben," 744–746.

[315] Chapter 3 (Catalogue), 3.2 Pauline monasteries in the Pilis. 2. Monastery of Holy Spirit, 158, Figure 57.

the result of the previous function of the buildings.[316] A few meters northwest of the ruins, several wild fruit trees (apple and pear) may represent a historical orchard at the site.[317] Here, the remains of a complex water management system were recorded. As sources did not mention this, the existence of any related structure is only a hypothesis.

Due to the attributes of the local soil, the fishponds (3.a-e) were first dug into the ground at a sharp angle, then the terrain of the valley ca. 200-250 m from the monastery was slightly elevated.[318] Today the moats and structural details are barely observable, only a circular area covered by reeds indicates their presence. The mill was identified by previous research, but the mill channel, which was mentioned in archaeological reports,[319] was destroyed by erosion and human activity. Although the medieval settlement in the valley near the stream is clearly identifiable, it also could be a manor, which was the nucleus of a later settlement.[320] There is no data on workshops connected to a water management system, but there were some buildings excavated to the south of the church, which served industrial purposes.[321]

There are only a few medieval documents on the monastery[322] but there is no strong evidence against the presence of the general characteristic features of an average Pauline monastery here. A telling event is that, acting together with the Holy Cross Monastery—which must have been a good financial decision—the Paulines could buy a house for 400 Florins, which was supposedly a moderately

---

[316] Torma, ed. (1979), *Magyarország Régészeti Topográfiája* 5, 298–299; Benkő (2015a), "Udvarházak és kolostorok a pilisi királyi erdőben," 744–746.

[317] This was clarified after the field surveys; here I would like to thank my father for calling my attention to the regularity of the apple and pear trees. After the field survey, László Ferenczi gave free run in a document on the plan of the surrounding landscape heritage management, which also marks the area as a historical orchard. Hereby I would like to thank his help as well.

[318] A landscape architectural survey detected three fishponds here, but according to the situation that our field surveys have revealed, the terrain—as it is in the humid bed of a valley—seems to be changing radically in a short period of time.

[319] For more on this see Chapter 3 (Catalogue), 3.2 Pauline monasteries in the Pilis. 2. Monastery of Holy Spirit, 153, 3.e.

[320] After the Ottoman period the uninhabited territories were settled by newly arriving people; therefore, it is problematic to connect the newly founded settlements with medieval origins. Although, if there ever was a settlement inhabited by the monks, it can be expected to be named after the monastery, as it was a general practice in such situations.

[321] Lázár (2012), "Pilisszentlélek műhelyház."

[322] See Chapter 3 (Catalogue), 3.2 Pauline monasteries in the Pilis. 2. Monastery of Holy Spirit, 154–155.

high-category building in the late Middle Ages. The strong connection between the two monasteries might have originated from the foundation of the Holy Spirit Monastery, which must have been a *filia* of the Holy Cross Monastery. Translating this to spatial language, the two monasteries were not far from each other, the ideal route between them was ca. 1 km.

Although it has been suggested that royalty was accommodated here, besides the written evidence, there are only a few archaeological sources that can be used to support this idea.[323] The present picture of the ruins shows the final (and supposedly less) period of the buildings, finished around the turn of the fourteenth and fifteenth centuries, which–based on the uncovered stone fragments of the monastic buildings–was no different to the typical rural architecture of early fifteenth-century Hungary.[324]

Monastery of Saint Ladislaus (Pilisszentlászló)

As the location of the monastery is unsure and the landscape features have not yet been recorded, written sources and historical maps are the basis for the conclusions discussed here. Examining the historical maps of the eighteenth and nineteenth centuries (usually drawn by Pauline monks[325]), several questions can be added to the whole issue of the St. Ladislaus Monastery. As the analysis on the structural dynamics of the Pilis has revealed, it is supposed to be situated in a

---

[323] For example, excavated stove tiles came from the refectory and the southern outbuilding. The foundation of a stove(?) in the chapter and a mold of a stove tile (decorated with the Madonna and Child Jesus) were also found in the monastery. Such motifs, or even stove tiles were rare in lay buildings until the late fifteenth century, thus they are usually regarded as luxury materials connected to royal and prominent ecclesial space. Sarolta Lázár, "A pilisszentléleki pálos kolostor kályhacsempéi" [The stove tiles of the Pauline monastery of Pilisszentlélek], *A Komárom-Esztergom Megyei Múzeumok Közleményei* 8 (2001): 167–180.

[324] The information from the material is enough to reconstruct some parts of the buildings, like the vestry and the apse of the church. Gergely Buzás, "A pilisszentléleki pálos kolostor kőfaragványai" [Stone fragments of the Pauline monastery of Pilisszentlélek], in: *Varia Paulina. Pálos Rendtörténeti Tanulmányok* [Studies on the history of the Pauline Order], vol. 1, ed. Gábor Sarbak (Csorna: Private Edition of Vince Árva, 1994), 182–183.

[325] After the Ottoman period, as part of the long consolidation, there were several attempts to restore medieval properties to the original religious order. This has raised many questions and misunderstandings up until contemporary scholarship. For an example see: Laszlovszky (2009), "Ciszterci vagy pálos?"

special location halfway between Visegrád and Óbuda, which may correlate with the foundation of the monastery.[326]

There are debates about to what extent the modern parish church of present-day Pilisszentlászló was built on the Pauline monastery, right above the settlement of Szentlászló on an abandoned hill (on the basis of a royal hunting lodge).[327] An early map (eighteenth century) representing the boundaries and inner structure of the settlement, interestingly marks a building, an ecclesial site or more likely a mill to the east-southeast (*Figure 24*). Some other features also appear, like boundary marks (probably *metae terrae*) from Szentlászló down to the settlement of Bogdány and the arable lands on the hill where later maps mark the St. Ladislaus Monastery, right above Szentlászló.

Although the above map cannot be georeferenced properly, the site of the marked building is identifiable on modern maps as well. Its location could possibly be around present-day St. Ladislaus Hill (Szent László-hegy), somewhere on the southeastern-eastern side of the map or (unlike the order of the hills on the historical map) more to the northwest, around Kis-Pap-hegy (lit. Little Priest Hill) (*Figure 25*).

Another historical map (*Figure 26*, directed to the east-southeast) marks a cross at the same location on the boundary ditch between the Szentendre and Szentlászló settlements, but it can be understood as the sign of intersecting roads.[328] On this map the (supposed) ruins (*rudera*) of St. Ladislaus are marked on the hill over the settlement, which is generally accepted by recent scholarship as the location of the monastery. This map also shows some hints about historical land usage: a vineyard (*vinea*) is present east of the settlement, near the cross.

These historical maps also contain information about the boundary of Szentlászló,[329] and though several reconstructions of the boundary have been suggested, due to the extensive debates around this topic, further, more detailed

---

[326] As was highlighted above, the foundation of the monastery raises many questions. The monastery was supposedly founded by King Ladislaus IV by 1291, as it was the contemporary practice to name the monastery after its founder, especially when the founder was the king. This argument is crucial because here it is clearly visible that the traditional history by Gyöngyösi and the data from original documents, also used by Gyöngyösi, do not correlate with each other. Therefore, in his *Vitae Fratrum* there is a significant discrepancy.

[327] Györffy (1956), "Adatok," 284.

[328] It is also interesting that on other maps this cross is duplicated, suggesting that something of importance could have really existed there. See other maps from the National Archive: S 86 No. 8 and 9, S 107 No. 19.

[329] Map S 86 No. 8, S 86 No. 4.

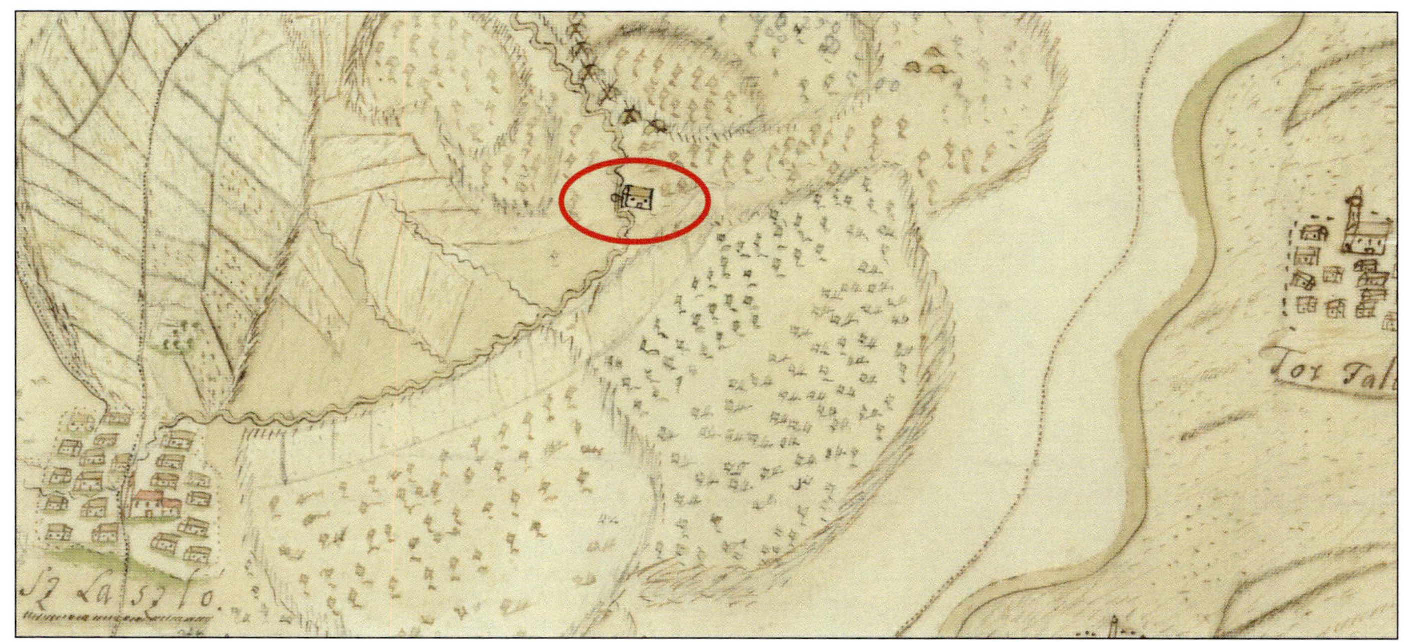

Figure 24. Detail from a historical map; Szentlászló settlement and its territory. (Eighteenth century) National Archive, S 86 No. 1.

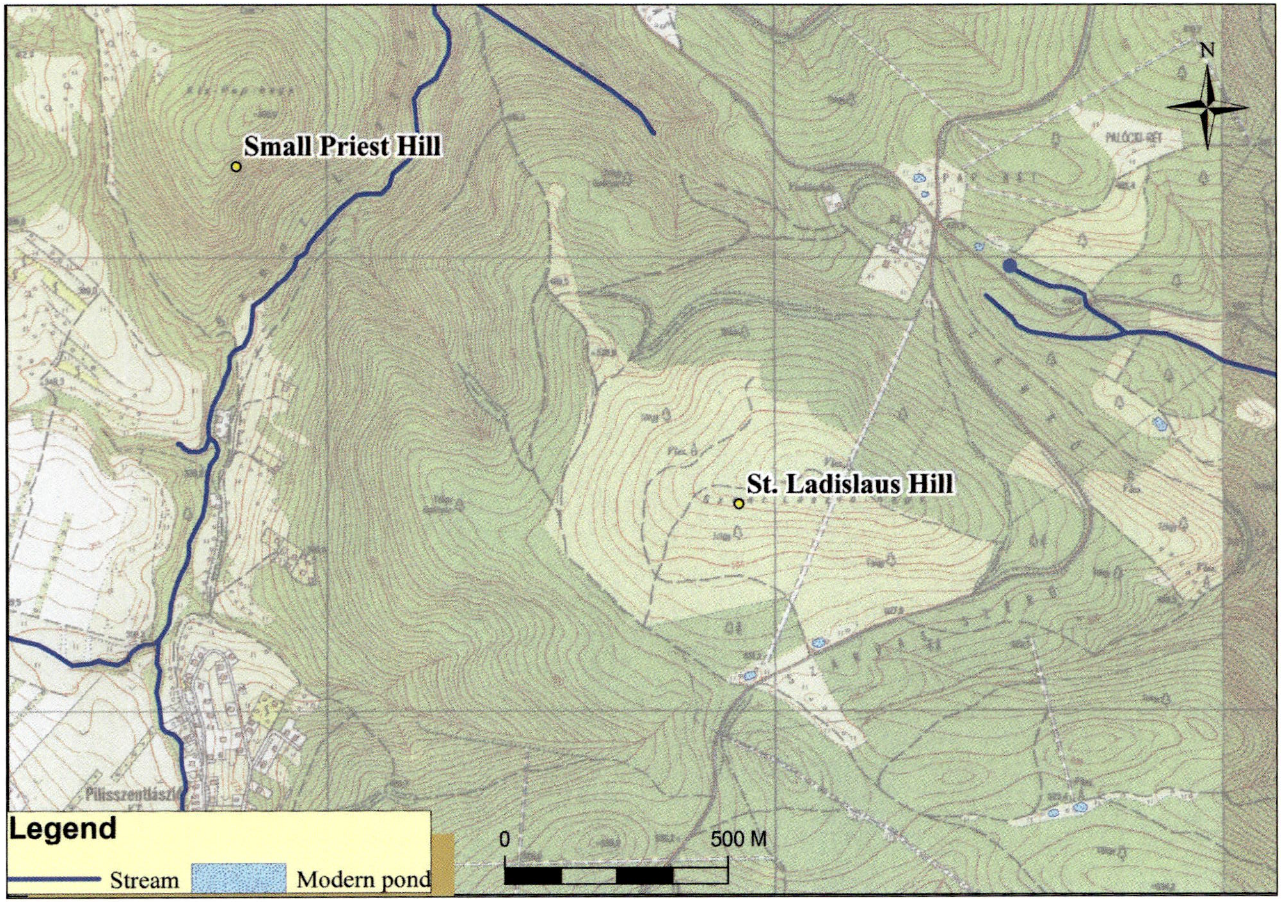

Figure 25. Present-day landscape of Pilisszentlászló. Detail from the map of the Unified National Map System (projection 1: 10 000)

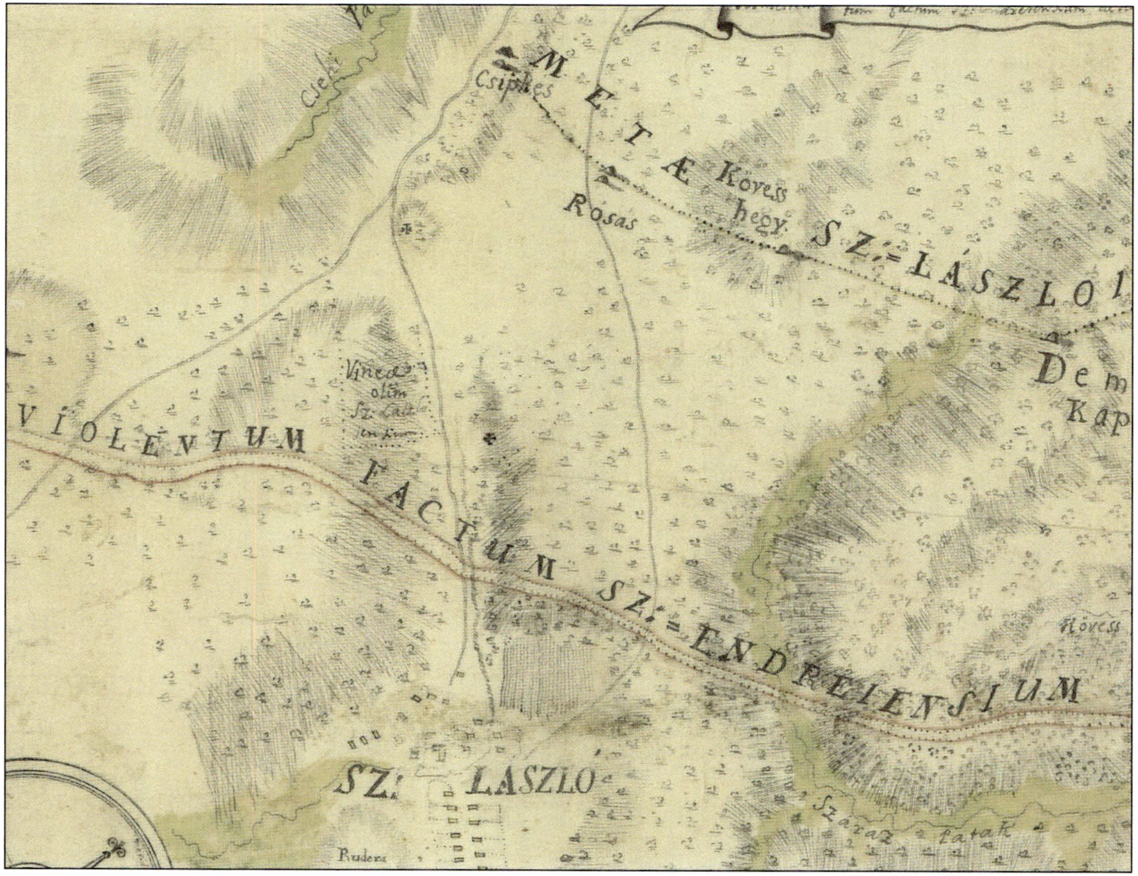

Figure 26. Detail from a historical map; the boundary between Szentlászló and Szentendre. (Map directed to the east; from 1760) National Archive, S 86 No. 5.

research is needed to compare the information.[330] Note that most of these maps support the idea that the arable lands were and still are located on the hill where the monastery was supposedly located.

Another map finely illustrates how complex the medieval landscape must have been. The details of the map shown below (*Figure 27*) illustrate the boundary between Szentlászló and Bogdány (the settlement to the northeast), where a garden, cultivated by the inhabitants of Szentlászló (*hortus molior Szt. László*), and two charcoal production sites (*carbonarium*) were located. What is more important is that the Kékes Stream can be identified as the present-day Apátkúti (lit. "Abbot's Well") Stream, where at least one mill was used by the Paulines. This identification, however, seems to contradict the sources, which describe this stream as being in the territory of the royal village in Szentendre, which is located east of Szentlászló. Furthermore, there is a stream from Szentlászló to the southeast, which floods into the Danube near medieval Szentendre, among the Kis- and Nagy-Kékes (lit. Small and Great Kékes) hills.

The written sources on the St. Ladislaus Monastery contain rich information on the late Middle Ages, suggesting that this monastery fits right into the conventional Pauline scheme, as the monks aimed to create a regular and stable income from vineyards and mills (as the most precious features), and by renting houses or sometimes receiving donations by alms.[331] Even empty sites that were suitable for building mills, moreover the ruined mills, such as those—close to the monastery on Kékes Stream—donated to the Paulines (in 1358) by the king, were valuable to the Paulines. It is unknown how often it was necessary to make repairs on mills, but more than a hundred years after the donation, a charter informs us that a mill still existed on the stream, but it needed to be repaired.[332] The monks' basic daily food could be supplied from the fishponds, of which two were at the disposal of the monks, situated "over the monastery" (most probably north to it): a larger one, which

[330] It is also a problem that these maps were drawn within a short period, containing different information and approaches.

[331] See the relevant data on these features in Chapter 3 (Catalogue), 3.2 Pauline monasteries in the Pilis, 3. Monastery of St. Ladislaus, 164–166.

[332] Peter of Tahi, in the name of his wife, sons, brother (Stephen, the provost of Dömös), and himself, offered a large donation to the monastery for the preparing of the larger fishpond and mill at Kékes Stream. In return, he likely asked for permission to be buried in the monastery. The donator also prospected more donations in the future and at the same time the monks of the monastery were obligated to celebrate a mass for the family on each Saturday in front of the Virgin Mary altar. Romhányi (2010), *Pálos gazdálkodás a középkorban,* 99, ref. 547.

had to be renovated at the time of the donation.[333] It is also known that a settlement (Kékes) existed near the monastery by 1301, settled by a castellan of Visegrád.[334]

Figure 27. Historical map; the boundary between Szentlászló and Bogdány (1760). National Archive, S 86 No. 5.

[333] DL 17454; Romhányi (2010), *Pálos gazdálkodás a középkorban,* 86.
[334] Györffy (1956), "Adatok," 254.

2.4 Conclusions on Spatial Analysis

When investigating the history and archaeology of the Paulines in the Pilis, several approaches can be used. On the level of the Pilis, by examining the locations and changing importance of the Pauline monasteries, a draft on the dynamics of the region can be drawn. With the discontinuation of itinerant kingship, the role of the hunting lodges or (a kind of) *curiae regales* had changed; they were not as important for the kings as before. Therefore—as the symbolic representation of royal power in the Pilis—the kings donated these buildings to religious orders (to the Cistercians in 1184, and the Paulines in the second half of the thirteenth century).

Royal power shifted from Esztergom to Buda and Visegrád in the mid-1200s; by that time Esztergom, as a place of royal representation, was entirely left. The Paulines "followed" the movement by their presence at the St. Ladislaus Monastery, halfway between Buda/Óbuda and Visegrád. By the end of the thirteenth century, the emphasis of royal power apparently moved to Buda, which was marked by the foundation of the St. Laurence Monastery nearby. This relationship of royal and ecclesial seats and the foundation of Pauline monasteries in the Pilis was revealed by the location of centers and the monasteries, also their geographical relations to the roads of the Pilis.

In the second half of the thirteenth century the Pauline Order was highlighted by their royal support, ensuring their somewhat stable presence and economy (or at the least, their self-sufficiency). Alongside royal support, their stable standing and the background of the order ultimately resulted in their official recognition by the highest ecclesial authority of medieval Hungary, the archbishop of Esztergom, in 1291.[335] After this event, another incident confirmed the importance of the eastern region of the Pilis, namely, the political meeting in the St. Ladislaus Monastery held in 1308.

Afterwards, the Pauline network and economy rapidly developed; a significant event in this development was the foundation of monasteries in the 1350s in the Börzsöny Forest (Nosztre and Toronyalja), north of the Pilis and Visegrád, on the other side of the Danube bank. Apparently, King Louis I sought to give new meaning to symbolic royal representation through the Paulines by his foundations and by settling them close to Visegrád, near the royal court situated around the Lower Palace, which was built around that time.

[335] In this context it is even more surprising that in 1270 the monks could already elect a general provost. At that time it is hardly correct to talk about the Paulines as an order; this title must have been symbolic and the provost had influence over just a few monasteries or eremitic communities.

The official papal confirmation of the order was a great success, but perhaps the translation of St. Paul the First Hermit's body in 1381 had a more significant impact on the Paulines. By that time, the royal curia had been built in Buda, which might have been essential in the decision about the final resting place of the relics. After all, the St. Laurence Monastery dominated not only the Pauline hierarchy, but had a strong influence in the royal court as well. King Sigismund I attempted to create another symbolic center near Visegrád, but it seems to have been unsuccessful. During the mid-1400s, mostly during the reign of King Matthias I, several monasteries were donated to the order that had been previously run by other religious orders unsuccessfully, but acquiring the San Stefano Rotondo in Rome shows that their expansion outside the Kingdom of Hungary was also highly fruitful.

By the sixteenth century, thanks to their brilliant self-management and strong royal (and ecclesial) support, the Pauline Order could stabilize its position and had overwhelming leverage in the Kingdom of Hungary. Analyzing the spatial attributes of medieval features and trying to discern the supposed logic behind them can help us to articulate or sometimes even reformulate the meaning and role of the Pauline Order, Pauline monasteries and hierarchy, and the dynamic changes within their primary spatial sphere, the Pilis.

Regarding the description of the monasteries, the Catalogue should be taken into consideration as well. Our main goal was to systematically list the known features of the space, and to record their condition. Another goal was to find new features in the targeted areas surrounding the monasteries. From the three monasteries, two were precisely identifiable in the landscape. Their systematic summary has revealed new features behind their foundation, and helped to outline the frame of their life and local history.

The Holy Cross Monastery is regarded as the first monastery of the Paulines, but it must be noted that there were related hermit communities and monasteries existing well before its appearance. Nevertheless, it had symbolic preeminence, as is attested by the traditional history of the order and several contemporary documents. This was likely true until general changes in the spatial network affected its role; changes in royal policy led to the end of the supposed leadership of the Holy Cross Monastery. Afterwards, from the beginning of the thirteenth century, it apparently became an average Pauline monastery with a complex water management system and some properties, as well as a regular income from their rented buildings that could sustain the community of ca. 15 monks living in the cloister. The decline of its symbolic role is quite evident from the fact that at the end of the fourteenth century the Holy Cross Monastery was not even considered as a potential site for the final emplacement of the relics of St. Paul the First Hermit.

The Holy Spirit Monastery seems to have had the smallest impact since its beginnings, but the site itself says a lot about the circumstances of its foundations. The archaeological and architectural evidence more or less proved the existence of an earlier (royal) curia. By the end of the fourteenth century its size and character was similar to the Holy Cross Monastery. The location of the St. Ladislaus Monastery could be indicated by a suitable landscape environment, but as the circumstances of its foundation and its precise whereabouts are not known, we can only form hypotheses. Nonetheless, where it was possible to pinpoint the area of analysis precisely, it was proven that the circumstances of the Pilis forest are exceptionally suitable for the examination of monastic space.

Conclusions and Further Possibilities of Research

Erst our fathers trod these lonely woods
Raising humble shacks among the rocks,
And delving deep into the scattered caves.
A hermit and a holy man, the priest Eusebius
has founded here the hall named for the Holy Cross.
Soon the brothers emerged from their caverns,
and all confined to a monastic life therein.
From here the order of Paul the hermit spread
Across the nations, spotlessly clad in strict virtues,
As the stream sprouts forth to become a great river.[336]
(Father István Varsányi.
On the founding of the Holy Cross Monastery. Before 1530)

Deseri quondam lustrantes invia patres,
Hinc humiles scopulis casas fixere sub altis,
Et latebras sparsim statuunt in rupe cavata.
Vir sacer hanc heremita Eusebius atque sacerdos
Sub titulo tandem Sanctae Crucis extruit aulam.

[336] The translation of András Szabó, based on the Latin and Hungarian versions. Hereby I would like to express my heartfelt gratitude for his help.

Mox ad eum fratres specubus fluxere relictis,
Caeperuntque simul claustralem ducere vitam.
Hinc heremitarum Pauli succrevit in orbe
Religio, morum probitate nitens et amictu,
aximus exiguo fluvius sic fonte redundat.
Vesprimius formam vivendi praesul habendam
Tradidit Eusebio, donec ab Urbe petat,
Hinc Augustini instanter concessa roganti
Pontifice a summo regula sancti patris.
(Distichon fratris Stephani Warsani super fundatione monasterii
Sanctae Crucis in Pilisio)

The Pauline Order had a career full of dynamic changes, closely connected to royal power and representation, and it can be regarded as an ideal subject for landscape studies. Research on the Pauline economy from a historical perspective has a good basis, thanks to recent research's gathering, evaluation, and analysis of the relevant data. However, scholarship also has to deal with the contradiction between the early modern traditional history of the Pauline Order (*Vitae Fratrum*) and the medieval sources (some traces even preserved in the *Vitae Fratrum*). All these sources should be reevaluated in a systematic way, because much of the contradictory information could reveal a more articulated difference between what had happened and what was supposed to happen.

Examining Pauline space from a landscape archaeological perspective does not have a long history, but the basic methods are well emphasized in this field by Hungarian scholars. Although there are significantly more general works on the research of the Pauline Order, individual studies have also been published in the last few years. In these circumstances the approach of this work is systematic; it requires the documentation of spatial features and the collection of sources, which is indeed a great task, but it is also crucial to apply, visualize, and analyze the information on a digital platform. This method results in a clearer picture on each level of space.

Turning to the basic question of this text, it is evident that the role of royal power was fundamental in the evolution of the Pauline Order from its very beginnings. Therefore, their location in the *desertum* reflects the spiritual and symbolic representation of royal power in the Pilis royal forest after the thirteenth century, which can be analyzed from the point of view of spatial features like roads and royal/ecclesiastical centers, or simply from the terrain (e.g., LCP analysis). A more complex approach including detailed research of the settlement system of the area would undoubtedly bring some new data into consideration.

Side by side with their growing political potency, the Paulines' economic management changed and developed, which formed a stable basis for ecclesiastical approval. The basic forms of economy were developed by the fourteenth century; they received donations predominately of arable land, vineyards, and mills—connected by fishponds (St. Ladislaus Monastery). Then, correlating with late medieval trends, they managed to develop a more stable monetary economy. Just as the Paulines' character changed from hermits to "unmade-mendicants," so did the monasteries' regional role change through the centuries. Spatially this meant a shift from the west (Esztergom) to the east (Visegrád, then Buda), from the Holy Cross Monastery to the St. Ladislaus Monastery.

Regarding the spatial sources, valuable data was found during field surveys, although the land-use systems—mostly the remains of past water management systems—were only partly discoverable. Simply revealing and registering this spatial data means a great deal and gives a basis for further research, but the precise reconstruction of their development, construction, and use requires more general results on the topic, not to mention the problem of chronology. All these features probably represent the last phase of the monasteries, the end of the late Middle Ages.

Another crucial goal for further research is the study and collection of other landscape features in the Pilis and their correlation with medieval sites. There are still unknown and unverified sites that could help clarify the picture of the medieval landscape of the Pilis with the use of traditional sources and new techniques based on a digital platform. Using the LiDAR technique for a survey would result in a detailed terrain model of the Pilis, which is absolutely crucial for a precise understanding of the landscape, not just to have an ideal resolution for digital models, but to identify new archaeological sites as well.

Geoarchaeological research (e. g., sampling fishponds) would help in reconstructing the past landscape regarding flora and fauna (including fish) and it could reveal some data on the structure of fishponds and details of the whole water management system of the Paulines. Each of the discussed monasteries would be an ideal place for such research, even the suggested locations of the St. Ladislaus Monastery could yield some results. In this case an elementary method would reveal information: the classic archaeological excavation. Probe trenches near the supposed site, the present-day parish church of the settlement, would reveal whether further archaeological investigations would be fruitful or not. The excavation of the fishponds would also be worthwhile.

Another future task would be to examine Pauline architecture in general by continuing the work of Tamás Guzsik. In this case, in addition to individual analysis it would be crucial to broaden the picture to a regional scale, where all the ecclesiastical buildings are integrated and evaluated as comparative features. Also, as the last source collection of the Paulines was gathered a few decades ago, as Beatrix Romhányi also suggests,[337] it would be timely to re-launch this increasingly important and just as difficult work. With the evolution of digital technology, the archives have flooded scholars with a large number of historical documents (e.g., charters and maps); therefore, it is suggested to integrate this way of collecting as well.

The increasing number of systematic studies with complex approaches will form the basis for comparative studies as well. Yet a true comparison is only reliable with the Abaúj region,[338] where the background of the foundations completely differs from the Pilis, although the general attributes that were highlighted in the Abaúj region are valid in the Pilis as well. The environmental circumstances of the locations are the same: they are both hidden, but not secluded from the lay sphere, the main economic sources, the local circumstances and use of a complex water management system are also the same. It is interesting that cooperation among the groups of monasteries in the Pilis is not as clear as it is in the Abaúj region; minimal cooperation is clear between the Holy Cross and the Holy Spirit Monasteries, as they possessed common properties and were geographically close to each other, but besides these facts, there is no other related evidence on this question.

This work is only the first step in a large enterprise, which—based on a spatial approach—reveals new aspects in the research of the Pauline Order. The Paulines in the Pilis were one of the main "attributes" of the royal forest; therefore, the more thoroughly they are researched, the more precise of a picture will be revealed about them and about their development and changing role in royal power and the Pauline hierarchy. This correlates with the need for systematic and individual studies on Pauline monasteries, which would affect the conclusions of general studies as well. In this case, a relevant way to continue the research is to expound on the conclusions made based on the excavated archaeological materials, through which the tools of daily life can suggest more about the Paulines' impact on the landscape.

---

[337] Romhányi (2010), *Pálos gazdálkodás a középkorban,* 10.

[338] Belényesy (2004), *Pálos kolostorok Abaúj-Hegyalján.*

3. Catalogue

3.1 Overview of the Significant Medieval Historical Events Regarding the Pauline Order and the Pilis Region[340]

Date	Event
972(–1240s)	Esztergom was the most important royal residence and ecclesiastical center of the Hungarian Kingdom.
Before 1046	The St. Peter Provostry at Óbuda was founded (most probably) by King Peter I (1038–1040, 1042–1046).
1055	The St. Andrew Monastery was founded by King Andrew I (1046–1060).
ca. 1107	Foundation of the Dömös Provostry in the Pilis by Prince Álmos, brother of King Coloman (1095–1116) on a *regale allodium*.
1184	The Cistercian Monastery was founded in the Pilis by King Béla III (1172–1196).
1187	The Pilis was mentioned as the King's very own Forest.
1198	King Emeric (1196–1204) donates the royal palace at Esztergom to the Archbishop; thereafter Esztergom developed mainly as a religious seat. Even so, the kings (mainly King Béla IV) stayed there for longer periods several times before the mid-1200s.
1200s	At the end of the twelfth, beginning of the thirteenth century the royal residence of Óbuda emerged in the *medium regni*.
1225	Bishop Bartholomew gave rules to the hermits living above the Patacs Hill (South Hungary, today Pécs-Jakabhegy in Baranya County)
1225	The *comes* of Pilis County was mentioned the very first time.
1241/42	The Mongol invasion.
1240s	The role of Esztergom as a capital decreased, while the Buda castle (fortified town with royal curia) was built.

[340] Data extracted from Altmann et al. (1999), *Medium Regni*; Belényesy (2004), *Pálos kolostorok Abaúj-Hegyalján*, 88–90; Szabó (2005), *Woodland and Forests*, 93–97.

1251	The construction work of the royal castles in Visegrád was partly completed. The Upper Castle was built to protect, in case of another invasion, the nuns of what is today Margaret Island (back then Rabbit Island) in Budapest. The Lower castle was built for the king.
1250s	Eusebius founds the community of the first hermits and the Monastery of Holy Cross in the Pilis, near Esztergom.
1255	The construction of Buda Castle had beenalready finished by this time. It was basically a fortified urban settlement with a royal curia.
1259	King Béla IV (1235–1270) donates "the castle [of Visegrád] with the county and district of Pilis" (*...castrum cum comitatu et districtu de Pelys...*) to the queen.
1263	Seven communities were recorded in the first inventory of hermits living in the territory of the Veszprém Bishopric. The hermitages were too poor to ask for religious allowances, so Paul, Bishop of Veszprém, ordered an individual rule for them.
1270	The first general provost was elected in the Holy Cross Monastery.
1291	In the Veszprém diocese Benedict, Bishop of Veszprém, issued the second inventory of Pauline monasteries, in which the Holy Cross and the St. Ladislaus Monasteries were mentioned. Lodomér, the Archbishop of Esztergom ratified the inventory and the existence of such hermit communities.
1290s	Construction of St. Laurence Monastery.
1297	Andrew, Bishop of Eger, gave a guideline of lifestyle for the hermits living in that Bishopric.
1301–1323	After the death of Andrew III (1301), the last ruler of the Árpádian dynasty, Charles Robert I of Anjou, the first Angevin ruler, spent many years to stabilize his reign (1308–1342). During this period his main centre was not located in the *medium regni* but in the eastern part of the kingdom.
1308	Cardinal Gentilis the Papal Legate supporting the fight of Charles I for the royal power, confirms the regulations of St. Augustine for the order (13th December), one month after the political meeting with Matthew Csák (10th November) in the Pauline Monastery of St. Ladislaus at Kékes.

1309	The first general chapter (*capitulum generale*) of the Pauline order was held at the St. Laurence Monastery (near Buda!), which shows that it took over the lead from the Holy Cross Monastery. Cardinal Gentile Papal Legate mentions the Order of Saint Paul the First Hermit (*fratribus S. de Heremo, O. S. Pauli primi eremite per Hungariam*) in a charter.
1323	After the death of Matthew Csák, Charles Robert and the royal court moved to Visegrád.
1327/1328	The inventory of Ladislaus, Archbishop of Kalocsa, mentions thirty monasteries in 1327, at some places with twelve or twenty monks. As a result, Pope John XXII (1316–1334) permitted the monks to follow the rules of St. Augustine and elect a prior general who had the right to visit, discipline, and absolve from excommunication. From then on, their lands were exempted from paying tithe, and they were separated from the local ecclesiastical organization.
1347	King Louis I (1342–1381) moved the royal court from Visegrád to Buda (to the so called *Kammerhof*, which is supposed to have stood northeast of the castle hill in the town).
1352	King Louis I founded the Pauline monastery at Nosztre, north of the Pilis and the Danube bank in the Börzsöny forest.
1355	King Louis I moved the royal court back from Buda to Visegrád.
1368	Pope Urban V (1362–1370), at the request of the King Louis I, approved and ratified the Pauline order.
Ca. 1377	The construction of a *curia regia*, a new castle/palace for the royal court was finished south of the Castle Hill at Buda.
1381	The relics of St. Paul the First Hermit were translated from Venice to Buda (royal palace), than to the St. Laurence Monastery. On this occasion, King Louis donated the old royal palace (*Kammerhof*) to the Paulines.
1405–1408	The royal seat moved from Visegrád to Buda by the order of King Sigismund I (1387–1437).
1417	The permission given by Pope Martin V (1417–1431) allowed the Paulines to do pastoral work.
1454	The Paulines managed the Santo Stefano Rotondo in Rome.
1523	The relics of St. Paul were unified (the skull of the saint was translated from Karlstein by King Louis II [1516–1526]).

3.2 Pauline Monasteries in the Pilis

Monastery of the Holy Cross (Kesztölc-Klastrompuszta)

Location: A few kilometers to west from the modern village of Kesztölc, Komárom-Esztergom Co., HU
Coordinate: (WGS84) φ = 47 42 01.67028 λ = 18 50 05.39829
Status: The monastic buildings, situated next to a group of wells, were destroyed by the Ottoman army and the ruins were abandoned. It was used as a quarry for building material until the first half of the twentieth century. Finally, it was covered by soil (erosion) until the first excavations were conducted by István Méri in 1959–1961. At this time some earthworks (a fishpond and dike) were identified nearby the monastery. The buildings were partly excavated then transformed into an open-air ruin garden; just next to the excavated church a modern road crosses the middle of the former area of the monastery.

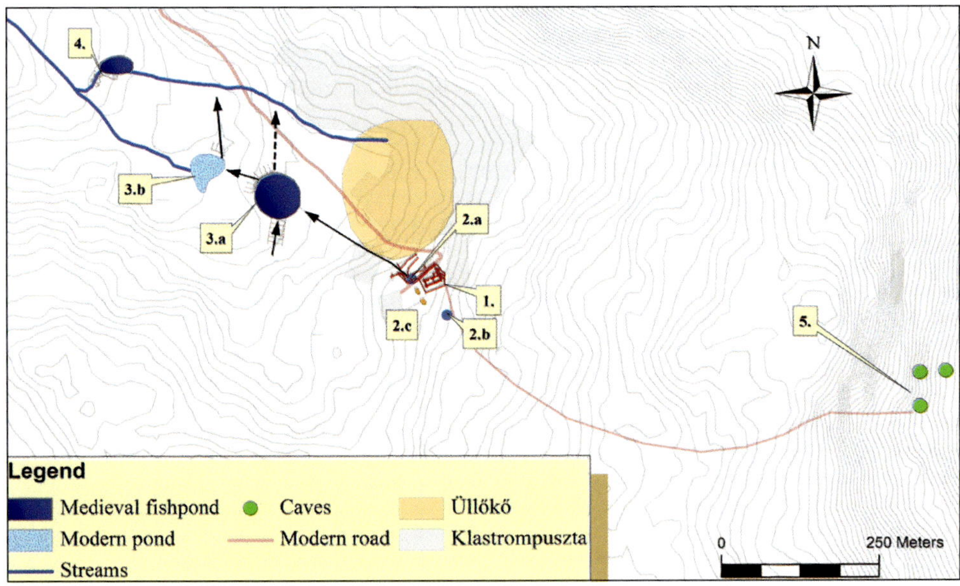

Figure 28. Summary of the spatial features detected around the Holy Cross Monastery. Drawn by the author

A. Spatial Features and Earthworks[341] *(Figures 28–30)*

1. Monastery (*Figures 30–32*). István Méri and his colleagues uncovered an 8 m wide and 26 m long Gothic church, the remains of the cloister attached to the north side of the church, and the apse of a chapel. The church was erected in the end of the fourteenth or the beginning of the fifteenth century, but archaeologists revealed the remains of earlier structures. The territory of the monastery (80 x 80 m) was enclosed by a precinct wall; several buildings were connected to each side of the wall, which functioned as workshops (slag, charcoal, and ovens were found there). The archaeological material covers the period from the tenth to the sixteenth century (e.g., ceramics, fragments of ornate stone carvings, roof tiles, metal tools, pieces of a bell, simple and decorated floor tiles, fragments of a baptismal font, pieces of painted window glass, codex mounts, and a terracotta sculpture of Saint Christopher). Based on the results of the excavations and also on historical sources, the monastery must have been destroyed around 1543–45.

2. Springs/wells.

2.a. Bence Well (*Figures 30 and 33*). A well exists in the middle of the supposed area of the monastery. It was recorded on an archive photo; today it is covered with concrete on the north side of a modern road which runs just next to the church. Based on its location, it is assumed to have supplied the monastery with water or even supplied the fishponds east of the monastery (see feature no. 4.). Digitized on 22 March 2014.

2.b. Unnamed well (*Figures 30 and 34*). The report on the first excavation mentions a group of wells next to the walls of the monastery on the southeast. Today there is a modern, poorly built well house on them.

2.c. Dual well (?) (*Figures 30, 35–37*). Southwest of the church, inside the monastic area (today just after the wall of the ruin garden), two deep holes were recorded, lined with stone slabs (?). These may be the remains of a collapsed cellar as István Méri supposed, but also could have been used as a well in the nineteenth or twentieth century. Digitized on 22 March 2014.

[341] Torma, ed. (1979), *Magyarország Régészeti Topográfiája* 5, 234–240, 300–303; Original documents (Méri, István (1959a-c). "Kesztölc-Klastrompuszta, pálos kolostor") and individual results.

3. Fishponds and dikes

3.a. (*Figures 30, 38–40*) The water, supposedly coming from Bence Well, was deepened with a dike into a pond, which—due to erosion and a strong human impact—could be detected only roughly, mostly the southern part of it. Here an inlet channel was also recorded, which let the water in from the south hilly area. The channel or other fishponds and dikes, which may have led to the pond from the monastery, were destroyed by agricultural activity in the early 1960s. Recently a hotel was built in the area and a part of the field has been opened for picnickers and campers. The first scientific recording and also the digitization of the features took place during the survey connected to the present work (22 March 2014). Based on the digitization, the pond's diameter was about 85 meters.
3.b. (*Figures 30, 42–44*) The next pond was significantly altered around the mid-1900s. A medieval spur[342] was found in 1959 during its clearing. At the same time, on the northwestern side, in the intersection of the pond's margin the original vaulted inlet(?) channel was uncovered.[343] A modern drainage pipe and the natural channel of the water are still visible.
4. Dike (*Figures 30, 45–50*). West of the second fishpond the remains of a dike were newly recorded during the field surveys related to the present work.[344] A wide plateau is visible in the bed of a natural stream to the northeast of the dike, which had a different water supply than the fishponds. This stream originates north of the monastery nowadays, (Where a small settlement lies) and flows east-southeast. At the dike it turns sharply south and a few meters lower the stream coming from the modern fishpond (3.b.) flows into this stream. The channel of the stream at this point turns east again and flows to the valley, where is the end of the research area, where a modern fishpond has been built. Digitized on 22 March 2014.

5. Caves (*Figures 51–53*). Leány (lit. "maiden"), Legény (lit. "lad/young man"), and Bivak (lit. "camp") Caves are the remains of medieval hermit life. A great variety of archaeological material was found there, dated from prehistoric times to the early modern age. In the Leány and Legény Caves archaeologists uncovered some archaeological material from the early Árpádian Era (eleventh to thirteenth century). Therefore, the archaeologists connected these caves with the hermits' presence in the area.

[342] Torma, ed. (1979), *Magyarország Régészeti Topográfiája* 5, 234, site 9/5. Catalogue number (Historical Museum, Dorog): 63.6.18.

[343] István Méri, *A klastrompusztai legendák nyomában* [On the track of legends in Klastrompuszta], (Dorog: József Attila Művelődési Ház, n.d.), 8–9.

[344] Here I say thanks to Professor József Laszlovszky, who suggested me this site for study.

B. History

1. Chronological data

Date	Issue	Source
ca. 1250	**Eusebius** and six other hermits build the Holy Cross monastery near Esztergom, close to a spring and three caves.*	Gyöngyösi (1988), *Vitae Fratrum*, Cap. 8; *ÁMTF* 4, 699–700.
1262	After his death, **Eusebius** was buried in the monastery.	Gyöngyösi (1988), *Vitae Fratrum*, Cap. 11; *ÁMTF* 4, 699–700.
After 1262 [1262/1263/ 1265]	King Béla IV (1235–1270) donated his **royal hunting lodge** in the Benedek Valley, near Dömös (*insula de Pilisio*), to Prior Benedict, the successor of Eusebius at the Holy Cross monastery. (*Nota bene*: this data is unclear and unverified. It is sometimes understood as the date of foundation of each three monasteries in the Pilis region. Ferenc Hervay argued that this donation refers to the Holy Spirit Monastery and recent research agrees with this.**	Gyöngyösi (1988), *Vitae Fratrum*, Cap. 14, 15; Eggerer (1663), *Fragmen*, 83; Pázmány (1629), *Acta*, 122, 126; Györffy (1956), "Adatok," 283–284. *DAP* 2, 409; *ÁMTF* 4, 699–700; *MRT* 5, 299; *MRT* 7, 167.
1270	The hermits held a synod and elected Benedict, the prior of the monastery as the **general provost of the Pauline Order.**	Gyöngyösi (1988), *Vitae Fratrum*, Cap. 11; *ÁMTF* 4, 699; *MRT* 5, 236.
1274	King Ladislaus IV (1272–1290) donated a part of the **woodland** in the Pilis Forest to the monastery.	Gyöngyösi (1522), *Inventarium*, 82; Györffy (1956), "Adatok," 283; *DAP* 2, 401; *ÁMTF* 4, 699–700; *MRT* 5, 236.
1285	The monastery was burnt down by the royal army.	Eggerer (1663), *Fragmen*, 75; *MRT* 5, 236.

* *Eusebius construe fecit monasterium Sanctae Crucis prope Strigonio anno 1250, regis Belae 4-ti 16... coadunatis sisi sex fratribus prope speculam triplicem, quam ipse alias incoluerat, iuxta aquam vivam in honorem Sanctae Crucis...quoddam monasterium, regularis observantiae sedem futuram inchoavit.*

** Szabó (2005), *Woodland and Forests*, 116.

1287	King Ladislaus IV donated the land of *Bendwelgye* or Benedekvölgye (again, which lies in *insula* Pilis) with a hunting lodge to the Paulines, namely, Father Peter of Hévíz (*Petro de Calidis Aquis*) and his fellows. At the same time, the king mandates Father Benedek, prior of the Holy Cross Monastery, to send some monks to settle at that monastery (supposedly the Holy Spirit Monastery).	Gyöngyösi (1988), *Vitae Fratrum*, Cap. 15; *ÁMTF* 4, 701; *MRT* 5, 299.
1289	King Ladislaus IV donated deserted lands (the **village of** Üllőkő?) to the monks at the Holy Cross monastery (a verification of an earlier donation by King Béla IV). Here the king also mentions that his predecessors founded the monastery. The donation was reconfirmed by Andrew III in 1291.	Gyöngyösi (1988), *Vitae Fratrum,* Cap. 14; Gyöngyössy (1522), *Inventarium*, 135; *ÁMTF* 4, 283, 699–700; *DAP* 2, 401.
1291	The monastery was listed in the second inventory of the Pauline monasteries of Veszprém Bischopric.	Gyöngyösi (1988), *Vitae Fratrum*, Cap. 10; *ÁMTF* 4, 699–700; *MRT* 5, 236.
1307	*Mikocha*, son of Elek donated a **piece of land** to the monastery (*Chazlow*) which was previously a part of a neighboring village, Csév (1332).	Gyöngyösi (1522), *Inventarium*, 82–83; Györffy (1956), "Adatok," 283; *ÁMTF* 4, 699–700; *MRT* 5, 236.
1308	Lady *Gewnghe* (lit. "weak") donated her **vineyard** to the monastery.	Gyöngyösi (1522), *Inventarium*, 82–83; Györffy (1956), "Adatok," 283; *ÁMTF* 4, 699–700; *MRT* 5, 236.
1327	King Charles Robert I (1308–1342) confirmed the possession of properties and lands of the monastery.	*ÁMTF* 4, 699–700.
1328	Michael, the Archdeacon of Komárom donated the **property of Teszér** to the monastery.	Gyöngyösi (1522), *Inventarium*, 82–83; Györffy (1956), "Adatok," 283; *ÁMTF* 4, 699–700.
1336	The Paulines of the monastery obtained a release from paying tax on their **vineyard** which lay at the foothills of Kesztölc by the chapter of Esztergom. (This was confirmed in 1396 by the chapter of Buda).	Gyöngyösi (1988), *Vitae Fratrum*, Cap. 23; Györffy (1956), "Adatok," 283; *ÁMTF* 4, 699–700; *MRT* 5, 236.
1358	A charter mentions the **lands** of the Paulines at Csév.	Bártfai (1891), *Pest megye*, 74; *MRT* 5, 236.

1376	John of Kesztölc donated his **vineyard** at Kesztölc to the monastery.	Gyöngyösi (1988), *Vitae Fratrum*, Cap. 33; Györffy (1956), "Adatok," 283; *MRT* 5, 236.
1393	Perambulation: data on the **boundary** between the village of Kesztölc and the Monastery of the Holy Cross.	DL 23 6647 (original, Archive of the Chapter of Esztergom, L. 28. f.1. n. 1.); *MRT* 5, 236.
1396	The monastery gained immunity from paying the decimal tax (*decima*) on their **vineyard** (and vines) at Kesztölc).	Gyöngyösi (1988), *Vitae Fratrum*, Cap. 38; *MRT* 5, 236.
1425–1513	The Holy Cross (Prior Andreas) and the Holy Spirit monastery (Prior Matthias) shared the ownership of a **house in Buda** (Mindszent [lit. "Allsaints"] Street), which they bought for 440 florins; their regular income from the rental charge is 8 florins. Later, in 1513, the two monasteries rented the house to a skinner, Sigismund Peiniczer, for 100 florins with a stipulation that he should pay 10 florins each year and keep the house in good condition.	1436, 1489: Gyöngyösi (1522), *Inventarium*, 82; *DAP* 2, 400–401; *MRT* 5, 237; Romhányi (2010), *Pálos gazdálkodás a középkorban*, 47.
1455	The Paulines had a **property** at Csév, next to the lands of the chapter of Esztergom. Brother Jacob was present at the registration of the domain.	Bártfai Szabó (1938), *Pest megye*, 209; *MRT* 5, 237.
1471–72	Ambrusius of Szántó, the provost of Esztergom sponsored the **construction** of an arcade at the monastery.	Gyöngyösi (1988), *Vitae Fratrum*, Cap. 59; Györffy (1956), "Adatok," 283; *MRT* 5, 237.
1476	The monastery owned a **house in Esztergom**, which was donated by magister Emeric Lovasi as an eternal alm; he requested regular masses for his peace in return.	*DAP* 2, 401; Romhányi (2010), *Pálos gazdálkodás a középkorban*, 189.
1526	The monastery was destroyed by the Turkish army.	Gyöngyösi (1988), *Vitae Fratrum*, Cap. 83; Békefi (1891), *A pilisi apátság*, 275.
1570	A *defter* mentions and locates *Szent Kereszt-puszta*, the deserted area of the monastery.	Györffy (1956), "Adatok," 283; *ÁMTF* 4, 699–700; *MRT* 5, 237.

2. Known priors of the monastery[345]

Eusebius (1256? –1270), Benedict (1270–1290), Stephen (1290–1297?), Laurence (1297–1317?), Kilián (1336–1346), Nicolaus (1346–1353), Tristan (1368–1369), Gregory – 1376, Stephen – 1393, Giles – 1396, Lawrence – 1421, Andreas – 1425.

3. Perambulation[346]

*...Primo et principaliter inciperet in proximitate declivii magni montis **Kewresmal** dicti, super dictas possessiones **Keztewlch et Chabÿa** vocatas existentis, quod videlicet declivium **Kewresmalerezteÿe** diceretur, ubi duas metas terreas erexissent. Abhinc directe ad meridiem de eodem monte non longe descendendo et quandam viam attingendo, secus ipsam viam duas metas terreas erexissent, hinc in ipsa via ipsis partibus pro meta derelicta, modice ad occidentem reflectendo in fine quarundam terrarum arabilum unam metam terream cursilem cumulassent, abinde per easdem paulisper ad dictum meridiem pergendo et quandam aliam viam de dicta Keztewlch. ad **clastrum dicte ecclesie Sancte Crucis** ducentem saliendo penes ipsam viam duas metas terreas fecissent, inde reflexive ad sinistram partem non multum in ascensu montis **Urdugkewehatha** dicti pergendo in latere ipsius montis unam metam terream cursilem erexissent, abhinc ulterius procedendo in cacumine ipsius montis duas metas terreas posuissent; inde ad dictum meridiem tendendo et de ipso monte im vallem **Zeketarla** dictam descendendo in ipsa valle duas metas terreas fecissent. Hinc amplius ad eandem plagam pergendo et quoddam Berch **Kezephwante** dictum attingendo circa cacuminem ipsius unam metam terream cursilem cumulassent, exhinc ulterius ad eandem plagam non longe eundo in quadam planicie prope fines quarundam terrarum arabilum **Gyurhegmegÿ** appellatarum duas metas terreas cumulassent, inde reflexive quasi inter occidentem et meridiem modice eundo in alia planicie **Mezewanthe** dictam secus terras arabiles unam metam terream cursilem fecissent. Exhinc ad eandem partem per ipsas terras arabiles ulterius procedendo, de ipsaque planicie **Mezewanthe** descendendo in latere ipsius descensus duas metas terreas fecissent. Abhinc ad ipsam plagam magis descensive tendendo in quandam magnam viam de Strigonio versus Budam transeuntem saliendo, et quuodam **Berch Balwanhat** dictum iuxta ipsam viam habitum attingendo in cacumine ipsius Berch unam metam terream cursilem fecissent. Inde de ipso Berch ad eandem plagam*

[345] Gyöngyösi (1988), *Vitae Fratrum*, Cap. 23; 25; 33. Györffy (1998), *Az Árpád-kori Magyarország történeti földrajza* 4, 699–700; Torma (1979), *Magyarország Régészeti Topográfiája* 5, 236–237.

[346] DL236647 – Original from 1393. DL 8014 – Copy, 1696.1 Transcription of the original charter with the kind help of Katalin Szende.

descendendo inter terras arabiles duas metas terreas posuissent. Abhinc per easdem terras arabiles ad eandem partem usque pratum ***Mycheletrethe*** *dictum eundo secus fines ipsarum terrarum arabilium et iuxta idem pratum unam metam terream cursilem fecissent. Deinde iret directe non longe ad eandem partem usque ad metas aliarum possessionum cometanearum et ibi terminarentur....*

C. Annotated Archaeological Research[347]

The first findings were listed in the catalogue of the Historical Museum of Dorog in 1955 by Géza Szepessy; La Tène, Roman, and medieval coins, ceramics, mainly medieval iron tools, spurs, knives, and horseshoes were found at the site.

During the field surveys for the *The Archaeological Topography of Hungary* series, after the report of Géza Szepessy and István Méri in 1959 István Horváth published about the remains of a supposedly medieval fishpond (3.b) in 1965, where Bronze, Iron, and Árpádian Age ceramic fragments were found. It has to be highlighted that István Méri was the only one who mentioned that a complete water management system was constructed in the valley which leads from Kesztölc to the Holy Cross Monastery. It is still clear in the system of the present-day terraces (*Figure 54*).

The first archaeological research at the monastery (church, chapel chapter, and workshops), lead by István Méri, took place in 1959 and 1961 (the results were published only in 1993 by Júlia Kovalovszki), which was continued sixty years later, in 2013 by Elek Benkő and Balázs Major. Many questions and unclear data were present in the research until the beginning of the first excavation, even the location of the monastery was in question.[348] Since the very first archaeological research, strong destruction of landscape features has been documented, only archive photos reveal the past landscape around the monastery (*Figures 55–56*).

Leány, Legény, and Bivak Caves (see 5. Caves) were excavated at different times by Lajos Bella, István Horváth, Géza Szepessy, László Vértes, and Dénes Jánossy. Besides these, less is known about another cave, Sármánka, near the monastery, where Péter Börcsök and László Vértes Jr. uncovered archaeological material from the twelfth and thirteenth centuries in 1968, which they believed was connected with the hermits of the Árpádian Era.

---

[347] Based on original documents from the Archive of the National Museum (Méri (1959a-c), "Kesztölc-Klastrompuszta, pálos kolostor"); Méri (n.d.), *Klastrompuszta*; Torma, ed. (1979), *Magyarország Régészeti Topográfiája* 5, 234–240, 300–303.

[348] On the research history of the monastery and the various evaluation of data, see Torma, ed. (1979), *Magyarország Régészeti Topográfiája* 5, 234–236.

The fishponds and the water management system were never documented precisely until 2014, when Katalin Tolnai and András Harmath digitized the area of fishpond 3.b and dike 4 (21-22 March 2014).

D. Selected Literature

ÁMTF 4, 699–700.
MTF 1, 15.
DAP 2, 400–407.
Méri (n.d.), *Klastrompuszta.*
Méri (1959a-c), "Kesztölc-Klastrompuszta, pálos kolostor."
MRT 5, 234–240.
MRT 7, 300–303.
Guzsik (2003), *Pálos építészet.*
Kovalovszki (1992), "Klastrompuszta."
Romhányi (2012a), "Pálos kolostorok."
Solymosi (2005), "Pilissziget.".

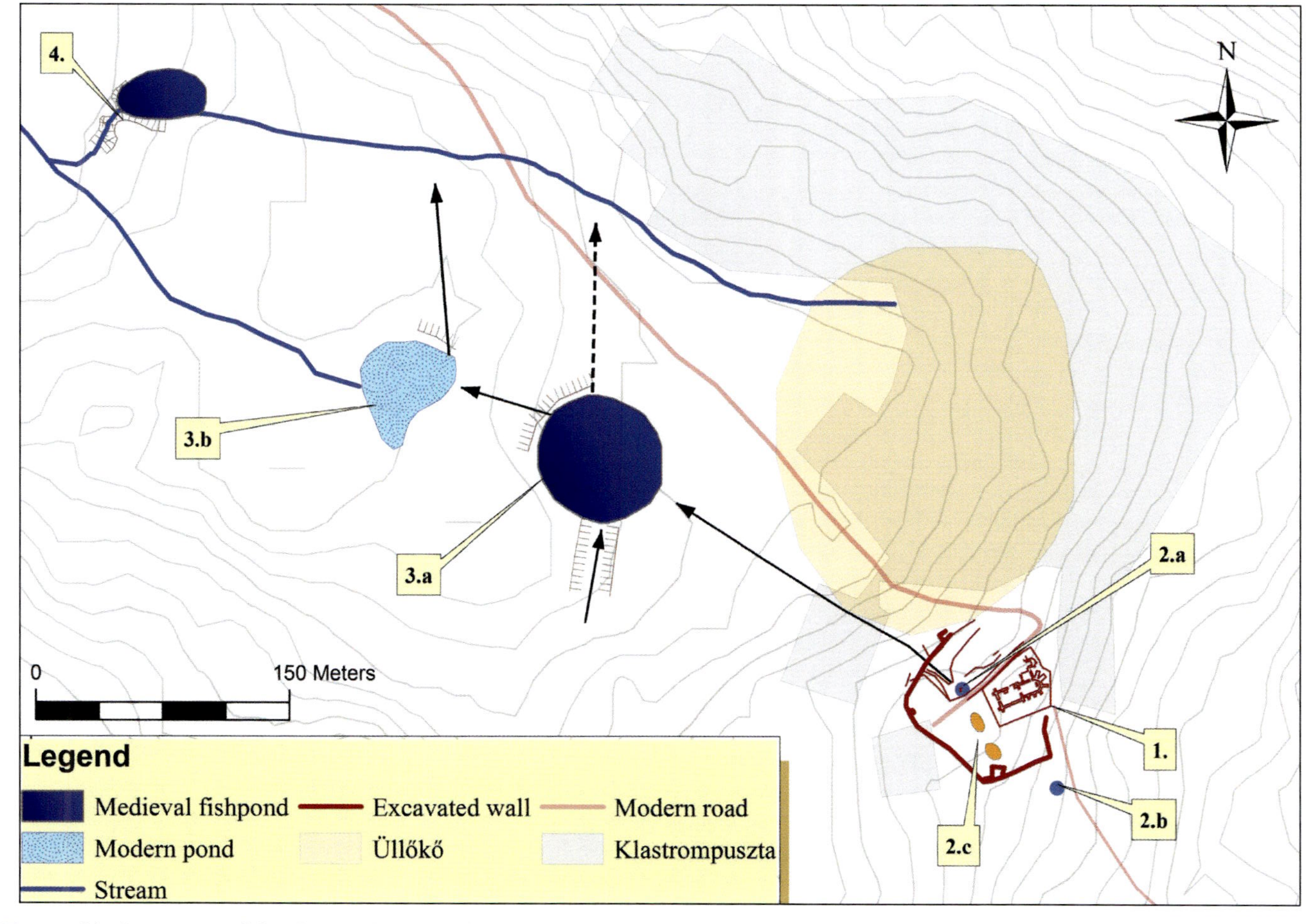

Figure 29. Summary of the detected spatial features around the Holy Cross Monastery, except the caves. Drawn by the author

Figure 30. The ruin garden at Kesztölc nowadays, behind the rocky hills to northeast. Photo taken by the author (22 March 2014)

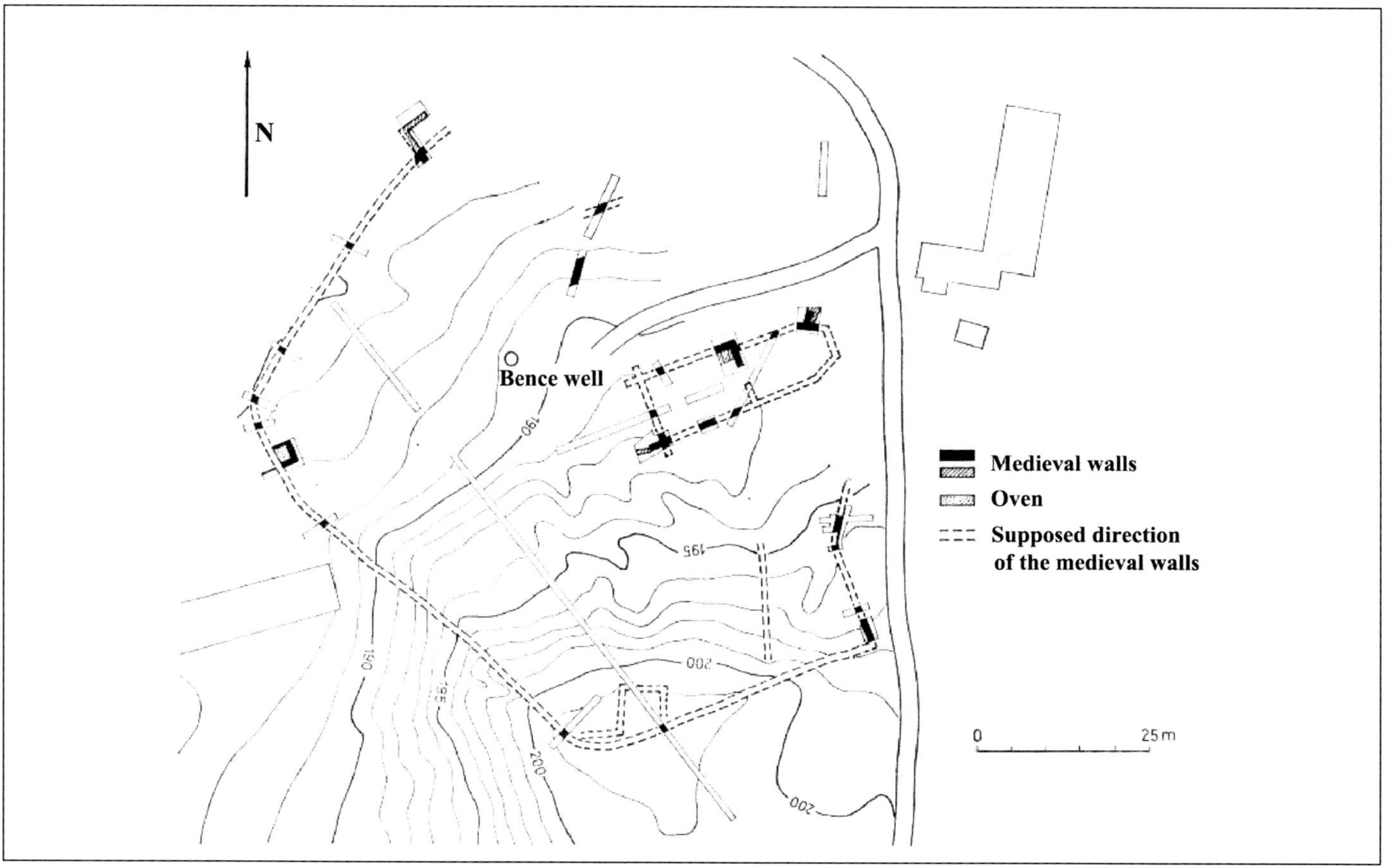

Figure 31. The plan of the site at the Monastery of Holy Cross. On the basis of the work of István Méri. Torma, ed. (1979), Magyarország Régészeti Topográfiája 55, 235.

Figure 32. The Bence well from the north.
Archive photo. Méri (1959c), "Kesztölc-Klastrompuszta"

Figure 33. An unnamed double well, southeast of the ruins.
Archive photo. Méri (1959c), "Kesztölc-Klastrompuszta"

Figure 34. Archive photo of the collapsed cellar/double well. Photo taken from the northeast. Méri (1959c), "Kesztölc-Klastrompuszta"

Figure 35. Present-day photo of the collapsed cellar/double well. Photo taken from the north by the author (22 March 2014)

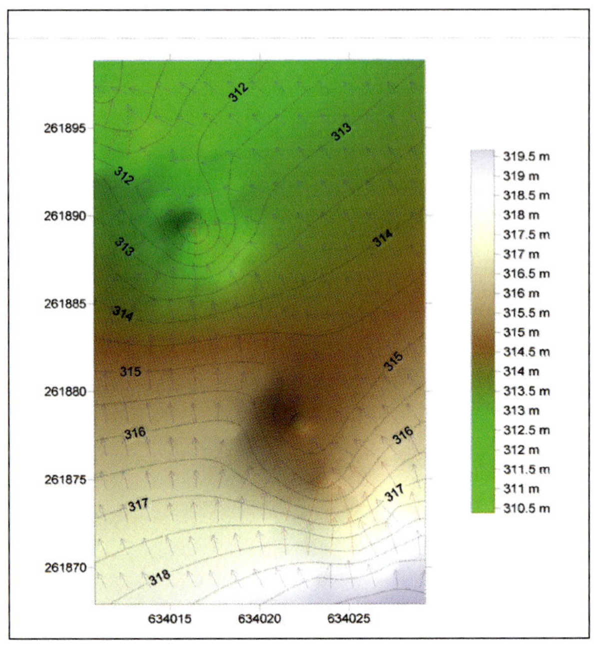

Figure 36. The digitized terrain model with the supposed double well/cellar. Digitization (22 March 2014) and terrain model by András Harmath and Katalin Tolnai

Figure 37. Fishpond 3.a nowadays. Photo taken from east by the author (22 March 2014)

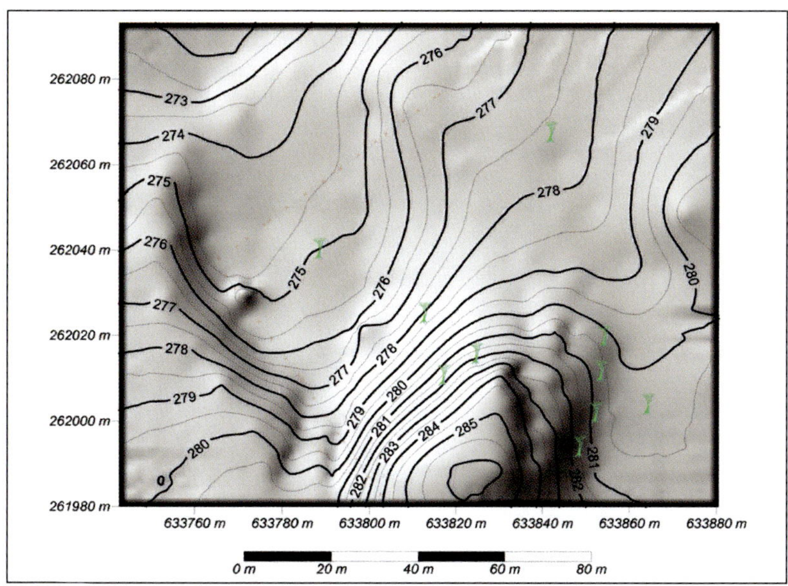

Figure 38. The digitized terrain model of Fishpond 3.a. Digitization (22 March 2014) and terrain model by András Harmath and Katalin Tolnai

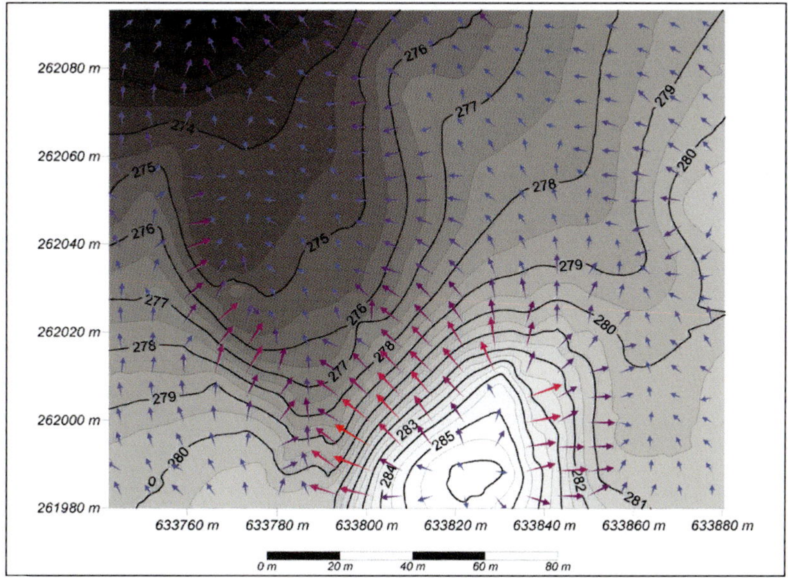

Figure 39. A digitized terrain model of Fishpond 3.a., presenting the elevation with arrows, which emphasizes the channel on the south. Digitization (22 March 2014) and terrain model by András Harmath and Katalin Tolnai

Figure 40. The probable remains of the dike between Fishponds 3.a. and 3.b. Photo taken from the northwest by the author

Figure 41. Fishpond 3.b. nowadays. Photo taken by the author (22 April 2014)

Figure 42. The remains of the medieval vaulted stone inlet on the west-northwest. Méri (1959c), "Kesztölc-Klastrompuszta"

Figure 43. The channel of the dike for Fishpond 3.b nowadays. Photo taken from the southeasteast by the author (22 March 2014)

Figure 44. The fishpond just above the dike (4.) to the north, which lies in the bushy area, in the lower part of the picture. The fishpond (blue oval) and the direction of the stream (green arrow) just before the dike were marked on the picture. The photo was taken by the author (23 March 2014)

Figure 45. The dike (4.) below the stream's turn to the south; photographed from south by the author (21 March 2014)

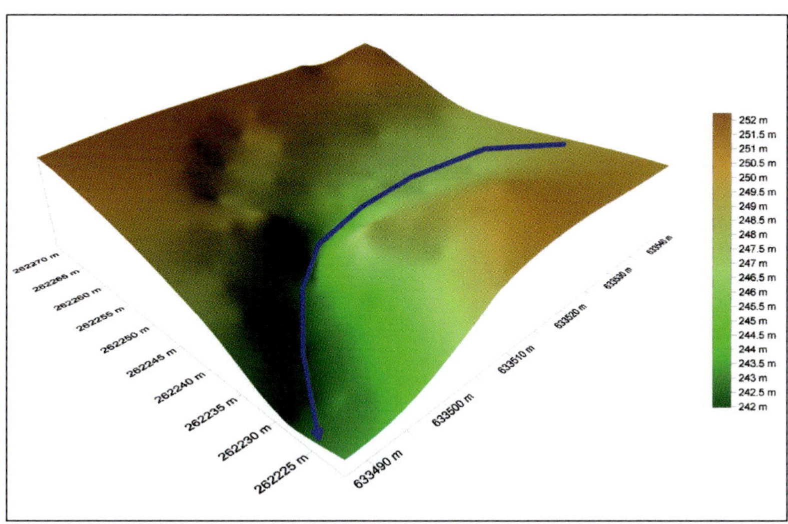

Figure 46. The digitized terrain of the dike (4.); a view from south. Digitization (22 March 2014) and terrain model by András Harmath and Katalin Tolnai

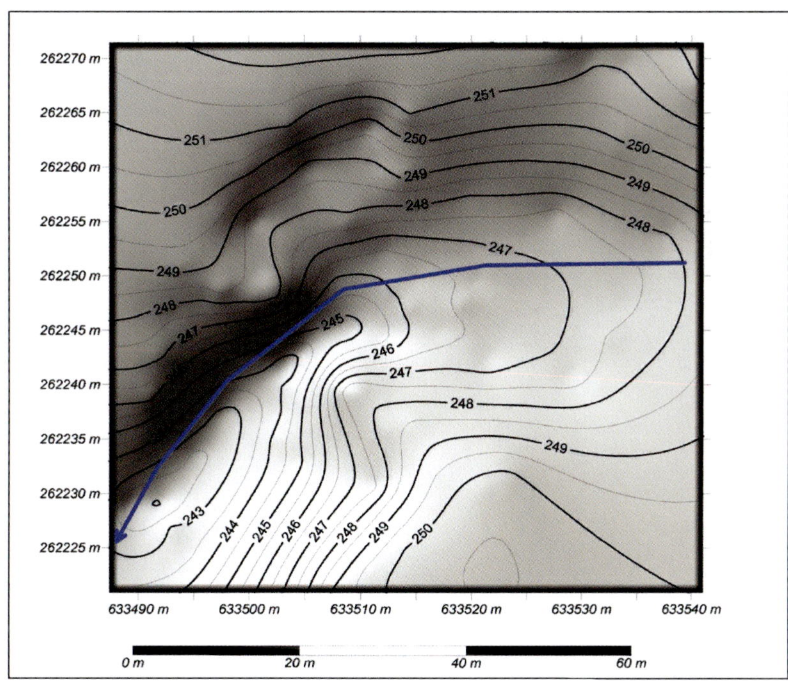

Figure 47. The digitized terrain model of the dike (4) with highpoints, directed to the north. Digitization (22 March 2014) and terrain model by András Harmath and Katalin Tolnai

Figure 48. The southern part of the dike (4.), documented from the north by the author (21 March 2014)

Figure 49. A view to the east of the area after the dike. Documented from the west by the author (22 March 2014)

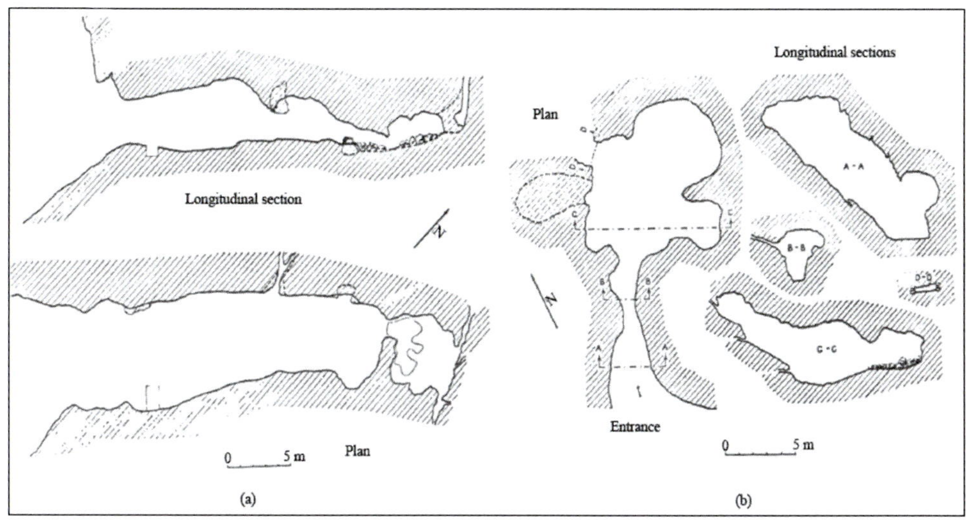

Figure 50. The vertical and horizontal cut of Legény (a) and Leány (b) Caves. Torma, ed. (1979), Magyarország Régészeti Topográfiája 5, 302.

Figure 51. The entrance of Legény Cave, documented by the author (22 March 2014)

Figure 52. The view from Legény Cave to the west. Documented by the author (2 March 2014)

Figure 53. Branches in the landscape from Fishpond 3.b. to the west, the direction of present-day Kesztölc. They may be part of a complex water management system of past centuries. Documented by the author (22 March 2014)

Figure 54. Archive photo of the surroundings of the ruins, photo taken from the east by István Méri (1959c), "Kesztölc-Klastrompuszta"

Figure 55. Archive photo of the terrain around the monastery, photo taken from southwest by István Méri (1959c), "Kesztölc-Klastrompuszta"

Monastery of the Holy Spirit (Pilisszentlélek)

Location: Over to the north of the modern village of Pilisszentlélek, Pest Co., HU
Coordinate: (WGS84) φ = 47 44 04.96190; λ = 18 50 36.75423
Status: Medieval monastic buildings were abandoned during the Ottoman period and the ruins were used as a quarry for building material. Almost completely excavated (1985–1992) by Sarolta Lázár, transformed into an open-air ruin garden with some identified earthwork features (fishpond) nearby.

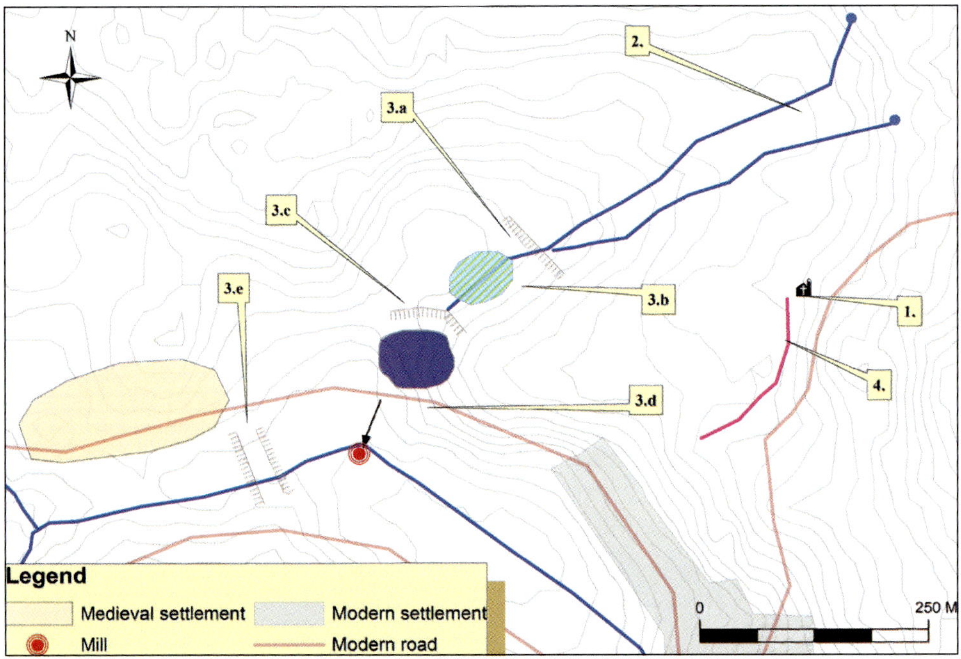

Figure 56. Summary of the spatial features detected around the Holy Spirit Monastery. Drawn by the author

A. Spatial Features and Earthworks (*Figure 56*)[349]

1. Monastery[350] (*Figures 56–58*). The church (20.5 x 10.7 m) has one nave, a straight apse at the end, and three altars inside. A vestry is connected to the north side of the church. On the eastern side of the cloister excavations revealed the

[349] Torma, ed. (1979), *Magyarország Régészeti Topográfiája* 5, 297–303. and new results.
[350] It should be mentioned that there was no available plan on a digital platform or any opportunity to gather precise spatial data.

remains of the corridor to the church, the stairway to the upper floors (where the archaeologist supposed the individual sleeping-quarters had been), the chapter, and the refectory. The main entrance was on the eastern part of the cloister. A one-story building was erected on the north side of the eastern cloister body. Some workshops must have operated in the southern buildings of the monastery. A reconstruction of the vault system was successfully implemented.

2. Spring and streams (*Figures 56, 59–60.* Near the monastery, about 200 meters to the north-northeast, a temporary spring was recorded in August 2013. An earlier survey (22 March 2014) revealed another spring in the bushy area about 50 meters to the northwest.[351] Following the stream channels, a complex natural system was revealed; the two stream beds running southwest-west after ca. 250 m continue in one single bed, where an earthwork seems to have existed.

3. Pond and dikes

3.a. Supposed dike (*Figures 56 and 61*). Just before the two streams unite, a narrow natural valley was recorded by recent field surveys (22 March 2014, 12 April 2014) on the southeastern stream. This may be the remnant of a half human-made, half-natural dike. Length: ca. 50 m. Direction: NW-SE.

3.b. Supposed fishpond (*Figure 56*). As the dike was detected, the wet area refers to a former pond, but no certain boundaries of this feature could be found. Diameter: ca. 80 m.

3.c. Supposed dike (*Figures 56 and 62)*. A shallow hump indicates the beginning of a lower layer which might have functioned as a dike in the past (most likely strong erosion destroyed the earthwork). In connection with the previous earthwork, this system is rather a suggested than a clear record. Length: ca. 70 m. Direction: SE-NW, than W.

3.d. Fishpond (*Figure 56*). At the end of the valley where the intermittant streams run, a large wet area exists, full of reed. It was not documented officially before the field surveys in this year. Diameter: ca. 75 m.

3.e. Dike (*Figures 56 and 63*). The highest point of it was almost 4 m in the 1960s; it was recorded at the deepest point of the valley by the field surveys connected to *The Archaeological Topography of Hungary* series. It was clear at that time that the dike had a floodgate. On the northern end there was a shoulder

[351] Also, it is supposed that the origin of the springs should be researched further to the northeast; some dry, shallow ditches in the landscape suggest this direction. A LiDAR record would surely help to decide this question.

dike (of the same height) with a drainage channel cut into the upper edge. The channel ran further to the east. Supposedly it was the channel of a medieval mill.

4. Pathway to the monastery. Next to the modern road, which lead to the ruin garden, an old road runs to the south. This might have been used in the Middle Ages because the entrance to the monastery was at the point where the old road reaches the ruins.

B. History

1. Chronological data

Date	Issue	Source
After 1262 [1262/1263/ 1265]	King Béla IV (1235–1270) donated his **royal hunting lodge** in the Benedek Valley, near Dömös (*insula de Pilisio*) to Prior Benedict, the successor of Eusebius at the Holy Cross monastery. (*Nota bene*: this data is unclear and unverified, and is sometimes understood as the date of foundation of each of the three monasteries of the Pilis region. Ferenc Hervay argued that this donation refers to the Holy Spirit Monastery and recent research agrees with this.* Also it is the closest to Dömös of all three monasteries.)	Gyöngyösi (1988), *Vitae Fratrum*, Cap. 14, 15; Eggerer (1663), *Fragmen*, 83; Pázmány (1629), *Acta*, 122, 126; Györffy (1956), "Adatok," 283–284. *DAP* 2, 409; *ÁMTF* 4, 699–700; *MRT* 5, 299; *MRT* 7, 167.
1287	King Ladislaus IV (1272–1290) donated the land of Bendwelgye or Benedekvölgye (again, which lies in *insula* Pilis) with a **hunting lodge** to the Paulines, namely, Father Peter of Hévíz (*Petro de Calidis Aquis*) and his fellows. At the same time the king mandates Father Benedek, the prior of Holy Cross Monastery, to send some monks to settle that monastery (supposedly the Holy Spirit Monastery).	Gyöngyösi (1988), *Vitae Fratrum*, Cap 15; *ÁMTF* 4, 701; *MRT* 5, 299.
1323	King Charles Robert I (1308–1342) stayed here and confirmed the document on the foundation of the monastery in the presence of the monks Nicolaus and Prichtold.	Gyöngyösi (1988), *Vitae Fratrum*, Cap. 20; Eggerer (1663), *Fragmen*, 113; *ÁMTF* 4, 701; *MRT* 5, 299.

* Szabó (2005), *Woodland and Forests*, 116, ref. 75; Gyöngyösi (1988), *Vitae Fratrum*, 209.

1378	King Louis I 1342–1382) spent Easter Passion week in the monastery, where he confirms the boundary of the monastery (the first perambulation) and donated new lands for the Paulines.	DL 6521 [Acta Paulinorum F. 5.N.2]; Gyöngyösi (1988), *Vitae Fratrum*, Cap. 34; *MRT* 5, 299.
1409	Pál Csupor erected an **altar** to the Holy Virgin and donated a **property** to support it.	Kürcz (1889), *Pálos*, 115; *MRT* 5, 299.
1425–[1443]–1513	The Holy Cross (Prior Andreas) and the Holy Spirit monastery (Prior Matthias) shared the ownership of a **house in Buda** (Mindszent [lit. "Allsaints"] Street), which they bought for 440 florins; their regular income from the rental charge was 8 florins (the house was mentioned again in 1443). Later, in 1513, the two monasteries rented the house to a skinner, Sigismund Peiniczer, for 100 florins and with the stipulation that he should pay 10 florins each year and keep the house in good condition.	Gyöngyösi (1522), *Inventarium*, 82 – DAP 2, 400–401; Romhányi (2010), *Pálos gazdálkodás a középkorban*, 47.
1443	The monastery gains some **properties** from the wife of Konrad Krusovecz.	Kürcz (1889), *Pálos*, 115; Kisbán (1938) , *Pálos* 1, 113; *MRT* 5, 299.
1467	At an installation in the property of **Bajon,** the monastery of Holy Spirit was represented as a **neighbor** by Father Nicolaus in person.	Bártfai (1938), *Pest megye*, 955. regesta; *MRT* 5, 299.

2. Known priors of the monastery[352]

Peter of Hévíz – 1287, Anthony – 1336, Nicolaus– 1342, Colomanus–1376, Matthias – 1425, Lawrence –1512

3. Perambulation[353]

*Quod **prima meta** incipit in **monte Kyrállesse** vocato a parte Aquilonari et deinde paululum in cacumine ad partem tendentur Orientalem, venit ad aciem ejusdem montis, a quo descendentur vadit ad quandam **viam**, per quam transitur **ad villam Marotis**, juxta quam est meta **Terrea**, abhinc versus eandem plagam gradientur*

[352] Based on Torma, ed. (1979), *Magyarország Régészeti Topográfiája* 5, 299.

[353] DL 6521 (*Acta Paulinorum*). Transcription of the copy.

jungitur cuidam loco ***Oh Remethe-Hely*** *appellato, secus rivulum* Örűmes ***Patak*** *nuncupatum et penes eundem in bono spatio directe transeundo, ac postmodum contra partem declinando meridionalem venit* ***ad fines jugerum, seu terrrarum arabilium Fratrum*** *praedictorum, et tandem paulisper girando, tendit ad radicem montis* ***Soklós*** *nominati, ab hincque transeundo quasdam alias particulas* ***Terrarum*** *actualium eorundem Fratrum ambiendo quendam alium* ***rivulum*** *salientur versus partem occidentalem, venit ad radicem alterius* ***Montis Fekete-Keő*** *nominati, et ad quandam* ***stratam*** *sub eodem existentem, juxta quam habet(ur?) quidam* ***grandis lapis*** *de predicto monte ruptus, a quo circulariter vergendo in latere ejusdem longi* ***montis versus Strigonium*** *adjacentis, penes viam in latere ejusdem Montis existentur immediate sunt erectae quatuor* ***metae terreae;*** *a quibus directe procedendo venit ad* ***montem Fejér-Keő*** *nuncupatum, juxta viam prenominatam, ab hincque transiens jungitur cuidam. Cuidam* ***Valli Vodnyoló*** *nominate: item abinde contra predictam* ***plagam Aquilonarem*** *flectens tendit ad quendam Monticulum, in cuius vertice habetur similis Meta Terreae et de ipso procedendo vadit rursum in predictum* ***Montem Király-Lesse*** *appellantum, ibique terminatur.*

C. Archaeological Research[354]

The first excavations were conducted in between 1928 and 1933, when amateur archaeologists clarified the main plan of the monastery. Research excavations took place from 1985 to 1992 by Sarolta Lázár, when the church, the cloister, the eastern part of the surrounding wall, and the southern outbuildings (workshops) were researched (the gate and the northern building are still not researched). As in the case of the Holy Cross monastery, here also earlier walls and foundations were discovered by Tamás Guzsik who pointed out that the plan has many dubious parts. In his theory it is acceptable that the center and origin of the whole church was the 13x13 m square shaped "tower," where the apse and the connected vestry/chapter were formed.

The *Archaeological Topography of Hungary* mentions a dike (3.c) on the stream Szentlélek (3.c). Nowadays, after the regulation of the stream, it cannot be identified clearly. Recently, field surveys (22 March and 12 April 2014) revealed another dike (3.c) and a fishpond (3.d), but the earthworks are just slightly visible (mostly 3.a and 3.b earthworks, which were also revealed) because of the high

[354] Based on Torma, ed. (1979), *Magyarország Régészeti Topográfiája* 5, 299; Lázár, Sarolta (1994). "A pilisszentléleki pálos kolostortemplom kutatása" [Archaeological investigation of the Pauline Monastery at Pilisszentlélek], in: *Varia Paulina. Pálos Rendtörténeti Tanulmányok* [Studies on the history of the Pauline Order], vol. 1, ed. Gábor Sarbak, (Csorna: Private Edition of Árva Vince), 177–180; Guzsik (2003), *Pálos építészet*, 59.

degree of erosion. The route of the water can be followed to the springs on the hill side near the monastery.

D. Literature

ÁMTF 4, 70.
MTF 1, 16.
DAP 2, 411–413.
MRT 5, 297–303.
Lázár (1994), "Pilisszentlélek kutatása."
Lázár (1997), "Pilisszentlélek kutatása 1985–86."
Lázár (2001), "Pilisszentléleki kályhacsempe."
Buzás (1994), "Pilisszentléleki kőfaragvány."
Guzsik (2003), *Pálos építészet.*
Romhányi (2012a), "Pálos kolostorok."

E. Illustrations

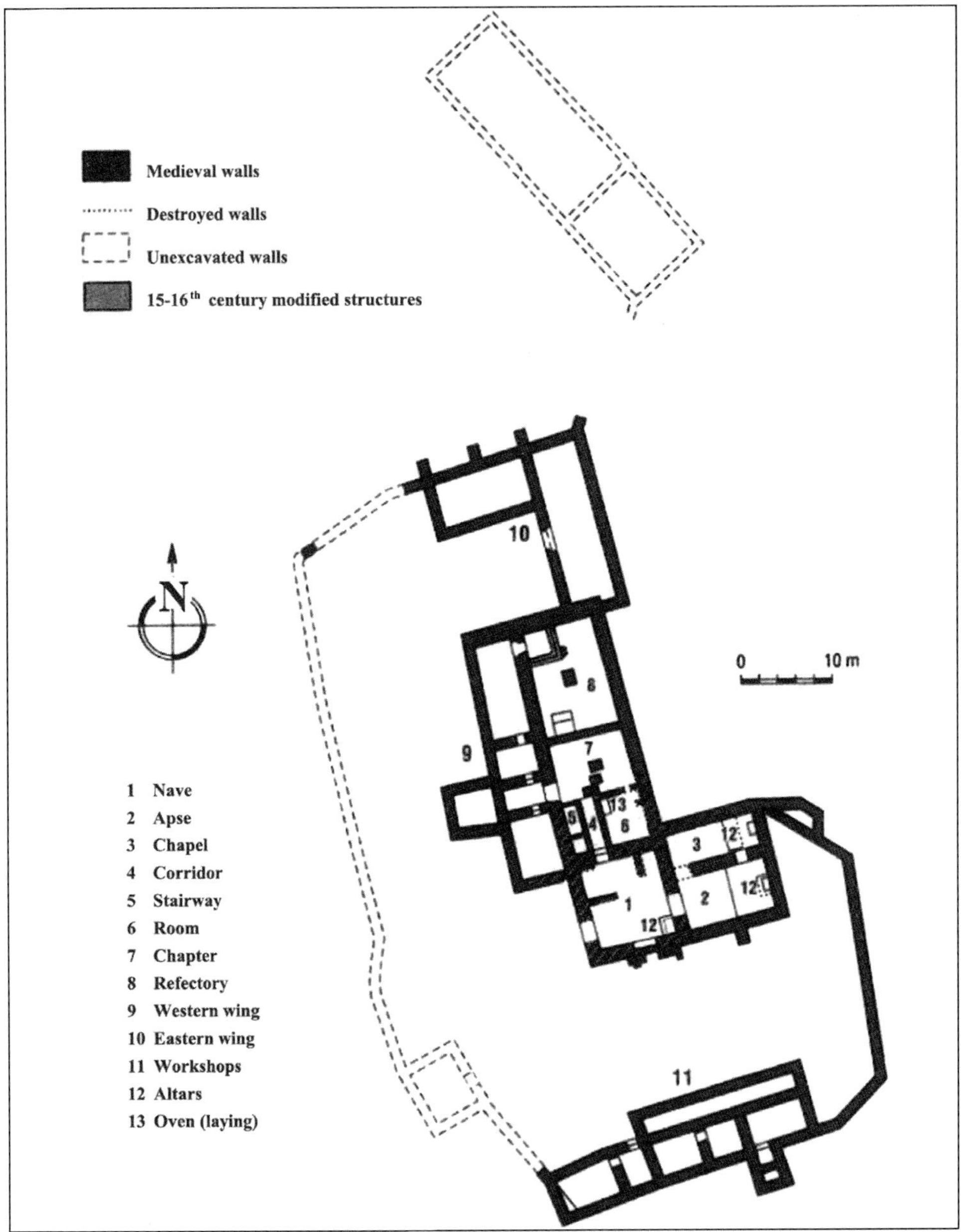

Figure 57. The plan of the Holy Spirit Monastery. On the basis of Lázár (2012), "Pilisszentlélek," 218.

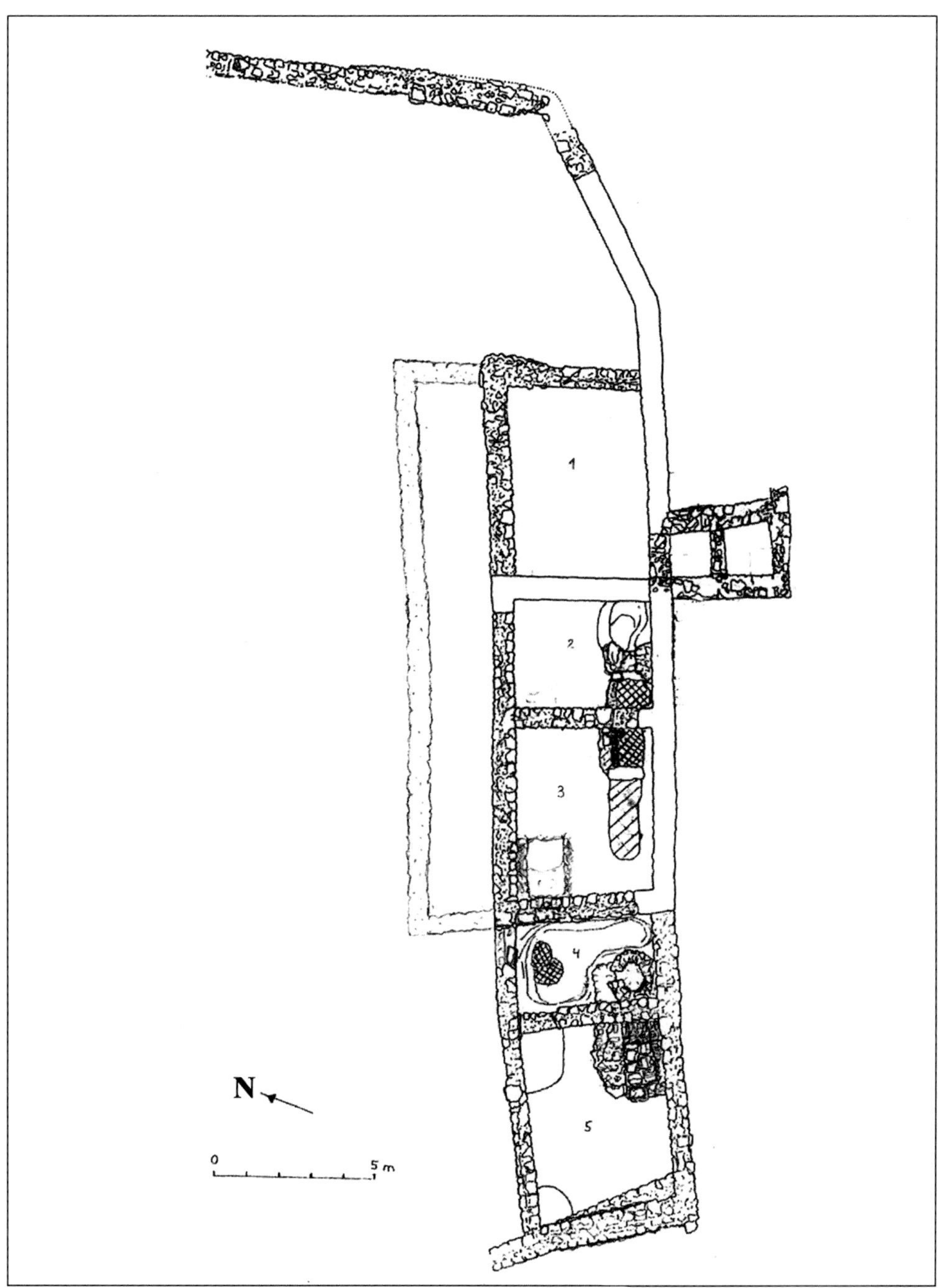

Figure 58. The excavated workshops in the Holy Spirit Monastery. Lázár (2012), "Pilisszentlélek," 219.

Figure 59. The spring (?) of the southern stream, just next to the hiking path. Documented by the author (12 April 2014)

Figure 60. The northern bed of the intermittant stream. Photo taken by the author (22 March 2014)

Figure 61. The probable dike 3.a.
Photo taken from the southwest by the author (22 March 2014)

Figure 62. The second fishpond that probably existed in the past.
Photo taken from the northwest by the author (22 March 2014)

Figure 63. Dike of a medieval fishpond in the 1960s(?) on Szentlélek (Holy Spirit) stream. Torma, ed. (1979), Magyarország Régészeti Topográfiája 5, 443 (Table 69, Picture 1)

Monastery of Saint Ladislaus (Kékes/Pilisszentlászló)

Location: Unidentified. The monastery is presumed to have stood on the hill over the modern village of Pilisszentlászló, Pest Co., HU.
Coordinate: (WGS84) φ = 47 43 36.39339; λ = 18 59 03.69130
Status: The medieval monastic buildings were abandoned during the Ottoman period, but the ruins are still not identified convincingly; there are arguments in support of the medieval origins of the present-day parish church on the hilltop and most scholars identify it as the church of the monastery.

A. Spatial Features and Earthworks[355] (*Figures 64-66*)

1. Monastery (*Figures 64–65*). The remains of the medieval monastery are supposed to lie under the present baroque church (built in the 1770s) on the top of the hill above the village. The ruins were noted in 1725 and they are marked on some eighteenth-century maps.

[355] Torma, ed. (1986), *Magyarország Régészeti Topográfiája* 7, 166–168.

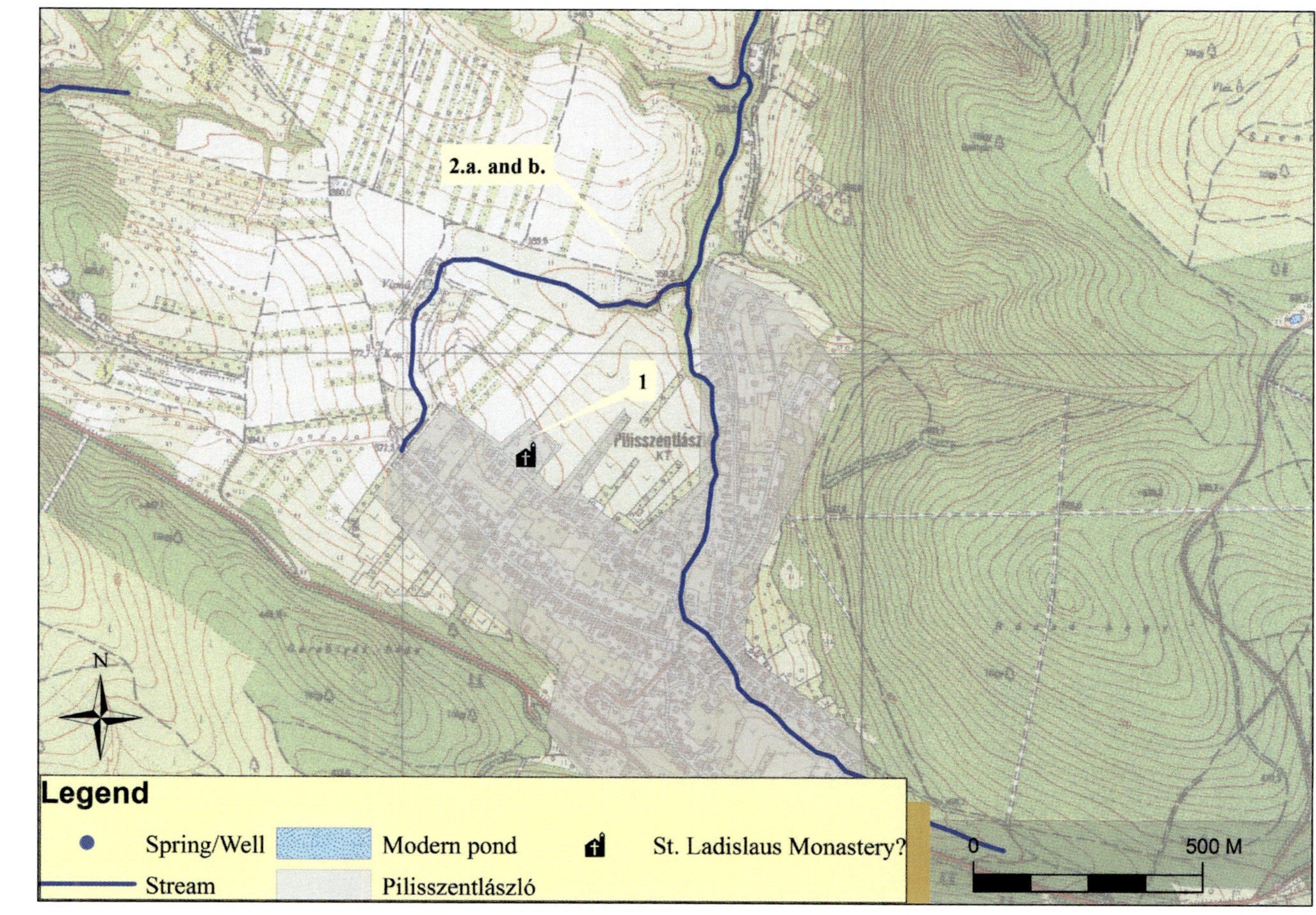

Figure 64. Summary of the spatial features detected around the St. Ladislaus Monastery on the cut of National Topographic Map

2. Dikes, fishponds

2.a. (*Figures 64–66*). From the settlement to the north, around 400 m, where a small stream flows into Apát-patak (Abbey stream), just before the confluence, a destroyed, 0,5-0,8m high, 15 m wide, and 30 m long dike closes the valley of the stream.

2.b. (*Figures 64–66*). About 60-70 m further to the west another dike was documented in the 1960s, it was 1.5-2.0 m high, 40-45 m long northwards and 20-25 m long southwards.

B. History

1. Chronological data

Date	Issue	Source
1046–1060	King Andrew I (1046–1060) donated his **hunting lodge** (built of stone) for religious purposes. Unverified data.	Eggerer (1663), 83; Pázmány (1629), *Acta*, 122, 126. Györffy (1956), "Adatok," 283–284; *ÁMTF* 4, 699-700; *MRT* 7, 167.
After 1262 [1262/1263/ 1265]	King Béla IV (1235–1270) donated his **royal hunting lodge** in the Benedek Valley near Dömös (*insula de Pilisio*) to Prior Benedict prior, the successor of Eusebius at the Holy Cross Monastery. (*Nota bene*: this data is unclear and unverified, and is sometimes understood as the date of foundation of each three monasteries in the Pilis region. Ferenc Hervay argued that this donation refers to the Holy Cross monastery and recent research also agrees with this.*	Gyöngyösi (1988), *Vitae Fratrum*, Cap. 14; Eggerer (1663), 83; Pázmány (1629), *Acta*, 122, 126; Györffy (1956), "Adatok," 283–284. *DAP* 2, 409; *ÁMTF* 4,
1291	The monastery was listed among the **clarified Pauline monasteries** by Benedict, the Bishop of Veszprém. (*In Pilisio ecclesiae ... Sancti Ladislai in Kekes*).	Gyöngyösi, *Vitae Fratrum,* Cap. 9, 16. Cited: Györffy, "Adatok," 285; *ÁMTF* 4, 700; *MRT* 7, 167.
1294	The monastery became an *exempt* ecclesiastical center; therefore it is **regulated directly by the archbishop** of Esztergom.	*DAP* 2, 409; *ÁMTF* 4, 700; *MRT* 7, 167.

* Szabó (2005), *Woodland and Forests*, 116.

1301	Before this year the archbishop of Veszprem argued that Trausulus, the castellan of Visegrád, settled the hospeses of Kékes on his properties at Szentendre. As the pope had ordered them to move but they were still there, the archbishop of Kalocsa excommunicated the settlers.	DF 200 075; *ÁMTF* 4, 700.
1308	Matthew Csák had the first **political talk** with Cardinal Gentile, papal legate, on the return of Visegrád and the homage of Charles Robert.	Cod. Dipl. VIII/7, 62; *ÁMTF* 4, 700; *MRT* 7, 167; Bakács (1982), *Iratok*, 313. reg.
1342	Georgius Gyöngyösi mentioned **King Charles Robert I** as the **founder of the church**.	Gyöngyösi (1988), *Vitae Fratrum*, Cap. 27; Györffy (1956), "Adatok," 284; *ÁMTF* 4, 700; *MRT* 7, 167.
1351	The Paulines sold their **vineyard** at "Barathkazelo," "Sumulmal" hill (Pilisborosjenő) to the nuns of Óbuda for 14 marks. With a *locus torcularis*, a wine press.	DL 4230, 4231; Bakács (1982), *Iratok*, 656–657; *MRT* 7, 142, 167.
1353	The church was consecrated by Prior General Peter.	*DAP* 2, 409.
1358 [1473]	King Louis I (1342–1382) donated a ruined **mill** to the St. Ladislaus monastery at Szentendre, *Kékes pataka* (the stream of Kékes) and also another upstream place for a mill.	DL 7121, (copy: DL 15116); *ÁMTF* 4, 700; *DAP* 2, 410; *MRT* 7, 167, 269; Romhányi (2010), *Pálos gazdálkodás a középkorban*, 75, 147.
–1412	The St. Ladislaus monastery owned a **parcel** in Visegrád. In 1412 Gregorius, the provost of St. Ladislaus Monastery (with the permission of Ladislaus, Pauline general provost) sold the parcel to Nicolaus Póré of Bogdány for 13 florins.	MOL DL 10021; Romhányi (2010), *Pálos gazdálkodás a középkorban*, 50, 145.
1456	Denis, the archbishop of Esztergom, donated a **mill** on the stream Rákos and a **parcel** (both parts of the property of Sződ) to the monastery.	*MRT* 7, 167.
1457	Péter Decan, citizen of Vác donated a **vineyard** called Bakos and located at "Pychewelgh" to the monastery.	*DAP* 2, 408; *MRT* 7, 167.
1458	The St. Ladislaus monastery exchanged a vineyard for a **mill (with semi-wheels)** at Sződ on the stream Rákos (the owner was originally Thomas Cristel; the value of the vineyard: 100 florins, the value of the mill: 114 florins).	DL 15203; *DAP* 2, 408, 410; *MRT* 7, 167; Romhányi (2010), *Pálos gazdálkodás a középkorban*, 75, 147.

1460	Elisabeth, mother of King Matthias I (1458–1490), ordered John of *Nysa* to give the mill at Sződ back to the Paulines, which he took from them by force.	DL 15513 (23 October).
1473	Peter of Tahi bequeathed to the monastery 100 florins to **repair the larger pond** and 50 florins to **repair the mill** on the Kékes stream.	DL 17454 (14th May) ; *MRT* 7, 167; Romhányi (2010), *Pálos gazdálkodás a középkorban*, 75, 150.
1488	Father Michael Futó bequeathed a **book** (a copy of Saint John's speeches) to the monastery.	Gyöngyösi (1988), *Vitae Fratrum*, Cap. 67; *DAP* 2, 409; *MRT* 7, 167.
[1493]-1498	János Fügedi, the prior of the St. Ladislaus monastery, sells the Pauline **house** in Olasz [Italian] Street in **Buda,** for 150 florins with the stipulation that the purchaser should pay extra 10 florins yearly rent to the Paulines.	DL 20034; Gyöngyösi (1522), *Inventarium* 87; *DAP* 2, 408; *MRT* 7, 167; Romhányi (2010), *Pálos gazdálkodás a középkorban*, 45.
1515	For the **other house** of the monastery in **Buda** (donated by Ladislaus of Szentpéter, next to the tight passage (Schüler Gasse) which leads to Olasz [Italian] Street) 6 florins was the yearly amount of rent.	Gyöngyösi (1522), *Inventarium* 87, *DAP* 2, 409; Romhányi (2010), *Pálos gazdálkodás a középkorban*, 45.

2. Known priors of the monastery

Weyce – after 1300;[356] Gregorius – 1412[357]

C. Archaeology

There have been no proper excavations. Around the baroque church, in the graveyard, local people often find the remains of some built structures. Inside the church Tamás Guzsik recorded some Gothic characteristics and features.

D. Literature

ÁMTF 4, 700–701.
MTF 1, 11–12.
DAP 2, 408–410.
MRT 7, 166–168.
Guzsik (2003), *Pálos építészet.*

[356] Györffy (1998), *Az Árpád-kori Magyarország történeti földrajza* 4, 700..

[357] DL 10021; medieval charter cited in Romhányi (2010), *Pálos gazdálkodás a középkorban*, 50.

E. Illustrations

Figure 65. Summary of the spatial features detected around the St. Ladislaus Monastery. Created by the author on a Google Earth cut

Figure 66. The remains of a dyke 2.b near the St. Ladislaus Monastery.
Photo taken by the author (10 March 2017)

Key to Abbreviations

ÁMTF 4
Györffy, György. *Az Árpád-kori Magyar ország történeti földrajza* [A historical geography of Hungary in the Árpádian period]. Vol. 4. Budapest: Akadémiai Kiadó: 1998.

Cod. Dipl.
Fejér, György. *Codex diplomaticus Hungariae ecclesiasticus ac civilis*. Vols. 1–11. Buda: Regiae Universitatis Hungariae, 1829–44.

DAP
Gyéressy, Béla et al. *Documenta Artis Paulinorum*. Vol. 1–4. Manuscript, ed. Melinda Tóth. Budapest: Hungarian Academy of Sciences, 1976–79.

KMTL
Kristó, Gyula, ed. (1994). *Korai magyar történeti lexikon* (9–14. század) [Early Hungarian historical lexicon (ninth-fourteenth century)]. Budapest: Akadémiai Kiadó.

MRT 5
Horváth, István, Mónika Kelemen and István Torma, ed. *Magyarország Régészeti Topográfiája* 5. Esztergom és a dorogi járás [The archaeological topography of Hungary. Esztergom and the district of Dorog].Vol 5. Budapest: Akadémiai Kiadó, 1979.

MRT 7
Torma, István, ed. *Magyarország Régészeti Topográfiája* 7. Pest megye régészeti topográfiája: A budai és szentendrei járás. [The archaeological topography of Hungary. The archaeological topography of Co. Pest: Buda and Szentendre districts]. Vol. 7. Budapest: Akadémiai Kiadó, 1986.

MTF 4
Csánki, Dezső and Antal Fekete Nagy, ed. *Magyarország történeti földrajza a Hunyadiak korában* [A historical geography of Hungary in the age of the Hunyadi family]. Vol 4. Budapest: Magyar Tudományos Akadémia, 1941.

Bibliography

Primary Sources

Bakács, István (1982). *Iratok Pest megye történetéből,* 1002-1437 [Documents on the history of Pest County, 1002–1437]. Budapest: Pest Megyei Levéltár.

Bártfai Szabó, László (1938). *Pest megye történetének okleveles emlékei 1002-1599-ig* [Charters of the history of Pest County from 1002 to 1599]. Budapest: published by the author.

Eggerer, Andreas (1663). *Fragmen Panis Corvi…* Vienna.

Fejér, György (1829–1844). *Codex diplomaticus Hungariae ecclesiasticus ac civilis*. Vols. 1–11. Buda: Regiae Universitatis Hungariae.

Gyéressy, Béla et al. (1975–1978). *Documenta Artis Paulinorum.* Vols. 1–3. Ed. Melinda Tóth. Budapest: Magyar Tudományos Akadémia.

Gyöngyösi, Gregorius (1532). *Decalogus de beato Paulo primo heremita comportatus*. Cracow: Florianum Unglerium.

Gyöngyösi, Gregorius (1522). *Inventarium privilegiorum omnium et singularum domorum ordinis eremitarum sancti Pauli primi heremite*. Manuscript. Budapest, Egyetemi Könyvtár Cod. Lat. 115 (Liber viridis) f. 1–89.

Gyöngyösi, Gregorius (1988). *Vitae Fratrum Eremitarium Ordinis Sancti Pauli Primi Eremitae.* Ed. Ferenc Hervay. Bibliotheca Medii Recentisque Aevorum. Series Nova IX. Budapest: Magyar Tudományos Akadémia.

Gyöngyösi, Gregorius (1983). *Arcok a magyar középkorból.* [Faces from the Middle Ages]. Ed. Ferenc Hervay. Budapest: Szépirodalmi Könyvkiadó.

Hadnagy, Valentinus (1511). *Vita Divi Pauli*. Buda: Matthias Milcher.

Sarbak, Gábor, ed. (2003). *Miracula Sancti Pauli primi heremitae. Hadnagy Bálint pálos rendi kézikönyve,* 1511 [The Pauline handbook of Bálint Hadnagy]. Debrecen: Kossuth Egyetemi Kiadó.

Pázmány, Péter (1629). *Acta et Décréta Synodi Diocesiana Strigoniensis*. Bratislava.

Romhányi, Beatrix, and Gábor Sarbak, eds. (2013). *Formularium maius ordinis Sancti Pauli primi Heremitae*. Budapest: Szent István Társulat.

Weinrich, Lorenz (2000). *Hungarici monasterii ordinis Sancti Pauli primi heremitae de urbe Roma. Instrumenta et priorum registra*. Roma, Budapest: Hungarian Academy of Rome.

Secondary Sources

Altmann, Júlia et al., eds. (1999). *Medium Regni. Medieval Hungarian Royal Seats*. Budapest: Nap Kiadó.

Aston, Michael (1985). *Interpreting the Landscape: Landscape Archaeology and Social Studies*. London: Batsford.

Aston, Michael, ed. (1988). *Medieval Fish, Fisheries and Fishponds in England.* British Archaeological Report, British Series, 182. Oxford: British Archaeological Reports.

Aston, Michael (2000). *Monasteries in the Landscape.* London: Tempus.

Bándi, Zsuzsanna (1986). "Északkelet-magyarországi pálos kolostorok oklevelei" [Written evidence about the Pauline monasteries in the friaries of Northern Hungary]. *Borsodi Levéltári* Évkönyv 5: 586–602.

Bencze, Zoltán and György Szekér (1993). *A budaszentlőrinci pálos kolostor* [The Pauline monastery at Budaszentlőrinc]. Budapest: Budapesti Történeti Múzeum.

Belényesy, Károly (2004). *Pálos kolostorok Abaúj-Hegyalján* [Pauline Friaries in the Abaúj Hegyalja Region]. Miskolc: Herman Ottó Múzeum.

Békefi, Remig (1891–1892). *A pilisi apátság története* 1184-1814 [A history of the Pilis monastery 1184-1814]. Pécs.

Benkő, Elek (2011). "Via regis – via gregis. Középkori utak a Pilisben" [Via regis – via gregis. Medieval roads in the Pilis]. In *"Fél évszázad terepen". Tanulmánykötet Torma István tiszteletére 70. születésnapja alkalmából.* Eds. Klára Kővári and Zsuzsa Miklós, 115–119. Budapest: Akadémiai Kiadó.

Benkő, Elek (2015a). "Udvarházak és kolostorok a pilisi királyi erdőben" [Manor Houses and Cloisters in the Royal Forests of the Pilis Region]. In *In medio regni Hungariae. Régészeti, művészettörténeti* és *történeti kutatások "az ország közepén".* [Archaeological, art historical, and historical researches "in the middle of the Kingdom"]. Eds. Elek Benkő and Krisztina Orosz, 727–753. Budapest: MTA Régészettudományi Intézet.

Benkő, Elek (2015b). “In medio regni Hungariae.” In *In medio regni Hungariae. Régészeti, művészettörténeti* és *történeti kutatások “az ország közepén”.* [Archaeological, art historical, and historical researches “in the middle of the Kingdom”]. Eds. Elek Benkő and Krisztina Orosz, 11–27. Budapest: MTA Régészettudományi Intézet.

Benkő, Elek (2016). “A Szent Kereszt remetéinek korai kolostorai a Pilisben” [The early cloisters of the hermits of the Holy Cross in the Pilis]. In *Pálosaink és Pécs* [Our Paulines and the town of Pécs]. Ed. Gábor Sarbak, 25–40. Budapest: Szent István Társulat.

Bernhardt, John W. (1993). *Itinerant Kingship and Royal Monasteries in Early Medieval Germany, c.* 936–1075. New York: Cambridge University Press.

Bertók, Gábor, and Csilla Gáti (2014). *Old Times – New Methods. Non Invasive Archaeology in Baranya County (Hungary)* 2005–2013. Budapest: Archaeolingua.

Bond, James (1989). “Water Management in the Rural Monastery.” In *The Archaeology of Rural Monasteries*. Eds. Roberta Gilchrist and R. Mytum, 83-112. Oxford: British Archaeological Reports 20.

Bond, James (2000). “Landscape of Monasticism.” In *Landscape: The Richest Historical Record*. Ed. Della Hooke, 63–74. Birmingham: Society for Landscape Studies Supplementary Series 1.

Bond, James (2004). *Monastic Landscapes*. Stroud: Tempus.

Butler, Lawrence (1989). “The Archaeology of Rural Monasteries in England and Wales.” In *The Archaeology of Rural Monasteries*. Eds. Roberta Gilchrist and Harold Mytum, 1–27. Oxford: British Archaeological Reports.

Buzás, Gergely (1994). “A pilisszentléleki pálos kolostor kőfaragványai” [Stone fragments of the Pauline monastery of Pilisszentlélek]. In *Varia Paulina. Pálos Rendtörténeti Tanulmányok* [Studies on the history of the Pauline Order]. Vol. 1. Ed. Gábor Sarbak, 181–183. Csorna: Private Edition of Vince Árva.

Buzás, Gergely, and Bernadett Eszes (2007). “XI. századi görög monostor Visegrádon” [Eleventh-century Greek monastery in Visegrád]. *Altum Castrum,* archaeological e-magazine. Last accessed December 6, 2017. http://archeologia.hu/xi-szazadi-gorog-monostor-visegradon, or In *Középkori egyházi építészet Erdélyben* (Arhitectura religiosă medievală din Transilvania) [Medieval ecclesial architecture in Transylvania]. Vol. 4. Eds. Péter Levente Szőcs and Adrian Andrei Rusu, 49–93. Satu Mare: Szatmárnémeti Múzeum.

Buzás, Gergely, Katalin Boruzs, Szabina Merva, and Katalin Tolnai (2014). "The Issue of Continuity in the Early Medieval Middle Ages in Light of the Most Recent Archaeological Research on the Late Imperial Period Fort in Visegrád." *Hungarian Archaeology*, Spring. Last accessed August 3, 2014. http://www.hungarianarchaeology.hu/wp-content/uploads/2014/05/eng_buzas_14TA.pdf.

Cabello, Juan, Csaba László, and Zoltán Simon (2008). "A Háromhegyi Boldogságos Szűz Mária Pálos kolostor régészeti kutatása" [Archaeological investigation of the Pauline monastery dedicated to the Blessed Virgin Mary at Háromhegy]. *A Hermann Ottó Múzeum Évkönyve* 47: 147–168.

Csánki, Dezső, and Antal Fekete Nagy, eds. (1941). *Magyarország történeti földrajza a Hunyadiak korában* [A historical geography of Hungary in the age of the Hunyadi family].Vol. 4. Budapest: Magyar Tudományos Akadémia.

DL. Magyar Nemzeti Levéltár – Országos Levéltár, *Diplomatikai Levéltár* [National Archive of Hungary, Section Q] Collection of Medieval Charters (1109–1526). Contains 108 362 charters. Arcanum Hungaricana Database. (Last accessed: 13 May, 2018). https://archives.hungaricana.hu/en/charters/.

Elm, Kaspar (1966). *Die Bulle "Ea quae iudicio" Clemens' IV. 30. VIII.1266. Vorgeschichte, Überlieferung, Text, und Bedeutung.* Heverlee-Louvain: Institut Historique Augustinien.

Elm, Kaspar (2000). "Eremiten und Eremitenorden des 13. Jahrhunderts." In *Beiträge zur Geschichte des Paulinerordens* (Berliner Historische Studien, Vol. 32, Ordensstudien 14.) Eds. Kaspar Elm, Dieter R. Bauer, Elmar L. Kuhn, Gábor Sarbak, and Lorenz Weinrich, 11–22. Berlin: Duncker und Humblot.

Elm, Kaspar (2016). *Religious life between Jerusalem, the desert, and the world.* Leiden: Brill.

Éri, István, ed. (1969). *Magyarország Régészeti Topográfiája. Veszprém megye régészeti topográfiája: A veszprémi járás.* [The archaeological topography of Hungary. The archaeological topography of Veszprém County. Veszprém district]. Vol. 2. Budapest: Akadémiai Kiadó.

Ferenczi, László (2009). "Észrevételek a topuszkói (toplicai) ciszterci apátság birtokstruktúrájával kapcsolatban" [Notes on the estate structure of the Cistercian abbey at Topuszkó (Toplica)]. In *A ciszterci rend Magyarországon és Közép-Európában*. Vol. 5. Ed. Barnabás Guitman, 277–292. Piliscsaba: Pázmány Péter Katolikus Egyetem.

Ferenczi, László (2014). "*Molendium ad Aquas Calidas*. A pilisi ciszterciek az állítólagos Fehéregyházán. Történeti, topográfiai és tájrégészeti kutatás a pilisi apátság birtokán" [The Cistercians in the Alleged Village of Fehéregyháza. Topographical and Landscape Archaeological Investigations on the Estate of the Pilis Abbey] *Studia Comitatensia* 1: 145–161.

Ferenczi, László (2018). "Water Management in Medieval Hungary." In *The Economy of Medieval Hungary* (Series: East Central and Eastern Europe in the Middle Ages, 450–1450, Volume: 49). Eds. József Laszlovszky, Balázs Nagy, Péter Szabó, and András Vadas, 238–254. Leiden: Brill.

Ferenczi, László, Márton Deák, Balázs Kohán, and Tamás Látos (2013). "Történeti útvonalak kutatása a Pilisben: tájrégészeti-tájtörténeti vizsgálatok térinformatikai háttérrel" [Research of historical pathways in the Pilis: landscape archaeological and landscape historical examinations with GIS]. Manuscript, Budapest.

Ferenczi, László, and József Laszlovszky (2014), "Középkori utak és határhasználat a pilisi apátság területén" [Medieval roads and landscape management on the estate of the Pilis Abbey]. *Studia Comitatensia* 1: 103–124.

Füzes, Miklós (1972). "Előzetes jelentés az 1967. évi pogányszentpéteri kolostor-ásatás XVI. század eleji gabonaleletéről" [Preliminary report on the sixteenth-century grainfind from the 1967 excavation of Pogányszentpéter cloister]. In *A Thúry György Múzeum jubileumi emlékkönyve* (1919–1969) [The Jubilee Volume of the Thúry György Museum (1919–1969)]. Ed. Gyula Kiss, 285–290. Nagykanizsa: Thúry György Múzeum.

Gerevich, László (1983). "The Royal Court (Curia), the Provost's Residence and the Village at Dömös." *Acta Archaeologica Academiae Scientiarum Hungarica* 83: 385–409.

Gerevich, László (1984). *A pilisi ciszterci apátság* [The Cistercian Abbey at Pilis]. Szentendre: Pest Megyei Múzeumok Igazgatósága.

Gerevich, László (1992). "Dömös." *Műemlékvédelem* 36: 73–80.

Gondán, Felícián (1916). *A középkori magyar pálos rend és nyelvemlékei (Festetich- és Czech-kódexek)* [The medieval Pauline order and its monuments (The Festetich and the Czech codexes]. Pécs: Printed by József Taizs.

Grimm, Gerald Volker, ed. (2011). *Kleine Meisterwerke des Bilddrucks. Ungeliebte Kinder der Kunstgeschichte. Handbuch und Katalog der Pfeifentonfiguren, Model und Reliefdrucke*. Aachen: Suermondt-Ludwig-Museum.

Guzsik, Tamás (2003). *A pálos rend építészete a középkori Magyarországon* [Pauline architecture in medieval Hungary]. Budapest: Mikes Kiadó.

Grynaeus, Tamás (1994). "A pálosok orvosló tevékenységének egy elfeledett emlékéről" [On the forgotten memories of the Pauline medical care]. In *Varia Paulina. Pálos Rendtörténeti Tanulmányok* [Studies on the history of the Pauline Order]. Vol. 1. Ed. Gábor Sarbak, 234–236, 294–298. Csorna: Private Edition of Vince Árva.

Györffy, György (1956). "Adatok a Pilis megyei monostorok középkori történetéhez" [Data on the medieval monasteries of Pilis County]. *Művészettörténeti Értesítő* 5/4: 280–285.

Györffy, György (1998). *Az Árpád-kori Magyarország történeti földrajza* [A historical geography of Hungary in the Árpádian period]. Vol. 4. Budapest: Akadémiai Kiadó.

Hervay, Ferenc Levente (1981), "A klastrompusztai rom eredete: Adatok a pálos rend történetéhez" [The origins of the ruins in Klastrompuszta: Data on the history of the Pauline order]. *Esztergom Évlapjai*: 59–76.

Hervay, Ferenc Levente (2005), "Pálosok" [Paulines]. In *Magyar Katolikus Lexikon*, 10. kötet [Hungarian Catholic Lexicon, Vol. 10]. Eds. István Diós and János Viczián, 484–489. Budapest: Szent István Társulat.

Hervay, Ferenc Levente (2007), "A Pálos Rend eredete" [The origins of the Pauline order]. In *Decus solitudinis: Pálos évszázadok* [Pauline centuries]. Eds. Gábor Sarbak and Sándor Őze, 57–65. Budapest: Szent István Társulat.

Holt, Richard (1988). *The Mills of Medieval England*. Oxford: Basil Blackwell.

Horváth, István (1974), "Klastrompuszta – a pálos rend bölcsője (Adatok a pálos rend kialakulásához)" [Klastrompuszta – the cradle of the Pauline order (Data on the evolution of the Pauline order)]. *Vigilia* 39/9: 611–615.

Horváth, István (1981). "A klastrompusztai rom eredete: Adatok a pálos rend történetéhez" [The origins of the ruins in Klastrompuszta: Data on the history of the Pauline order]. *Esztergom Évlapjai*: 59–76.

Keevill, Graham, Michael Aston, and Teresa Hall, eds. (2001). *Monastic Archaeology: Papers on the Study of Medieval Monasteries.* Oxford: Oxbow Books.

Kelényi, Ottó (1936). "A Buda melletti Szent Lőrinc pálos kolostor történetének első irodalmi forrása (1511)" [The first literary source (1511) on the history of the St. Laurence Pauline Monastery near Buda]. *Tanulmányok Budapest Múltjából* 4: 87–110.

Kékedi, Andrea (2008). "Középkori pálos kolostorok környezetátalakítása a nagyvázsonyi történeti táj példáján" [The impact of medieval Pauline monasteries in the landscape on the example of the historical landscape at Nagyvázsony]. MA Thesis in Landscape Architecture: Budapesti Corvinus Egyetem, Budapest.

Kisbán, Emil (1938-1940). *A magyar pálos rend története* [The history of the Hungarian Pauline Order]. 2 vols. Budapest.

Knauz, Ferdinand (1882). *Monumenta Ecclesiae Strigoniensis.* Vol. 2. Esztergom: Horák.

Kovalovszki, Júlia (1992). "A pálos remeték Szent Kereszt-kolostora (Méri István ásatása Klastrompusztán)" [The Pauline monastery of the Holy Cross (the excavation of István Méri at Klastrompuszta)]. *Communicationes Archaeologicae Hungariae*: 173–207.

Kubinyi, András (1962). "A király és a királyné kúriái a XIII. századi Budán" [The curiae of the kings and queens at Buda in the thirteenth century]. *Archaeologiai Értesítő* 89: 160–171.

Kubinyi, András (1994). "Főváros, rezidencia és az egyházi intézmények" [Capital, residence and ecclesial institutions]. *Magyar Egyháztörténeti Évkönyv* 1: 57–70.

Kubinyi, András (1996/1999). "Előszó. Az 'ország közepétől' a fővárosig." In *Medium Regni.* Eds. Júlia Altmann et al., 5–8. Budapest: Nap Kiadó.

Kubinyi, András (2002). "A királyi vár és lakói a középkorban." *História* 9–10: 14-18. http://www.tankonyvtar.hu/en/tartalom/historia/02-0910/ch04.html.

Kürcz, Antal (1889). *A magyarországi pálos rend története* [The history of the Hungarian Pauline order]. Budapest: Hunyadi Mátyás Printing-house.

Laszlovszky, József (1999). "Field systems in medieval Hungary." In *The man of many devices, who wandered full many ways: Festschrift in honor of János M. Bak.* Eds. Balázs Nagy and Marcell Sebők, 432–444. Budapest: CEU Press.

Laszlovszky, József (2004). "Középkori kolostorok a tájban, középkori kolostortájak" [Medieval monasteries in the landscape, medieval monastic landscapes]. In *Quasi liber et pictura: Tanulmányok Kubinyi András hetvenedik születésnapjára* [Studies for the seventeenth anniversary of András Kubinyi]. Ed. Gyöngyi Kovács, 337–349. Budapest: Eötvös Loránd Tudományegyetem.

Laszlovszky, József (2006). "The Medieval Royal Seat and Forest at Visegrád: A Proposed World Heritage Site and its Heritage Aspects". In *Archaeological and Cultural Heritage Preservation: Within the Light of New Technologies*. Eds. Erzsébet Jerem, Zsolt Mester, and Réka Benczés, 83–94. Budapest: Archaeolingua.

Laszlovszky, József (2008a). "Az Európai Táj Egyezmény és a hazai tájrégészet" [The European Landscape Convention and the national landscape archaeology]. *Műemlékvédelmi és Építészettörténeti Szemle* 52/2: 101–104.

Laszlovszky, József (2009). "Ciszterci vagy pálos? A Pomáz-Nagykovácsipusztán található középkori épületmaradványok azonosítása." [Cistercian or Pauline? Interpretation of the medieval architectural remains at Nagykovácsipuszta, Pomáz]. In *A ciszterci rend Magyarországon* és *Közép-Európában*. Vol. 5. Ed. Barnabás Guitman, 191–208. Piliscsaba: Pázmány Péter Katolikus Egyetem.

Laszlovszky, József (2013). "The Royal Palace in the Sigismund Period and the Franciscan Friary at Visegrád. Royal Residence and the Foundation of Religious Houses." In *The Medieval Royal Palace at Visegrád.* Eds. Gergely Buzás and József Laszlovszky, 207–218. Budapest: Archaeolingua.

Laszlovszky, József (2018), "Agriculture in Medieval Hungary". In *The Economy of Medieval Hungary* (Series: East Central and Eastern Europe in the Middle Ages, 450–1450, Volume: 49). Eds. József Laszlovszky, Balázs Nagy, Péter Szabó, and András Vadas, 79–112. Leiden: Brill.

Laszlovszky, József, and Péter Szabó, eds. (2003). *People and Nature in Historical Perspective*. (CEU Medievalia 5.) Budapest: Central European University, 2003.

Laszlovszky et al. (2014). "The 'Glass Church' in the Pilis Mountains". *Hungarian Archaeology*, Winter. Last accessed August 3, 2017. http://www.hungarianarchaeology.hu/?page_id=279#post-5582

Lawler, Jennifer (2004). *Encyclopedia of the Byzantine Empire*. London: McFarland.

Lázár, Sarolta (1994). "A pilisszentléleki pálos kolostortemplom kutatása" [Archaeological investigation of the Pauline Monastery at Pilisszentlélek]. In *Varia Paulina. Pálos Rendtörténeti Tanulmányok* [Studies on the history of the Pauline Order]. Vol. 1. Ed. Gábor Sarbak, 177–180. Csorna: Private Edition of Vince Árva.

Lázár, Sarolta (1997). "A pilisszentléleki volt pálos kolostortemplom kutatása 1985-86" [Archaeological investigation of the Pauline Monastery at Pilisszentlélek, 1985–1986]. *A Komárom-Esztergom Megyei Múzeumok Közleményei* 5: 493–518.

Lázár, Sarolta (2001). "A pilisszentléleki pálos kolostor kályhacsempéi" [The stove tiles of the Pauline monastery of Pilisszentlélek]. *A Komárom-Esztergom Megyei Múzeumok Közleményei* 8: 167–180.

Lázár, Sarolta (2012). "A pilisszentléleki pálos kolostor műhelyháza [The workshop of the Pauline monastery at Pilisszentlélek]. In *Laudator Temporis Acti – Tanulmányok Horváth István 70 éves születésnapjára* [Studies for the seventeenth birthday of István Horváth]. Ed. Edit Tari, 213–222. Esztergom: Balassi Bálint Múzeum.

Le Goff, Jacques (1985). "Le desert-forêt dans l'Occident medieval". In: *L'imaginaire medieval*. Paris: Édition Gallimard.

Lovag, Zsuzsa (2014). *Az Esztergom-prímás szigeti apácakolostor feltárása* [The excavation of the nunnery at Esztergom-Prímás sziget]. Budapest: Magyar Nemzeti Múzeum.

Luckhurst, David (1964). *Monastic Watermills: a study of the mills within English monastic precincts*. London: Society for the Protection of Ancient Buildings.

Majorossy, Judit, ed. (2013)*"A királynét megölni nem kell félnetek jó lesz...". Merániai Gertrúd emlékezete,* 1213-2013. *Történeti vándorkiállítás, kiállításvezető* [The queen to kill you must not fear, will be good .... Commemorate Gertrude of Merania, 1213-2013. Historical Touring Exhibition, Museum Booklet]. Szentendre: Ferenczy Múzeum.

Mályusz, Elemér (1945). "A Pálos rend a középkor végén" [The Pauline order at the end of the Middle Ages]. *Egyháztörténet* 1: 1-53.

Mályusz Elemér (1971). "Remeterendek" [Hermit Orders]. In *Egyházi társadalom a középkori Magyarországon*, 254-274. Budapest: Akadémiai Kiadó.

Méri, István (n.d.). *A klastrompusztai legendák nyomában* [On the track of legends in Klastrompuszta]. Dorog: József Attila Művelődési Ház, n.d.

Méri, István (1959a). "Kesztölc-Klastrompuszta, pálos kolostor. Ásatási jelentés 1959" [Kesztölc-Klastrompuszta, Pauline monastery. Report on the excavations of 1959]. Hungarian National Museum, Archive, 334.K.IV.

Méri, István (1959b). "Kesztölc-Klastrompuszta, pálos kolostor. Ásatási napló 1959" [Kesztölc-Klastrompuszta, Pauline monastery. Field diary 1959]. Hungarian National Museum, Archive, III/196/53.

Méri, István (1959c). "Kesztölc-Klastrompuszta, pálos kolostor. Fotódokumentáció 1959" [Kesztölc-Kalstrompuszta, Pauline monastery. Photo documentation 1959]. Hungarian National Museum, Archive, II/1960/73.

Meyvaert, Paul (1986). "The medieval monastic garden". In *Medieval Gardens*. Ed. E. D. Macdougall, 23–53. Washington DC: Trustees for Harvard University.

Miskolci, Melinda, and Gábor Szörényi (2013). "A miskolc-szentléleki pálos kolostor története és 2012. évi kutatása" [The history of the Pauline friary near Miskolc and its archeological excavation in 2012]. In *A Kaposváron 2012. november 22–24. között megrendezett Fiatal Középkoros Régészek IV. Konferenciájának tanulmányai. A Kaposvári Rippl-Rónai Múzeum Közleményei* 2. [Study Volume of the 4th Conference of Young Medieval Archaeologists. Studies of the 4th Conference of Young Medieval Archaeologists, 22–24 November 2012, Kaposvár]. Ed. Máté Varga, 83–91. Kaposvár: Rippl-Rónai Múzeum.

Müller, Róbert (1972). "A pogányszentpéteri ásatás" [The excavation at Pogányszentpéter]. In *A Thúry György Múzeum jubileumi emlékkönyve* (1919–1969) [The Jubilee Volume of the Thúry György Museum (1919–1969)]. Ed. Gyula Kiss, 265–282. Nagykanizsa: Thúry György Múzeum.

Nagy, Szabolcs Balázs (2014). "A bakonyszentjakabi pálos kolostor feltárásának első eredményei" [The first results of the excavation at the Pauline monastery of Bakonyszentjakab]. *Várak, kastélyok, templomok.* [Forts, castles, churches]. Annual Studies. Ed. Pál Kósa, 56–59. Pécs: Talma Kiadó.

Neitmann, Klaus (1990). "Was ist eine Residenz? Methodische Überlegungen zur Erforschung der spätmittelalterlichen Residenzbildung." In *Vorträge und Vorschungen zur Residenzfrage*. Ed. Peter Johanek, 11-43. Sigmaringen: Jan Thorbecke.

Nováki, Gyula (1985). Szántóföldek maradványai a XIV–XVI. századból a Sümeg-Sarvalyi erdőben [Remains of arable lands from the fourteenth-sixteenth century in the woods of Sümeg-Sarvaly]. *Magyar Mezőgazdasági Múzeum Közleményei*: 19–32.

Orosz, Krisztina (2010). "Várak és kolostorok konyhái a középkori Magyarországon" [Kitchens of Castles and Monasteries in Medieval Hungary]. In *A középkor és a kora újkor régészete Magyarországon* 2. [The archaeology of the middle ages and the post middle ages in Hungary] Vol. 2. Eds. Elek Benkő and Gyöngyi Kovács, 562–596. Budapest: MTA Régészettudományi Intézet.

Ortvay, Tivadar (1891). *Magyarország földrajzi leírása a XIV. század elején* [The geographical report of Hungary in the fourteenth century]. Vol. 1. Budapest: s.n.

Pusztai, Tamás (2007). "A gönci pálos kolostor 2004-2005. évi kutatása" [The research of the Pauline monastery at Gönc in 2004-2005]. In *Decus Solitudinis. Pálos évszázadok* [Pauline Centuries]. Ed. Gábor Sarbak, 515–536. Budapest: Szent István Társulat.

Rackham, Oliver (1996). *Trees and Woodland in the British Landscape*. London: Phoenix, revised edition.

Rainer, Pál (2016). *Ádám Iván veszprémi kanonok pálos kolostorokról készült rajzai a veszprémi Laczkó Dezső Múzeumban* [The drawings of Iván Ádám Canon of Veszprém on Pauline monasteries, located in the Lackó Dezső Mueum at Veszprém]. Veszprém: Lackó Dezső Múzeum.

Roberts, B. K. (1988). "The Re-discovery of fishponds". In *Medieval Fish, Fisheries and Fishponds in England.* Ed. Michael Aston, 9-26. Oxford: British Archaeological Reports.

Romhányi, Beatrix (2000). *Kolostorok és társaskáptalanok a középkori Magyarországon* [Monasteries and collegiate Chapters in Medieval Hungary]. Budapest: Pytheas.

Romhányi, Beatrix (2007). "Pálos gazdálkodás a 15-16. században" [Estate management of the Pauline order in the fifteenth and sixteenth centuries]. *Századok* 141: 299–351.

Romhányi, Beatrix (2008). "A pálos rendi hagyomány az oklevelek tükrében. Megjegyzések a Pálos Rend középkori történetéhez" [The tradition of the Pauline Order as reflected in charters. Remarks on the medieval history of the Pauline Order]. *Történelmi Szemle* 50/3: 289–312.

Romhányi, Beatrix (2010). *A lelkiek a földiek nélkül nem tarthatóak fenn – Pálos gazdálkodás a középkorban* [Spirits cannot be sustained without earthly goods – Estate management of the Pauline order in the Middle Ages]. Budapest: Gondolat Kiadó.

Romhányi, Beatrix (2011). "A pálos élet forrásai a középkorvégi Magyarországon" [Sources of the Pauline life in Hungary at the end of the Middle Ages]. *Az Egyetemi Könyvtár Évkönyvei* 14–15: 323–330.

Romhányi, Beatrix (2012a). "Pálos kolostorok a Pilisben" [Pauline monasteries in the Pilis]. In *Laudator Temporis Acti – Tanulmányok Horváth István 70 éves születésnapjára.* [Studies for the seventeenth birthday of István Horváth]. Edit Tari, 223–227. Esztergom: Balassi Bálint Múzeum.

Romhányi, Beatrix (2012b). "Life in the Pauline Monasteries of Late Medieval Hungary." *Periodica Polytechnica* 43: 53–56.

Romhányi, Beatrix (2015a). "Kolostorhálózat – településhálózat – népesség. A középkori Magyar Királyság demográfiai helyzetének változásaihoz" [Monastic network – settlement system – population: on the demographic changes of the medieval Hungarian Kingdom]. *Történelmi Szemle* 57: 1–49.

Romhányi, Beatrix (2015b). "Ceperuntque simul claustralem ducere vitam. A pálos rend és a Medium Regni kapcsolata" [The relationship of the Paulien Order and Medium Regni]. In *In medio regni Hungariae. Régészeti, művészettörténeti és történeti kutatások "az ország közepén"* [Archaeological, art historical and historical researches 'in the Middle of the Kingdom']. Eds. Elek Benkő and Krisztina Orosz, 756–764. Budapest: MTA Régészettudományi Intézet.

Romhányi, Beatrix (2016). "Heremitae – monarchi – fratres. Szempontok a pálos rend történetének újragondolásához" [Perspectives for rethinking the history of the Pauline Order]. In *Pálosaink és Pécs* [Our Paulines and the town of Pécs]. Ed. Gábor Sarbak, 9–24. Budapest: Szent István Társulat.

Sarbak, Gábor, ed. (1994). *Varia Paulina. Pálos Rendtörténeti Tanulmányok* [Studies on the history of the Pauline Order]. Vol.1. Csorna: Private Edition of Vince Árva.

Sarbak, Gábor (2001). "Pálosaink írásbelisége a középkor végén" [Pauline scripts at the end of the Middle Ages]. *Vigilia* 66/2: 112–119.

Sarbak, Gábor, ed. (2007). *Decus Solitudinis. Pálos évszázadok* [Pauline Centuries]. Budapest: Szent István Társulat.

Sarbak, Gábor, ed. (2010). *Der Paulinerorden. Geschichte-Geist-Kultur*. Budapest: Szent István Társulat.

Solymosi, László (2005). "Pilissziget vagy Fülöpsziget? A pálos remeteélet 13. századi kezdeteihez" [Island of Pilis or Island of Philip Island? Additions to early Pauline hermit life in the thirteenth Century]. In *Emlékkönyv Orosz István 70. születésnapjára*. Eds. János Angi and János Barta, Jr., 11–23. Debrecen: Debreceni Egyetemi Kiadó.

Stegena, Lajos, ed. (1982). *Lazarus secretarius. The First Hungarian Mapmaker and His Work*. Budapest: Akadémiai Kiadó.

Szabó, Péter (1998). "Pilis: A Hungarian Forest in the Middle Ages." MA Thesis in Medieval Studies: CEU, Budapest.

Szabó, Péter (1999) "Pilis: Changing Settlements in a Hungarian Forest in the Middle Ages". *Annual of Medieval Studies at the CEU for* 1997–1998: 283–293.

Szabó, Péter (2005). *Woodland and Forests in Medieval Hungary*. BAR International Series 1348. Archaeolingua, Central European Series, Vol. 2. Oxford: Basingstoke Press.

Szepesy, Géza (1959). "Levél a Magyar Nemzeti Múzeumnak (1959. február 9.)" [Letter to the Hungarian National Museum – Report on the archaeological findings at Kesztölc-Klastrompuszta, 9th February, 1959. Hungarian National Museum, Archive, 456. K. VI.

Tari, Edit, and Endre Tóth, eds. (2012). *Laudator temporis acti. Tanulmányok Horváth István 70 éves születésnapjára* [Studies for the seventeenth birthday of István Horváth]. Budapest: Martin Opitz.

Taylor, C. C. (1988). "Problems and possibilities". In *Medieval Fish, Fisheries and Fishponds in England.* Ed. Michael Aston, 465–474. Oxford: British Archaeological Reports.

Torma, István (1981). "Mittelalterliche Ackerfeld-Spurenim Wald von Tamási (Komitat Tolna)." *Acta Archaeologica Academiae Scientiarum Hungaricae* 33: 245–256.

Torma, István ed. (1979). *Magyarország Régészeti Topográfiája. Komárom megye régészeti topográfiája* [The archaeological topography of Hungary. The archaeological topography of Komárom County: Esztergom and Dorog districts]. Vol. 5. Budapest: Akadémiai Kiadó.

Torma, István, ed. (1986). *Magyarország Régészeti Topográfiája. Pest megye régészeti topográfiája: A budai* és *szentendrei járás* [The archaeological topography of Hungary. The archaeological topography of Pest County: the Buda and Szentendre districts]. Vol. 7. Budapest: Akadémiai Kiadó.

Urbán, Máté (2009). "Pálos zarándokhelyek a későközépkori Magyarországon" [Pauline pilgrimage sites in late medieval Hungary]. *Vallástudományi Szemle* 5/1: 63–85.

Urbán, Máté (2010). "Puszta sivatag és Paradicsom kert – Táj és természet a remeterendek és a ciszterciták középkori felfogásában" [Abandoned desert and Paradise – Landscape and nature in the understanding of hermit orders and Cistercians]. *Vigilia* 75: 2–9.

Végh, András (2006). *Buda város középkori helyrajza* 1 [The Medieval map of Buda]. Vol. 1. Budapest: Budapesti Történeti Múzeum.

The aerial photographs of this volume have been provided by Civertan Graphic Studio for which we express our thanks.

Wheatley, David, and Mark Gillings (2002). *Spatial Technology and Archaeology: the archaeological applications of GIS*. London: Taylor & Francis.

Zatykó, Csilla (2005). "People beyond landscapes: past, present and future of Hungarian landscape archaeology." *Antaeus* 33: 369–388.

Zólyomi, Bálint, and István Précsényi (1985). "Pollenstatistische Analyse der Teichablagerungen des mittelalterlichen Klosters bei Pilisszentkereszt." *Acta Archaeologica Academiae Scientiarum Hungaricae* 37: 153–158.

Zupka, Dušan (2011). *Ritual and Symbolic Communication in Medieval Hungary under the Árpád Dynasty (1000 - 1301)*. Oxford: Brill.